W9-AAX-571

IN THE RED ZONE

IN THE
RED ZONE

A Journey into the Soul of Iraq

STEVEN VINCENT

SPENCE PUBLISHING COMPANY • DALLAS

2004

To those whose lives were taken

on September 11, 2001

Published in the United States by
Spence Publishing Company
111 Cole Street
Dallas, Texas 75207

Library of Congress Control Number: 2004114371

ISBN 1-890626-57-0

Printed in the United States of America

Contents

Acknowledgments

I T HAS BEEN OVER A YEAR since I made my first trip to Iraq—a year that has completely transformed my life. My first trip took place from late September to mid-October, 2003; my second from mid-January to late March, 2004. My total time traveling through Iraq, in addition to reporting work from Jordan, was around four months. I paid my own way, went where I wanted, and drew my own conclusions, unhampered by media or institutional bias.

I had more help in writing this book than I could have ever imagined. I cannot thank enough my lifelong friend, Jonathan Roth, professor of history at San Jose State, for his support, encouragement, and general handholding. I must also thank my mother and father and friends like Charlie Finch, Susan Heidenreich, Alan Jones, and Grace Roselli, and of course, Steve Mumford, for inspiring me to go in the first place. I'd also like to express my gratitude to Kathryn Lopez of *National Review Online*, Jamie Glazov of *Frontpage*, and Karl Zinsmeister of *American Enterprise*, as well as *Commentary* and *Reason* magazine for printing my articles while I was in the Middle East. Thanks also to the many people who read my daily emails and encouraged me to write a book about my experiences. Further thanks goes out to my agent Andrew Stuart, as well as my editor, Mitchell Muncy, and the people at Spence Publishing.

The list of Iraqi friends I would like to thank would fill an entire page. But I must mention Esam Azizawy, Ahmed al-Safi, Moham- mad Rassim, Haider Wady, Qasim al-Septi, Yahya Batat, and Rand Petros, as well as Dhia, Samir, Sabah, and the countless other drivers and guides who looked out for me in dangerous times. My special thanks go to Nasser Flayih Hasan for exquisite insights into the soul of Iraq—and, of course, to Nour—I only wish I could reveal her real name, so people could know this wonderful young woman, and what the face of liberated Iraq will look like once, *insha'allah*, peace comes to her country.

Lastly, I must express my deepest gratitude to my wife, Lisa Ramaci, for the unwavering support she offered in helping me to make this journey, starting with that terrible morning of 9-11 and extending to this day. Without her courage and resolute assistance, my travels, this book, and the self-knowledge I gained from both would not have been possible.

IN THE RED ZONE

The View from the Roof

The purposes of the Almighty are perfect,
and must prevail, although we erring mortals
may fail to accurately perceive them in advance.

Abraham Lincoln, 1863

"KEEP ALERT, MAN."

The tall, gangly sergeant from Milwaukee seemed concerned. Adjusting his Kevlar vest, he rested his weapon on his knee and spoke in a calm and knowledgeable tone. "When you leave here, look out for IEDs"—Improvised Explosive Devices, or roadside bombs set by anti-Coalition fighters. "The bad guys put 'em in the carcasses of dead dogs or drop 'em from freeway overpasses."

"You got a flak jacket or helmet? You carrying a weapon?" asked the second soldier, a linebacker-sized specialist from North Carolina. I shook my head, a little distressed to see a shadow cross both their youthful faces.

To the east, across a gently rising plane strewn with rocks and small boulders, the sky was just beginning to brighten with the dawn. A nice bit of timing, seeing how Fahdi and I had left Amman, Jordan, at 1:00 AM, hurtling through the darkness as fast as three hundred miles of pitted roadway and numerous police checkpoints would allow. Now as my driver submitted our passports to one last set of border officials, I stood on the soil of liberated Iraq, before a pair of American GIs so big and heavily armed they seemed to have been conjured from some Aladdin's lamp.

"Who you with, anyway?" asked the specialist, glancing at my Suburban as if expecting to see additional travelers.

This meant "What news agency?"—the *New York Times*, CNN, ABC, and so on. As I soon discovered, soldiers, officials from the Coalition Provisional Authority (CPA), and even many Iraqis assumed all reporters were part of big organizations—as if no one could be foolish enough to wander around the country by himself.

"Just a freelancer," I explained. "Out here totally on my own."

"*On your own?*" the specialist gawked in disbelief. "You mean you came by *choice*? Jesus, man, at least we *had* to come to this shit-hole."

Fahdi called to me and, a little embarrassed, I nodded to the GIs and clambered inside the Suburban. As we rumbled out of the checkpoint, the Jordanian pointed to a large cement pedestal, in front of which lay a tangle of steel rods and concrete debris. "*Maaku Saddam*," he grunted—no more Saddam—referring to the toppled statue, and regime, of the hated tyrant. Seeing "two vast and trunkless legs of stone stand in the desert," I couldn't help thinking of Shelley's parable of despotic vanity, *Ozymandias*: "Look on my Works, ye Mighty, and despair!"

As we cleared the last curlicue of concertina wire, a sliver of orange rose over the horizon to break the pre-dawn symmetry of the landscape. I settled back in my seat, feeling my heart pound. This was the moment I'd been heading toward since the morning of September 11, 2001—and perhaps even before that. I had quit my job as an art reporter and critic to do this, driven by conscience, support for the war, and some reawakened moral impulses I had yet to understand. What my journey would bring, whether it would answer my political and personal questions—or if I'd even survive the damn thing—I did not know. All I knew was that I had embarked on an experience of a lifetime, something I imagined would change me forever.

Shaking myself from my reverie, I asked Fahdi if I could replace his tape of Arabic pop with something I had brought from home. A private joke, I tried to explain. He shrugged, nodded, and I slipped in a cassette. Soon, as the sun burst over the horizon, pouring light into the sky, we were rocketing down Iraq's Highway 10, swaying to the happy strains of Nelson Riddle's "Route 66."

Next stop, Baghdad.

—

Had We sent down this Koran on a mountain,
you would certainly have seen it falling down,
splitting asunder because of the fear of Allah,
and We set forth these parables
to men that they may reflect.

The Koran, 59:21

A TERRORIST, A PRESIDENT, AND A NEW YORK ARTIST convinced me to go to Iraq.

The terrorist, of course, was Osama bin Laden. I had heard a sharp, plangent clang that morning, but with an innocence that has become an artifact of another era, thought nothing of it. After all, you hear a lot of strange noises in New York; it wasn't reasonable to consider this one any different. A few minutes later, I received a phone call from my neighbor Jane, who was standing on the roof of our Lower East Side building. "You should come up and see this," she said.

What I saw was what the entire world would soon witness: the north tower of the World Trade Center spewing black smoke from a rupture in its northeast corner. *Terrorists*, I thought, rushing downstairs to grab my cell phone. Back on the roof, I called my wife, Lisa, and was relieved to find her safe at work in her uptown office. A plane had gone off course, striking the building, she said. Possibly, possibly—that's more reasonable than any other explanation. I phoned a fellow journalist with whom I often talked politics: "Charlie, turn on your TV, man, you won't believe what—"

Out of nowhere it emerged, the swift black silhouette of a second airliner, flying impossibly low. In my memory, the image of that plane morphs into a black bird, a vulture, a symbol of death—but of course, the whole moment was unreal, hallucinatory, or perhaps more than real, like a dream: the blue clarity of the sky, the gleaming facade of the World Trade Center, Jane's scream as United Airlines Flight 175 disappeared behind the South Tower, followed an instant later by billowing orange fire that girdled the building. *Oh my God, dear God*, I screamed—then the phone slipped from my hand. And the world slipped with it.

It is all so vivid, even today. The silence that fell across the city as the structures burned. The wind that blew the smoke southeast, over Brooklyn, giving us an unimpeded view of the catastrophe, less than three miles away. The glowering black voids that moments before had been filled with offices—and office workers. Then, the unthinkable: gray clouds of ash and debris as first one building, then the other, fell. "It's gone, Lisa," I reported as the North Tower vanished from the horizon. "There is no more World Trade Center." Who could imagine ever saying something like that?

It didn't stop there, of course. The news from the Pentagon and the field near Shanksville, Pennsylvania; the smoke that rose for days from Ground Zero; the faces of the "missing" taped to bus stops; candles burning in makeshift shrines on street corners; the realization that hundreds of firemen, police officers, and paramedics were gone, vanished, dead—events kept unfolding, each bringing a fresh wound. And though no one Lisa or I knew was injured or killed in the attacks, the wounds went deep nonetheless. They still hurt.

We all had our reactions to that day; mine were no different from those of millions of other Americans. But after the numbness of the shock and horror, after the grieving over our losses, after the anxiety that the terrorists might return—didn't Mohammad Atta have his eye on a crop duster at one point?—after facing the possibility we might perish in New York ("Do we want to leave?" I asked Lisa. "Hell no!" was her immediate reply—I don't think I've ever been more proud of her)—after all that came rage. How dare these terrorists attack my city, my country; how dare they put my wife, our friends, and me in fear for our lives? Who do these maniacs think they are? Like many of us, I had little knowledge—then—of Islam, Wahabbism, the splintered Caliphate, Sunni-Shia divisions, the intra-Muslim politics that contributed to the Trade Center's destruction (though I became a *very* fast student). I wanted revenge, I wanted to see an injured nation claim just retribution for the violence inflicted upon it. When the bombs fell on Afghanistan and the Taliban regime that October, I cheered; when the Islamofacist regime collapsed, I exulted. This is what we had to do, I thought. Take the fight to the turbaned mullahs and the cave-dwelling terrorists. *Project American power into the heart of the evil that attacked us.*

Evil. Before that September morning, I hadn't though much about it. Evil was something for horror movies—or far-away places like Auschwitz or the Killing Fields. Evil was what happened to other people—and besides, it was a matter of interpretation, historical, cultural, or psychological factors, all very reasonable when you analyze it. But I think differently now. I saw something evil take place before my eyes, on the burning rim of Manhattan. I sensed its hatred of humanity, civilization, prosperity, and self-reliance—anything that helps us to lift ourselves above nothingness and despair. It was not a presence I could define, or prove, or analyze, any more than I could define, prove, or analyze love. I just felt it. Evil was real, palpable, frightening.

But it was not beyond analysis or definition. The more I reflected on what I saw on 9-11, the more I realized that radical evil—metaphysical Evil—differs from the merely bad, tragic, even catastrophic by its unlimited malevolence. In the case of the Trade Center attack, men, women, children, combatants and non-combatants, Muslims and non-believers alike, none of these distinctions mattered to bin Laden. In raising the standard of war, he and his fellow jihadists may have articulated a fanciful set of demands (withdraw from the Middle East, abandon Israel, and so on), but their deeper motives lack even the qualification of being unrealistic. They see their motives as sacred, absolute, beyond profane negotiation or worldly compromise. The scope here is non- (or perhaps in-) human: *Dar-al-Islam*, the House of Islam, must someday, somehow overcome *Dar-al-Harb*, the House of War, that is, the non-Islamic world, the place you and I call home. As Sayid Qutb, the radical Egyptian intellectual and great influence on bin Laden wrote in his book *Milestones*, a kind of Muslim version of *Mein Kampf*, "The earth belongs to God and should be purified for God, and it cannot be purified for him unless the banner 'La ilaha illa Allah' ['There is no God but Allah'] is unfurled across the earth."[1]

That is their narrative, their apocalyptic script. It's what gives meaning to what they consider their struggle and sacrifices, and fuels the obscenity of their homicidal martyrdoms. And ours? What myth, what storyline does America and the free world use to sustain our morale in this conflict? Even before work crews had cleared the debris from Ground Zero a fear began to trouble—then torment—me: that the deaths of thousands would go unanswered, that the West could provide no opposing narrative to balance bin Laden's victory, that the terrorist's megalomania would be the only legacy of murdered innocents, that we would do nothing beyond destroying a few pathetic mullahs and chasing *hadith*-quoting fascists from one tribal sanctuary to the next. *It's not enough, it's not enough*, I kept thinking as the "hunt for bin Laden" continued. A few victories here and there are not enough to give meaning and purpose to the deaths on 9-11. Worse, President Bush refused to call for national sacrifice, declining to put the country on a war footing. Where was the sense of larger purpose, a rallying concept commensurate with the terrorist attack itself, something that would consecrate the dead to a reawakening of the American spirit?

Although it has grown infamous of late, the idea of democratizing the Middle East seized my imagination. What better way to use American power—and ensure our own safety—than with such a grand strategic effort? How better to finish what bin Laden had started than to transform America's post-9-11 trauma into a secular crusade for freedom and democracy? And the place to start?

1 Sayyid Qutb, *Milestones* (Kuwait: International Islamic Federation of Student Organizations, 1978), 44.

One of the key regions of *Dar-al-Islam*, the veritable crossroads of the Muslim world: Iraq. I cared little about "weapons of mass destruction," less about Al Qaeda links with Saddam Hussein. Nor, I must admit, did I really concern myself—then—with the tyrant's genocidal record. No, I envisioned the liberation of that country as a way to cure the Arab stagnation that had increasingly begun to infect the world. A nation's just wrath, harnessed to a righteous cause, seemed to me the proper way to ensure that the victims of 9-11 "shall not have died in vain."

Although I hadn't voted for him, I grew to admire George W. Bush and his commitment to the liberation of Iraq. I applauded his challenge to the dithering United Nations. I supported his stand against our erstwhile European allies. I yearned to hear him call for sacrifice on the part of the country, and to frame the war as a moral conflict, rather than a search for WMDs, to exhibit some Lincolnesque humility and ironic self-awareness. But I was confident it would come. It had to. American presidents, like America herself, always rise to great occasions, don't they? When the Administration launched Operation Iraqi Freedom, I felt strangely excited. I wanted to join the conflict.

But how? I hadn't considered this aspect of the issue. At forty-seven, I was too old to enlist. Seeking an "embed" slot with military units seemed out of the question as well—the high-gloss art and culture magazines I wrote for were not about to send me to a war zone, nor were mainstream publications likely to assign an arts correspondent to Iraq. These practical considerations—the bane of moral fervor—seemed insurmountable. Over there, the greatest event of my lifetime was taking place, and I was here, missing it. I was stuck.

It was while in the depths of this personal quandary that I got a phone call from a New York artist named Steve Mumford. It was

April of 2003; the statue of Saddam that once marred Firdousi Square in Baghdad was still being dragged through the streets. "I'm flying to Kuwait next week, and from there I plan to cross into Iraq and make my way through the country," he told me. I was shocked, though I shouldn't have been. War, I knew, fascinated Steve. Not necessarily actual combat, but the way—as he put it once—"soldiers try to establish some sense of normalcy to their lives." His model is the great nineteenth-century American painter Winslow Homer, who during the Civil War made several trips to the Virginia front to record the war for *Harper's Weekly*. Politically neutral, perhaps ambivalent about the conflict in Iraq, Steve was going mainly to duplicate Homer's achievement, to create a body of art based on life in a war zone.

He returned in July and we arranged to have lunch together at a Lower East Side café. He looked older, grayer, more grizzled than I remembered him: he'd begun to resemble the senior military offic- ers he depicted in his drawings. As our meal progressed, he related tales of roaring around Baghdad in a Bradley Fighting Vehicle, of going on patrol with soldiers in the slums of Sadr City, of the friend- ships he'd made with Iraqis throughout the country. Basra, Samarra, Sulimaniya, Dohuk—the names of Iraqi cities rolled off his tongue like incantations from some magical text. And through it all, I kept hearing an inner voice challenging my complacency: Do you want to participate in this world-historical event? *Participate!* Do you want to enlist in the war against Islamofascism? *Enlist!* Do you want to help give meaning to the victims of 9-11? *Go to Iraq!*

With Lisa's patience, understanding, and financial assistance, I planned my first trip in the fall of 2003. I won't pretend I wasn't afraid—actually, there were moments when my nerve seemed to fail me and I wondered what the hell I was doing leaving my com- fortable position as a art journalist to venture off into a war. I had no military experience—unless you count my three years during the mid-1980s driving a New York cab at night (back then it was one of the most dangerous jobs in the country). Nor did I plan to bring a helmet or flak jacket: unlike Steve, I didn't intend to link up with the troops, not out of any ideological opposition (far from it), but simply because that journalistic vein seemed well-tapped by other writers. Still, as with most adventures, once the preparation and waiting ended and I boarded the flight to Amman, Jordan, my anxiety vanished. When I saw how many other journalists were also in Baghdad, my fears seemed almost—but not quite—foolish.

Once in the so-called City of Peace, I linked up with Steve, already several weeks into his second journey. We actually spent only a few days together. He embedded himself with the troops to make his drawings and sketches, while I sought to embed myself in Iraqi society. I traveled for nearly two months by myself all through Iraq—Baghdad, of course, with trips south to Karbala, Najaf, and Basra. Then, reluctantly, I returned to New York. I say reluctantly, because I knew that one trip was not enough. Even before I set out across the desert back to Amman and the flight home, I knew I'd barely scratched the surface of Iraq and its people, and that I'd have to return.

Steve and I did just that in early January, 2004, staying on until spring. Although I'll refer to my first trip in this book, it was the second that taught me the most about Iraq, the war, America, and myself. Nor—as Scheherezade would say—is the story over. As I write this, Steve is currently on his fourth trip to Iraq, and I plan to return as well. For me—for our entire generation—this is our moment in history.

But this is the story I have to tell now, a story that bears witness to events that are forming the legacy of America at the dawn of the twenty-first century. I saw much hope, beauty, and grace in Iraq, along with much—too much—that was irrational, brutal, and obscene. I learned some painful lessons: our great nation and its leaders are indeed fallible; good intentions are often not enough; words like "democracy" and "freedom" roll easily off the tongue, but land on the ground of the Middle East with unpredictable results. I still support the war, but I'm more sober in my views than I was that first morning when I stood on the Iraqi border, looking at the pre-dawn desert landscape, eager, anxious, to participate in the most noble cause I could imagine.

— 2 —

City of Peace

In days of yore and in times
and tides long gone before . . .
The Arabian Nights

ICNIC TABLES. Of all the things I imagined I'd first see upon
entering Iraq, these were not on the list. Yet there they were,
just over the border, three or four sand-colored metal tables
and umbrellas, with additional groups every fifty miles or so down
the highway. Surrounding them were nothing but small craggy boulders and hard, dun-colored earth that stretched off to the horizon.
Who would eat here, I wondered, enveloped in clouds of exhaust
and dust, with temperatures heading this September day above 120
degrees?

A small detail, perhaps, but it fascinated me. Here was Iraq, a
nation with a reputation for brutal repression and violence, greeting
visitors with absurdly impractical picnic tables. Placed there by the
former regime, their purpose, no doubt, was to create a facade of

geniality. But surely *everyone* knew the nature of Saddam Hussein, I thought; no one was fooled. And why so many tables? Their redundancy deepened the cynicism of the masquerade, as if mocking the very idea of normalcy. Nothing had been normal in Saddam's Iraq, it seemed, not even the joy of picnicking. I felt a sad distress each time we passed these marooned emblems of civility, our Suburban rushing ninety miles an hour down Iraq Route 10.

This was the part of the trip I had dreaded most. Not knowing what to expect in Iraq, I'd spent many sleepless nights in New York worried by reports of thieves and carjackers on the six-hour drive from the Jordanian border to Baghdad. The danger was particularly acute in the so-called Sunni Triangle, the area west of Baghdad where most anti-American violence was taking place. There, towns like Ramadi, Khaldiya, and Fallujah had become centers of operation for highwaymen adept at using BMWs and Mercedes to force travelers off the road. The bandits—known in Iraqi parlance as "Ali Baba"—were particularly interested in media people, whose modern-day caravans yielded rich troves of passports, money, computers, satellite phones, and other valuable gear.

This is why traffic on Route 10 would periodically lurch to the right to allow speeding convoys of SUVs to barrel past, their payloads of journalists guarded by sunglassed security men. On a small budget, I could rely only on the caution and experience of Fahdi, whom I'd selected, qualifications unknown, from among numerous drivers gathered beside their vehicles on a dark Jordanian highway, waiting to take passengers on the six-hundred-mile trip to Baghdad. A thin, bony, chain-smoking young man with an exhausted look in his eyes, Fahdi had insisted on leaving Amman at 1:00 AM. The idea was to hit the Sunni Triangle no later than mid-day: it was never good to be on Iraqi highways past 2:00 PM, he explained, when the Ali Baba began to prowl. I felt no inclination to argue.

But now that I was on the road, my anxieties vanished. The well-paved, four-lane highway was cluttered with cars, eighteen-wheelers, orange-striped taxi cabs, SUVs, buses, and pick-up trucks loaded with precariously-balanced mountains of cargo. Men, women, children, hundreds of people were on the move into and out of Baghdad. Lulled by the uneventful miles, I dozed, wakening when Fahdi made an unexpected stop: a Bedouin shepherd was leading his flock of goats across the roadway, beside two American M-1 tanks parked back-to-back on the median.

Outside of Ramadi, the first major town in the Sunni Triangle, we pulled into a truck stop, a collection of broken-down food stalls, oily black gravel, and grease-splattered mechanics in olive green robes. An occasional Bradley Fighting Vehicle rumbled past. As we were drinking tea in this post-apocalyptic environment, a thin, silver-haired Iraqi man dressed in a blue and white striped dress shirt and black slacks approached us. The GMC in which he was driving had broken down, he explained in English. Could we give him and his family a lift into Baghdad? Of course, I replied.

The man, Mohammad, was a computer specialist who lived in Vienna with his Iraqi wife, Soasa, a painter with numerous gallery exhibitions to her credit. They were returning to their native country, he said, to participate in its reconstruction, and to show their two small boys, both of whom had been born in Austria, "the land they came from." This was interesting, I thought: the UN and every anti-war group on the planet had estimated that the invasion would cause around one million refugees; as far as I could see, Iraqis were pouring back *into* the country.

Even more encouraging, Mohammad was a staunch supporter of America and the liberation of Iraq. "Those peace activists who took to the streets were fools," he remarked, referring to the worldwide protests that took place before the invasion. "If they saw for five minutes what went on this country under Saddam, they would not have tried to stop the war."

As if to prove his point, he leaned forward from the back seat and pointed out my window. "We're on the outskirts of Fallujah," he noted. "See the greenery around us?" It was true: although I hadn't noticed before, I now saw on both sides of the highway bluish-green palm groves, hedges, shrubs and dark green grasslands. "This area should be desert, like everything else we've seen. But Saddam diverted irrigation waters from the Euphrates River in order to turn it into a new Garden of Eden for his supporters. But at the same time, he turned thousands of acres of fertile marshlands in southern Iraq into desert in order to punish the rebellious Shia. In this way," Mohammad concluded, settling back into his seat, "Saddam turned a wasteland into a paradise—and a paradise into a wasteland. He corrupted even the geography of Iraq."

Mohammad and Soasa were the first Iraqis I met. They were an intelligent and good-looking couple and—despite the black shawl that covered Soasa's hair—seemingly Westernized and bourgeois. Their two boys were well-behaved. I felt comfortable with them. Sure, Mohammad tended to hog the conversation, but that was probably because his language skills were better than his wife's. All in all, they didn't seem much different than Americans.

But I was naïve. Soasa, it turned out, spoke perfectly good English. When I mentioned that I was interested in her art and might contact her in Baghdad, Mohammad stiffened. "Contact *me*, you mean," he interjected. "You must make arrangements with me," adding, with an indignant smile, "I am an old-fashioned Iraqi man." Embarrassed, I apologized for my gaffe and henceforth restricted my comments to Mohammad. He seemed pleased by my adjustment.

As Baghdad appeared on the horizon, I realized I had much to learn about Iraq.

—

The state of this city is greater than can be described.
But ah, what is she to what she was! Today we may
apply to her the saying of the lover: You are not you,
and the houses are not those I knew.

Ibn Jubayr, *The Travels of Ibn Jubayr*, 1184 AD

BAGHDAD IS AN UNLOVELY PLACE. Thirty-five years of war, economic sanctions, and terrorist attacks have filled the city with gutted buildings, pitted streets, and open fields filled with concrete debris and piles of garbage. The dominant color is brown: brown buildings, brown people, and brown skies, the last from the persistent smog that chokes the metropolis.

There is no real skyline or architectural focal point to this city of six million. Instead, it spreads from horizon to horizon in irregular clusters of habitations, as if the desert itself had coalesced into flinty structures of square-angled plaster and poured concrete. Many buildings, particularly former supermarkets, lie in ruins, victims of looters; others, such as the multi-storied Ministry of Communications, exhibit the awesome effects of cruise missile attacks: "surgical" holes in individual floors through which sunlight pours and pigeons fly.

The streets themselves are filled with trash, debris, and snarls of concertina wire. Cars either career down the roadway, heedless of pedestrians, or are frozen in traffic jams. Trees are few—there are no inner-city parks—leaving the avenues exposed to the merciless sunlight that seems to penetrate every niche. The heat can reach

145 degrees in August. The smell during these times is a throat-rasping combination of automobile exhaust and rotting garbage. In the rainy months of January and February, sewage facilities back up, creating muddy sidewalks periodically flooded by stagnant, oil-streaked water. During this time, a low, dense fog clings to the streets and outlying areas, casting a turbid gloom over the city. Car bombs detonate by day; gunshots crackle by night. Murders, kidnappings, robberies, carjackings, and other criminal activities occur with alarming frequency.

When I was there, the only remotely secure part of the city was the "Green Zone," the heavily fortified encampment that comprised the headquarters of the CPA. (Now called the "International Zone," the area contains the U.S. Embassy.) Only rarely did CPA people venture past the armed guards, concrete barriers, and barbed wire into the chaos and violence of the city proper. Through its long history, Baghdad has had numerous appellations, from the Round City to the Dome of Islam. Befitting the city's current condition and their own penchant for security jargon, Americans have given Baghdad a new name.

The Red Zone.

A crossroads city with no natural defenses, Baghdad's history has not been easy. The city was founded in 762 AD by Abu Ja'far al-Mansour, who sought to establish a new seat of government for his caliphate. The Abbasid monarch chose a fertile and relatively mosquito-free site on the west bank of the Tigris River, where caravans traveling the Khorasan road often met. He designed the city as a double-walled circular fort, some two miles in circumference, which he optimistically dubbed *Madinat al-Salaam*, or City of Peace.

Baghdad peaked early, hitting its golden age during the reign of the great Caliph Haroun al-Rashid (786-809). A patron of the arts and a reoccurring character in *The Arabian Nights* (many of

whose stories take place in Baghdad), al-Rashid oversaw what was
then the greatest city in the world, the New York of its time, boast-
ing wealth, religious piety, architectural wonders, and according to
some writers, ample opportunities for sin. Baghdad's decline began
almost immediately after his reign. In 813, al-Rashid's son Mamun
besieged the City of Peace, the first in an endless series of military
onslaughts that included multiple sackings by the Mongols (1258,
1393, and 1401) and the Ottoman Turks (1534 and 1638), and ending
with the Anglo-American invasion in 2003.

As far back as the twelfth century, the great Moorish traveler, Ibn
Jubayr, wrote that Baghdad "is like an effaced ruin, a remain washed
out, or the statue of a ghost. It has not beauty that attracts the eye,
or calls to him who is restless to depart to neglect his business and
to gaze." With few exceptions, a twenty-first century traveler might
say the same.

Fortunately, one of those exceptions is the south-central district
of Karada. Fortunately, I say, because that is where my hotel, the
Orient Palace, is located, and where I later rented an apartment on
Saddoun Street, a major thoroughfare. Situated on a tongue-shaped
spit of land created by a switchback of the Tigris River, Karada
is washed by river-borne breezes that carry with them the sweet,
perfume-like smell of the ancient waters. An ecumenical quarter of
the city, it is home to Armenians, Assyrians, and Chaldeans, not to
mention Arabs, Kurds, Sunnis, and Shia, making the neighborhood
a rare example—and model—of Iraqi integration.

By day, Baghdad is a tumultuous mass of crowded roadways
and bustling stores. Indeed, one of my greatest surprises in arriving in Baghdad was the intensity of street life. Karada, in particular,
teems with markets, small hotels, internet cafés, and appliance stores
selling everything from televisions to washing machines to electric
generators. Especially popular are satellite dishes, stacks of which

splay out across the sidewalks, blocking pedestrian traffic. In the early evening, the streets gleam with neon signs—PANASONIC, AIWA, LG—and the bright lights of restaurants such as the White Palace, Candles, and Il Paese (an Italian eatery serving a respectable cheese pizza). Here, too, you can find the necessities of life: newsstands, money exchanges, grocery stores, pharmacies, and a row of Christian-run liquor stores doing a brisk business despite the lengthening shadow of Islamic fundamentalism.

By night, however, the situation changes. Given the lack of electricity, a still-rampant crime rate, and an early morning curfew, no one with any legitimate interests goes out after dark, leaving the streets deserted save for American military vehicles and wandering packs of feral dogs.

The magic hour is dusk, when the softness of the light disguises Baghdad's wounds. I would leave the Orient Palace and wander through the neighborhood's upscale environs, angling toward the brightly lit shopping district of Karada Dakhil ("Inner" Karada) to the southwest. The surroundings were interesting—everything in Baghdad is interesting—but somewhat tawdry and sad. From the late 1950s into the 1970s, Baghdad underwent a process of modernization, during which much of the picturesque "old" city, with its narrow paths and decrepit brick houses, was replaced with straight, wide, automobile-friendly roadways. At the same time, Baghdad's nouveaux-riches demanded homes with such Western touches as carports, sleek facades, and flat roofs. Often combined with incongruous affectations like extravagant windows, mirrored tiles, and overly ornate gate decorations, their houses had an awkward Palm Springs-meets-Middle-Eastern-oil-money look.

But sprinkled amidst these gaudy structures, you can still find remnants of former times: small two-story houses with latticework balconies and grated windows, flanked by weather-beaten shutters and stone carvings worn with age. Here, memories of the proverbial "Moslem quarter" and its sealed homes and labyrinthine alleyways linger on. In the winter, when the sun sets earlier, you wind along cobblestone lanes, the cries of the muezzins sounding from different directions, people rushing home before the light fades entirely, a rusting iron gate pushed open to reveal a small inner courtyard and wooden door lit by a garish fluorescent tube before closing again, sealing off the mystery of its occupants forever. At this hour, I especially liked to walk to a mosque in Karada Dakhil whose facade gleamed with floral tiles and whose twin sky-blue minarets were linked by strings of brilliant white lights. There, in this setting, half majestic Islam, half Arabian Nights, I would discuss the intricacies of Shia theology with Hasam, a stocky, muscular man who stood at the front gate, guarding worshipers with a Kalashnikov rifle.

—

He echoed our unpopularity because
we had allowed our unpopularity
to be the fashionable cry.

Freya Stark, *Baghdad Sketches*, 1927

IF BY SOME WHIM OF ALLAH you could visit the City of Peace but meet only one person, I would nominate Qasim al-Septi, a handsome, loquacious, silver-haired artist, teacher, and father of three. Possessed of immense charisma—and political survival skills to match—Qasim runs the Hewar (Dialogue) Gallery, a combination art space, teahouse, and gossip nexus located in the Waziriya District northwest of the city center. It is without doubt the brightest spot in Baghdad's cultural life. If in *Casablanca*, "everyone goes to Rick's," in the Red Zone, everyone goes to Qasim's.

Here, within a backyard patio garden shaded by citrus and palm trees, poets, actors, and artists rub elbows with embassy officials, foreign journalists, ex-Baath party members, and former spies for Saddam's dreaded secret police, the *Mukhabarat*. (The unspoken rule regarding such people is unless they actively tortured or killed people, Iraqis forgive and try to forget.) Occasionally, guards from the nearby Turkish Embassy stroll through the grounds, machine guns dangling from their hands.

Qasim loves every bit of it. Hobbled by a clubfoot, the blue-jeans-wearing impresario limps around the gallery kissing visitors on the cheeks and calling everyone *habibi* (my love)—all the while issuing a stream of orders to factotums and fetch-it-men who scurry off to do his bidding. To entertain "special people"—foreign journalists and dignitaries—he grills fish caught in Tigris River to make mazgouf, a traditional Iraqi delicacy. His English is good, spoken in a high-pitched mellifluous voice. He is an expert in *hija'a*, the traditional art of composing spontaneous verses to lampoon an adversary, but I have never heard him practice it.

Ask Qasim his age, and he'll say, "I am ten thousand years old. I am Mesopotamian, Assyrian, Jewish, Islamic, and Christian." (He was born in Baghdad in 1953.) Ask him about his passion in life and he'll reply, "Like the man who loves dice and drink, I love art." While Qasim does respectable abstract paintings and mixed-media work involving the covers of discarded books whose pages he first tears out (a superb metaphor for Iraq, I think: a battered text violently shorn of content), his real art is the oasis of comity and secular culture he created at the Hewar.

The gallery's roots go back twenty years. Graduating from Baghdad's Academy of Fine Art in 1981, Qasim was unable to serve in the Iraqi army because of his deformed foot. Instead, he stayed back while friends marched off to the carnage of the 1980-1988 Iran-

Iraq War, and saw those who returned home shattered in mind and body. "I wanted to do something for them," he told me one stifling afternoon, as we sat in the gallery lunching on chunks of bread and lamb dipped into a spice-rich tomato sauce. "I wanted to create a gallery with beautiful art that could lead my friends to gardens, not graves." He tried to establish such a place in 1990, "but the first Gulf War ended that dream."

Qasim's narrative grew a little vague at this point, having something to do with a former art school teacher who became an official in the *Mukhabarat*, and a "rich man" who in 1992 mysteriously gave him $30,000 to buy the house, built in the 1940s for Iraq's Minister of Defense, in which he lives and works. I took this circumspection to mean that the artist had made his accommodations with the Baath Party, as so many Iraqis of his generation had to do, and I didn't press the issue. In any case, with the Hewar, Qasim found his métier. "From 1992 to 2003, we put on 105 exhibitions," he recounted. "We had no problems with the regime, because we showed 'pure' art, not propaganda. Those were good years, even with the economic embargo."

Because of the economic embargo, Qasim should say. As I was surprised to discover, the final decade of Saddam's rule was a golden age for Baghdadi culture. The sanctions placed on Iraq in the wake of Gulf War I may have crippled the overall economy, but they provided the city's artists with a stream of patrons in the form of embassy officials, U.N. personnel, and NGO workers, who flooded the country during this period. At the same time, the Baath Party, always eager to cultivate artistic expressions of *turath*, or "heritage," offered artists plenty of awards and competitions, cushy teaching jobs, and lucrative portrait commissions of Uncle Saddam.

As a sculptor in his fifties, Abdul Jabar, declaimed to me one day at the Hewar, "I'm proud I did portraits of Saddam! We all did,

I'm not going to lie about it! And we lived well on what he paid us, too!" Qasim also did at least one portrait of the tyrant, crowing that he "took friends out to dinners for weeks on the money."

But while Baghdad's older artists made their accommodations with Saddam, their art atrophied. The combination of government largesse and repression, in addition to non-critical acceptance by foreigners, had reduced most Iraqi art to Baath Party propaganda, bland abstraction, and third-rate sculpture, with little sense of personal identity. "For years Saddam told us we represented Arabs and Muslims," a young painter, Ahmed al-Safi told me. "Gradually, we lost an idea of who we were as Iraqis."

But not Qasim, it seems. "Our nation is a mosaic of Assyrian, Babylonian, and Sumerian culture. It has a noble soul, filled with suffering and love of beauty." I noticed he didn't add "Islam" to his description of *turath*, nor did he give much shrift to religious piety. Qasim is an old-fashioned secular nationalist. By the same token, though, he places little value in the New York-style contemporary art one finds in so many Baghdad galleries. "American art has no roots," he remarked. "Artists there just play on the surface and concern themselves mostly with technique. They have no feeling or soul."

You hear this a lot in Iraq, criticism of the shallowness of America, as opposed to the profound depth of the Land Between the Rivers. It's no use trying—as I did, many times—to suggest that the very newness of America, its lack of psychological or historical baggage, is its great source of strength; no, we are barbarians, fueled by technology, money, and greed. I once ran across an interview with Qasim (on the website of the North American Mennonite and Brethren in Christ Churches) in which he bitterly denounced Bush as the "first thief in the world" and seemed to take heart in the casualties suffered by American troops (thereby proving that "Iraq is not easy"). On the website of the American Friends Service

Committee, a Quaker organization, he reflected on the failure of American soldiers to stop the looting of Iraqi museums: "I think America wants to cancel the roots of Iraqi art and culture to make way for globalization."

Qasim never expressed such sentiments to me personally. Instead, he simply said that "life was much better before the Americans. Before, we had peace, art, life—now, we have nothing. No security, no electricity, nothing." Another time, he complained that "America has no sense of justice," a rare frown clouding his smooth, vulpine face. "She is always against the Arab. You liberated us, fine. Now, go home."

Still, for all his crypto-Baathism and Saddamite leanings, it was impossible to dislike the sly rogue. His cheer was infectious, his hospitality impeccable, and I knew that if I ran into trouble I could always turn to him for help—no small thing in Baghdad. Besides, Qasim once made a large, and perhaps unguarded, concession to me while we discussed the invasion and liberation of Iraq. "Yes, it is true. Sometimes I look at my boy and think of his future." Then, in a pensive tone, he added, "And I say to myself, 'Maybe God has truly worked His will through the United States of America.'"

—

IF THE HEWAR GALLERY offered me one perspective of life in post-invasion Baghdad, I discovered another in the dingy, crowded, yet somehow charming Shahbandar Café, one of the oldest, and perhaps best known, of the city's innumerable "coffee" houses (they only serve tea). But this perspective was quite different from the anti-American, soft-on-Saddam attitude that pervaded Qasim's place.

There is actually a sort of ritual involved in going to Shahbandar,

named after the a tenth century Iraqi-born poet. On Fridays, the
Muslim Sabbath day, you start at the top of Mutinabi Street (named
after yet another poet) and wander among the booksellers who for
decades have lined both sides of the narrow thoroughfare with their
offerings. You can find everything here—volumes in Arabic, Russian,
French, and, of course, English—spy novels, medical texts, technical
manuals from the 1970s, translated sermons by Ayatollah Khomeini,
back issues of *Maxim* magazine, political musings penned by Saddam himself and, not surprisingly perhaps, an inordinate number
of books about Hitler and Nazi Germany. Iraq has a proverb: "In
Cairo they write books, in Beirut they print books, and in Baghdad
they read books." Though decades of war and economic sanctions
has reduced Iraq's educated classes, judging by the numbers of Friday strollers packing Mutinabi Street, the appetite for the written
word is still strong. Being a bit of a bibliophile myself, I picked up
a number of tomes, among them a 1955 edition of Ameer Ali's 1889
A Short History of the Saracens, the autobiography of Harry St. John
Philby, the man who sold the West out to Wahabbism, Freya Stark's
1927 *Baghdad Sketches*, and British General Aylmer Haldane's 1922
memoir, *The Insurrection in Mesopotamia*.

At the end of the street, where the aging buildings give way to
Baghdad's old covered bazaar and a line of ochre-colored buildings—once the seat of Ottoman governance in Iraq, now a madrasa,
or Islamic school—you find a low, shabby awning and entranceway leading to a high-ceilinged room, the Shahbandar. Here, surrounded by faded photographs of pre-Saddam Baghdad and framed
Koranic inscriptions, middle-aged men sit on narrow benches and
drink lemon tea from small glasses called *stiikaan*, while smoking
aromatic tobacco from water-pipes, or *narghiles*. The atmosphere
between these turquoise walls seems unchanged since the days of

Abdul Karim Qasim, the army officer who ruled Iraq from 1958 to 1963, before being deposed by the Baath Party and who today is something of a folk hero in Iraq.

Arab intellectuals and artists, foreign correspondents, self-described members of the "resistance," NGO personnel, and anti-war activists—the Shahbandar was filled with a varied crowd whose tumultuous chatter was underscored by the constant bubbling of *narghiles.* The crowd was mostly male, I should add: the only women you saw in the café were Western journalists, often in *hejab*, dropping by to glean some local color to enliven their reports.

One of the most colorful characters, and a Friday afternoon fixture at the café, was a tall, burly Iraqi man in his late twenties, whose onyx eyes and thick black beard made him resemble Mullah Omar—or would have, if not for his contagious smile. His name was Esam Pasha Azizawy—the Pasha, he maintained, is an honorific title deriving from his grandfather, Nuri Said, who once served as Prime Minister of Iraq before being overthrown by General Qasim in the 1958 revolution.

Striking, gregarious, fluent in English, Spanish, and French, with a working knowledge of Russian and German, Esam trolled the crowd at the Shahbandar, chatting up Western journalists—especially the ladies—who were only too happy, as I was, to interview someone able to speak them in their native language. Along with his linguistic skills, Esam is also a self-taught artist (he painted the first Coalition-funded mural in Baghdad, a thirteen-foot depiction of traditional Iraqi images that replaced a portrait of Saddam Hussein) and a national judo champion. He also served for several months in the highly dangerous position of translator for the U.S. military.

He was but one of several young, talented, Westernized artists I met at the Shahbandar. Others included Haider Wady, a fashion-model-handsome sculptor who hides his long pony-tail beneath a *khaffiya*-like head scarf to escape harassment by Iraqi thugs; painter Mohammad Rassim, a gentle bear of man with an abiding interest in Iraq's Sumerian past and a deep love for children, for whom he designs books and magazines; and Ahmed al-Safi, an easy-going, sloe-eyed southern Iraqi whose shamanistic paintings of stick-like figures set in desert landscapes are among the best work you'll find in Baghdad today.

To my initial surprise, these "Baghdad Bohemians," as I liked to call them, expressed remarkably pro-liberation, pro-American views. "We were afraid America *wouldn't* invade," Mohammad said. "We chose war to finish Saddam." Or, as Haider put it, "When I saw the statue of Saddam fall, I couldn't believe it—it was like a dream. We used to pray to live for five minutes without his regime, now we have the rest of our lives." Esam found U.S. soldiers very impressive. "They called me 'sir!'" he enthused. "Do you know what it's like for an Iraqi to hear someone in uniform called him 'sir'? They didn't even call each other that!"

But of all the Bohemians I met in Baghdad, the one who had the greatest impact on my view of Iraq and the Iraqi people was poet, engineer, and former Olympic chess master Naseer Flayih Hasan. A tall, solidly built forty-year-old with a thoughtful, melancholic air, Naseer offered haunting insights into his nation's soul—and what Saddam inflicted on it. If Qasim and the older artists at the Hewar spoke with ill-concealed nostalgia for the Baath Party days, Naseer limned for me the psychological darkness of that era.

"Our recent past has been so bleak, so alienating, we felt nothing but hopelessness, as if we were lost to history," he told me one Friday afternoon at the Shahbandar. "Our whole relationship to the world was as if an iron hand separated us from life."

One of Naseer's poems captures the despair and lost years of the Saddam generation.

Theft

When he woke up from his dream
He stood by the window;
The war was gazing at him.
When he returned from his sadness
....
....
He was forty.

Yet now there was hope, something Naseer and millions of other Iraqis could never have imagined only a few months before. "Just when you can't take it any more, and you think you're about to throw yourself off the balcony, something happens," he related. "You discover that life can actually smile. April ninth was like a second birthday to me. I couldn't believe the shadow of Saddam was removed from my soul. I wanted to run naked in the street with joy." As for the fedayeen and pro-Baathist attacks that were ramping up in the autumn of 2003, "We expected such violence against our society and infrastructure," the poet averred. "Now we are adjusting ourselves. We have a second battle, this time against the terrorists."

I don't want to put too fine a point on this. It wasn't that the Hewar formed a pocket of Baathist support while the Shahbandar was a stronghold of pro-liberation feeling: the two cultural centers were far too complicated for such reductions, and besides, I saw the same faces at both. It is fair to say, however, that among Baghdad's "cultural elite," the over-forty crowd tended to view the Saddam years more favorably than those under forty—especially those in their twenties and early thirties, who did not grow up in the orderly, prosperous 1960s and 1970s, but came of age after Saddam took complete control of the country in 1979 and initiated over two decades of war. Naseer once put it in stark terms for me: "For most of my life, I've seen only oppression, violence, and death."

But now he was seeing something else: hordes of foreigners, whose presence further shattered the "iron hand" that once separated them from life. How strange it was for these Iraqis: Once alienated from the world, unable to speak their minds without threat of imprisonment or worse, they now found themselves blinking in the floodlight of international attention. Major news organizations and independent freelancers alike were coming to *them*, eager—on the surface at least—to solicit *their* opinions and feelings, and glean knowledge about their lives and homeland. Their surprise and exhilaration about standing on a global stage was palpable. "We have no frontiers now, everything is possible!" Haider enthused. I felt fortunate to witness their happiness, even though it made the disappointments to follow all the more painful.

—

BUT WHAT OF IRAQ'S WORKING CLASS? What did they think? How did the fall of Saddam affect them? Fearful of forming my own "Green Zone"—where an echo chamber of like-minded friends and acquaintances would reinforce my opinions and observations about Iraq until they gained an illusion of objectivity—I knew I had to venture beyond this charming, if *louche*, circle of artist and intellectuals and try to see the situation through other eyes. And here, my lack of resources and connections served me well. Rather than thundering around town in the dreadnought-sized SUVs favored by high-profile journalists, I turned to the city's enormous fleet of taxicabs. After a hundred or more cab rides and nearly as many conversations with cab drivers, I learned more about Iraq's mercurial attitude toward America and American power than I could have ever imagined I would.

When I asked their opinion of the U.S., for example, many drivers smiled, brushed their palms together in a "good riddance" gesture and crowed, "Saddam gone! America good!" Others flashed the thumbs-up gesture and exclaimed, "Amrikiyya thank you!" One cabbie became so worked up over the liberation of his country, he exclaimed, "We love U.S.A., do you believe me? They bring us freedom! We need U.S.A.!" Worried, perhaps, that I was not American (I refrained from revealing my nationality unless directly asked), he added, "We also need Britain, Poland, Spain"—this was before Al Qaeda's Madrid attack induced the heirs of the Reconquista to flee Iraq—"even Turkey!"

Some cabbies, however, took a more temperate view of the U.S. "America not good, not bad," one driver mused, as if discussing the weather. "Right now good, because they want what we want. But in the future—?" Another told me, "Bush finish Saddam, good. Now, America, go home"—once again, the "Thanks, Yanks, now beat it," syndrome you heard everywhere in Iraq. Other drivers expressed qualified support for the presence of U.S. troops, but complained about the seemingly intractable crime and terrorism problem. "Iraqi people very tired. When will America bring peace?"

Occasionally, I met drivers who were straightforwardly anti-U.S. "America no good," one maintained. "We thought when American people come, we sleep safe in our homes. But no, Iraqi people very afraid. When I drive, my mother prays I have no troubles with thieves, fedayeen, the U.S. army." The more critical the hack, I found, the greater chance he was a Sunni Muslim. The Sunnis, as we know, were long favored by Saddam and stood to lose the most in a democratic Iraq. This fear of the future explained, in part, one Sunni's diatribe: "America good only for America, not Iraqi people. Where are their promises of security, jobs, peace? Where is freedom?" When I asked what in his mind constituted "freedom," he replied, "Good government respectful of Islam—not when people drink alcohol on the street or believe what they want or when women do want they want." I had the feeling that last possibility was what he really feared.

Who were these guys? They ranged from working-class Joes to teachers and other professionals forced by economic hardship to drive for a living. They worked twelve-hour shifts, making around $7.50 to $8.00 a day—a "good" amount, one driver told me. Fares were cheap: to travel the three miles from my hotel to Coalition headquarters, I offered eight thousand dinars, or between $2 and $3 (depending on the dinar's strength), a fare some hacks refused, claiming it was too much. (Fortunately, gas, which was subsidized by the Coalition, was also inexpensive, costing less than 5 cents a gallon.) As in most Arab countries, in Iraq single passengers ride in the front seat—to sit in the back, Western-style, implies, or so I was told, that you are subservient to the driver, a gaffe abhorrent to the Arab sense of egalitarianism and hospitality.

But perhaps the most amazing aspect of Baghdad's cabbies were the variety and condition of the cars they drove. They were everywhere, these groaning, rattling, overheating Volkswagen Passats, Chevy Malibus, and Nissan Sunny Super Saloons, each a marvel of mechanical persistence in the face of ten years of crippling sanctions. Windows failed to open, upholstery was torn or nonexistent, shocks were gone, while exhaust fumes seeped into the vehicle's interior, adding another nuance to Baghdad's palette of odors. The windshields of many cabs were spider-webbed with cracks and bul-

let holes from the war and subsequent looting: in one car, you could
actually trace the trajectory of projectiles as they pierced the front
window and, just missing the driver, burrowed into the upholstery
of the backseat. ("Allah was with me that day," the driver mused.)
By the same token, even as newer cabs increasingly appeared on
Baghdad streets, many drivers—and their fares, as well—preferred
the broken-down jalopies, believing they made less attractive targets
for Ali Baba.

What drivers in new or old cars couldn't escape, however, was
the nightmarish traffic of Baghdad. All major cities are traffic head-
aches, of course, and those in the Third World most of all. But
Baghdad's *deyhams* were in a class by themselves. Imagine being
tied up in knot of trucks, automobiles, buses, donkey carts, and
the occasional patrol of American Humvees manned by overheated
and ill-tempered soldiers, your own car an unairconditioned, car-
bon monoxide-stinking wreck whose windows won't open in temperatures climbing to 125 degrees. Imagine, too, total disregard for
traffic laws: cars forcing themselves down the wrong sides of streets,
over cement medians, down the opposite side of freeway on-ramps,
ignoring red lights and the shouts of cops or civilian volunteers attempting to untangle the mess. Many times I spent thirty minutes
or more creeping inch by inch through an intersection, only to hit
a similar mess of blasting horns, irate drivers, and soaring heat a
few blocks later. *Y'allah*, I'd often hear my driver mutter—which,
loosely translated, means, "Oh my God . . . "

These *deyhams* had many causes. One was the lack of traffic
cops. Another was the lack of electricity, leaving many traffic signals
inoperative (not that Iraqi drivers would have heeded them anyway).
But a third reason was the surfeit of cars congesting the streets. As
people flooded back into Iraq, so did vehicles from such export hubs
as Jordan and Dubai. Everywhere you looked on the streets, you saw

the English designation "Export" on license plates; on Route 10 from Jordan, tractor trailers roared by laden with sparkling new BMWS, Mercedes or Chevy Caprice Classics. There was clearly money in the City of Peace, and people were spending it—often, it seemed, on automobiles.

Given the deplorable conditions under which Baghdad's cabbies worked, I was surprised at how generally upbeat they were about their post-liberation lives. And indeed, some people thought I was being fooled. One older woman I met at the Hewar argued that "Iraqis always favor whoever's in power. If Saddam ever came back, the taxi drivers would all sing, 'Oh, Father Saddam, we love you.'" Perhaps. Still, how would she explain this cab ride I had in October, the most memorable of all I experienced in Iraq?

The cabbie was an oversized, genial fellow, with thick black hair and a scraggly beard, who picked me up on al-Rashid Street, his Super Saloon festooned with strips of artificial flowers and images of the Shia Muslim icons Hussein and Ali. When I asked for his opinion of America, he shouted, "U.S. good! U.S. fantastic!" After I revealed my nationality, he cried, "I pray every night for President Boosh! God bless George Boosh!"

Over the tape-recorded sermons of a Shia cleric booming from his car stereo, my driver told me how in May, he took his two children on a pilgrimage to the holy cities of Karbala and Najaf, something he couldn't do under the regime of Shia-hating Saddam. "I was so happy, my family was happy!" His comments then began tumbling out one after another. First, he criticized the Arab media: "Al-Jazeera and Al-Arabia TV only say bad things about U.S., only talk about bombs and killing Americans. Never about how things are growing in Iraq, getting better." Then he turned to the entire Arab world: "They fear Iraq will become a democracy, then every country will want to become democratic, and the rulers will be in trouble: they only want people with one thought, one mind." As for Iraq's future, my driver had great optimism, provided that the new constitution including "religious freedom for everyone—Muslim, Christian, Jew. Mohammad said, 'Let there be no forcing of religion.' Mohammad said we are all brothers and to kill a man is to kill your brother."

By time I reached the Orient Palace, I had a Koran-sized lump in my throat. I peeled off a wad of dinars, but the cabbie refused to take it. After I implored him to accept payment, he took the bills, slipped them into his shirt pocket, then took them out and handed them back to me. "You give me money, now I give it back to you—a gift to my friend from America." Then, turning up the volume on the imam's sermon, he gave me a big gap-toothed smile and drove off in a cloud of exhaust. Watching him disappear into traffic, I had tears in my eyes, and they weren't from the Baghdad smog.

—

AMIABLE BOHEMIANS and affable cab drivers aside, the Red Zone remained a very dangerous place.

On a sweltering day in mid-October, I accompanied soldiers from the Florida National Guard as they laid down orange traffic cones and concertina wire to divert traffic from the Turkish Embassy, located in Waziriya. As the patrol commander, Captain Gil Petruska of Pensacola, Florida, explained, military intelligence believed that terrorists had targeted the embassy for attack. (Turkey was contemplating sending ten thousand troops to support the Coalition, a move that most Iraqis condemned.) This concerned me, for the Hewar lay directly behind the embassy and could suffer serious damage in an explosion. When I told Qasim about the threat, he simply shrugged. *Insha'allah*—whatever God wills.

Two days later, I dropped into the Hewar again, noticing as I went past the Turkish Embassy that construction crews had replaced the concertina wire with concrete barricades, protecting the Turks, but creating in the process a ferocious *deyham*. About three that afternoon, preparing to leave after chatting with Qasim, I debated whether I should stop by for a closer look at the barricades and to see if Captain Petruska was still around, or return to the Orient Palace to finish an article I was writing. Since I was meeting a Canadian peace activist for coffee later that evening, I decided work had to come first and caught a cab for the hotel.

I didn't hear the blast that erupted fifteen minutes later. Exploding directly in front of the Turkish Embassy, the suicide car bomber killed one passerby and injured thirteen others. (The damage would have been worse, but, as CPA authorities estimated, the concrete barricades absorbed ninety percent of the explosion.) In fact, I didn't know it had occurred until around 8:00 that night, when, in the midst of debating the morality of the invasion of Iraq with the Canadian, he mentioned the bombing. As it was too late to travel to Waziriya, I spent a sleepless night in the Orient Palace, imagining what might have happened to the Hewar and its occupants.

As early as possible the next morning, I took a cab over to the gallery. The street in front of it was crowded with Humvees, Bradleys, and tense American soldiers. Threading through multiple checkpoints, I came across Qasim surveying the damage to his house. He had just been serving tea to the French cultural attaché, he told me, when the bomb exploded, blowing out some windows in the gallery and sending car parts and burning palm fronds over the embassy building into the backyard garden. The bomber's leg had flown over the embassy building and landed beside the house.

After doing a few time computations, I realized that had I made the other choice the previous afternoon—had I gone over to inspect the barricades—I probably would have been in the radius of the explosion. That didn't really faze me, though: with bombs going off on a regular basis, you realize that a miss is as good as a mile. What did strike me, however, was the Iraqi reaction to the blast. Everyone in the Hewar's garden was talking about it; many seemed amused. I asked Qasim for a translation. It seems they were chuckling at a rumor that Al-Jazeera had shown a GI stepping on the bomber's blown-off face, which was laying like a discarded mask on the street. Someone else was telling a story about a poor man who had lost a shoe and had stopped behind the Turkish Embassy to pray for a replacement—when suddenly, there came a great clap of thunder and a shoe plummeted from heaven, the owner's leg still attached.

The humor shocked me. I couldn't imagine making jokes at such a horrific event, but within a few moments, I was laughing, too. The whole scenario, from the real fact of someone blowing themselves up in a car to the imaginary tale of the falling shoe, seemed the blackest kind of absurdity. Such things just didn't—couldn't—happen, I kept thinking, trying to suppress my laughter. It was my first inkling that history would not unfold in Iraq in the *reasonable* manner we'd expected—that peace and democracy would not rise phoenix-like from the ashes of the old regime. For the situation in Iraq was sliding in the one direction capable of defeating American power and idealism. It was becoming *unreasonable*.

"We have to laugh about our lives now or we'll go mad," Qasim said.

I was beginning to understand.

An Image of Hadeel

Perhaps the most evil aspect of religious terrorism
is that it aims to destroy moral distinctions themselves.
Its goal is to confuse not only its sympathizers,
but also those who seek to fight it.

Jessica Stern

On the day when crime dons the apparel
of innocence—through a curious transposition
of our times—it is innocence that is
called to justify itself.

Albert Camus, *The Rebel*

ONE DRIZZLY DAY IN LATE JANUARY, I dropped by the Green
Zone to visit the brother of a high school friend, now a
colonel in the U. S. Marine Corps. Jack had been stationed
in the city since December, overseeing a high-level office of the CPA.
A former fighter pilot, he now found himself shuffling papers and

attending meetings (many with CPA administrator Paul Bremer), experiencing all the frustrations of bureaucrats around the world. But *his* frustrations involved the fate of twenty-five million Iraqis and a major front of the war against Islamic terrorism. I was intrigued by his work, but I restrained myself: the CPA had warned its people not to discuss matters with journalists, and this included freelancers from northern California, where Jack and I grew up.

Instead, the colonel toured me around the "GZ." A fortified city-within-a-city on the banks of the Tigris in central Baghdad, the area that winter contained the offices of the Iraqi Governing Council, the Supreme Court, the Convention Center, and U.S. troop barracks. But its most notable attractions were Saddam's two presidential palaces, which the CPA had appropriated for its headquarters. With their cavernous banquet halls, gilded chandeliers and gaudily-painted rooms the size of basketball courts, these despotic citadels were at once grandiose, kitsch-ridden, and despicable—much like their former resident. In one gargantuan chamber, for example, a large painting of Jerusalem's Dome of the Rock faced a mural depicting Iraqi Scud missiles soaring heavenward, a perfect rendition of the tyrant's failed dream of becoming a modern-day Salah-ad-Din. That this room now housed American soldiers, their bunks draped with military-issue socks and underwear, seemed a delicious irony.

But what really caught my attention was not Saddam's delusions of power, nor the hum and buzz of bureaucrats involved in similar, if more benign, fantasies of controlling Iraq, but a photograph taped to a wall. The photo—actually a color xerox—showed a pretty, rather plump, reddish-haired Iraqi woman smiling at the camera, a Santa Claus cap perched atop her head. Her name, according to an inscription printed beneath her image, was Hadeel; she had served the CPA as a translator. At the time of the photograph, the twenty-nine-year-old had just gotten engaged, the nuptials set for mid-February. Caught in an unguarded moment of laughter, hair mussed, eyes gleaming, the silly mirth of an office Christmas party behind her, Hadeel seemed like any young woman the world over who was anticipating marriage, children, and a happy future growing old with her husband.

But Hadeel was dead. Three weeks after the party, a flatbed truck carrying a thousand pounds of plastic explosives and several 155-mm. artillery shells exploded in traffic outside the "Assassins' Gate" entrance to the Green Zone. Trapped inside the car as she waited to enter for work, Hadeel burned to death. Twenty-seven Iraqis and two Americans died along with her, making it one of the worst suicide bombings of the war.

"Hadeel's family wouldn't let any of us attend the funeral," Jack said. "They felt it might be dangerous if people discovered their daughter worked for the Americans."

Shocked into a kind of numbed fascination, I stared at the photocopy, the layers of tragedy unraveling before me. Innocence slain, youth destroyed—these are difficult to accept anywhere, at any time. More painful yet was the realization that in cooperating with the CPA, Hadeel had entrusted her safety to the United States of America—and it had failed her.

But worse—to my mind, at least (Hadeel, of course, was beyond caring about these distinctions)—was that terrorists had taken her life. It made the meaninglessness of her death, and her image before me, more bitter to contemplate. I asked myself the same questions that had troubled me after 9-11, that torment anyone who witnesses, or has lost loved ones in, a terrorist attack: Why? For what purpose? Who will answer for this crime? Nor was it just Hadeel I thought of. Happy, enthusiastic, ignorant of the fate that would soon claim her, she could have been anyone killed by terrorists—a stockbroker in the World Trade Center, a bus rider in Tel Aviv, one of hundreds of Iraqis killed by nihilistic men who, by their own admission, love death more than their victims love life.

Muttering "What a shame," or something equally banal, I forced myself to look away from the simple memorial. But I knew I'd never forget it—not Hadeel's face, nor the presence that seemed to have occupied the already-fading image of her smile. For I'd felt that presence before, in the photocopies plastered all over Manhattan in the days after 9-11—those same washed-out colors, the same mundane, non-heroic appearance of people whose faces represented an atrocity beyond all imagining. And I was reminded once again of all that had happened that day. Death without purpose, without necessity, without limit, was here, too. Saddam was gone, but the evil that had characterized his regime was not. Rather, it had taken a new form, rooting itself in the very heart of this land, supplanting the dictator as the new ruler—and occupier—of Iraq.

⸺

I HAD HEARD THE EXPLOSION that killed Hadeel. As I stepped into the shower on the morning of January 18th, a dull thump echoed across Baghdad. Even then, I wasn't sure how far away the blast had occurred, or if it had been a blast at all—perhaps I'd mistaken the noise of a door slamming shut in the hallway of the Orient Palace. A terrorist attack is like that. Bombs erupt so suddenly, so unexpectedly, and are such brutal transgressions of daily life, that until you grow accustomed to their presence—and God help the land in which you do—the mind has difficulty placing them in a proper context. You hope for another explanation: nearby workmen, a traffic accident, cargo falling off the back of a truck—something, at all costs, *reasonable*.

Even when a thick white haze enveloped my hotel, I still wasn't sure what had happened. BBC World News was not reporting an incident in downtown Baghdad; perhaps I had imagined the sound. Not until I met Steve Mumford at the hotel restaurant did I hear the news: an explosion had taken place at an entrance to CPA headquarters; casualties were high. Steve, by now an experienced embed "veteran," surmised that the haze was probably smoke and debris from the blast, drifting southwest from the Green Zone. I looked at the pall of ghostly white dust clinging to the windows of the Orient Palace—included in there, I realized, were atomized body parts.

Steve and I had planned to drop into CPA headquarters that very morning; because I had arrived in Baghdad the day before and needed to catch up on sleep, we got a late start. Another what-if: had we kept to our original schedule, we might have been caught in the explosion. If Hadeel, or any of the other twenty-nine innocents killed that morning had not kept to theirs, they would have missed it. The random, indiscriminate nature of bombings in the Red Zone plays havoc with the imagination, increasing their impact, their terror.

By the time we reached the Assassin's Gate, the fires from the burning cars and bodies had died out. Beyond a yellow strip of tape stretched across the road sat a Bradley manned by Tennessee National Guardsmen. Fifty yards beyond that lay a dozen or so vehicles twisted and smashed as if by a fist, and a blue and white city bus ripped apart by the blast. Roadblocks had halted traffic on both ends of the street, giving the devastation a peculiarly theatrical feel.

"We were the first on the scene," said a Guardsman, cautioning a group of women in abiyas to stand behind the tape. "There's nothing down there now but charred body parts." The bomb, he added, had been the most powerful he'd seen since the attack on the UN workers at the Canal Hotel in August. "This one left a crater in the ground half the size of a Humvee," he said. Steve asked if it had been a suicide bomber. "Oh yeah," the soldier confirmed, sunlight reflecting off his wrap-around sunglasses. "The guy's arm's still hanging out of the truck cab, along with part of his torso."

It seemed the *shaheed* had intended to ram his truck into the CPA compound, but had prematurely detonated the device in rush-hour traffic. A second car bomb had been defused further down the street, but the Guardsman wouldn't elaborate. As Steve took some photographs of the scene, I asked the soldier what he did in the States. He was a machinist from Nashville, he said. He'd been in Iraq for twelve months, had seven more to go, and couldn't wait to get home.

Steve and I crossed the street to an outdoor café. The day was surprisingly clear and warm for winter, with a soft breeze rising from the Tigris. Birds chittered in the eucalyptus trees, children played in the unexpectedly empty street, shopkeepers swept up glass from windows shattered by the explosion. Sipping tea in the pleasant sunlight—everything seemed so normal, like a Sunday afternoon in Greenwich Village—we looked down the road at the blast site. "Hard to believe, isn't it, that just a hour before . . . ?" I began, for no other reason that to disrupt the sense of reasonableness I found distressing. Of the kind of New England stock that considers it unnecessary to comment on the obvious, Steve aimed his camera at the Bradley and clicked the shutter. "Yeah," he said.

My more emotional, half-Armenian temperament couldn't let it go at that. I wanted to *feel* something, anything. Watching the body recovery teams, their faces wrapped in gauze, probe the wreckage of human remains, I wanted to experience anger, outrage. After all, right *there*, right in front of me, thirty-one people had died. Once

again, it was 9-11; once again, I was on the roof of my building wit-
nessing the obscene. There has to be an acknowledgement of such
atrocities that goes beyond mere mental registration and respectful solemnity, I thought. Some sliver of understanding or meaning
that we can wrest from the abyss. The answer was out there, just
beyond the threshold of reason, if only my soul were large enough,
broad enough, to encompass the unreasonable without shrinking
from fear. But try as I might, my attention kept turning towards
the beautiful day, the clouds drifting over Baghdad, various tasks I
needed to complete that afternoon . . .

Finally, abandoning the effort, I asked Steve if I could borrow
his satellite phone to call Lisa and tell her I was okay. That, at least,
I could do.

—

BUT THE IMAGE OF HADEEL STAYED WITH ME.

That evening, I went down to dine alone in Fifties, the restaurant of the Orient Palace. By chance, I found myself sitting next to
a group of three American anti-war activists (I'd met one the day
before), accompanied by an aging, white-haired man whom the
activists treated with unusual deference. I'd seen *him* earlier, too,
posing before a tripod-mounted video camera as he responded to
a reporter's questions.

"I've come to Baghdad to investigate disturbing reports of American human rights abuses," the man proclaimed, his tone suggesting
that Iraqis could sleep better now that he was on the scene. And
though I couldn't place him, his portentous manner—not to mention the presence of a reporter—made me think *celebrity*. Asking
around, I discovered he was the very famous Canadian folksinger
Bruce Cockburn. Ah.

Winter, 2004, was the time for what I came to think of as "pity tours" of Baghdad. The situation had briefly stabilized enough so that a flood of academics, documentary filmmakers, religious activists, rock stars, performance artists, and other compassionate souls felt safe enough to drop into the city for a short time and wring their hands over post-invasion conditions. My cynical Iraqi friends, accustomed to the initial wave of these do-gooders during the sanctions period of the 1990s, called them "The People of the Slogans," or the "'Oh My God!' Club"—the last moniker coined by Esam and Ahmed as a kind of running joke. As they told the story, they once witnessed an American activist in Baghdad, who, in the midst of an anti-embargo rally, turned to the TV cameras and cried—and at this point, the two Iraqis would imitate her voice before collapsing into laugher—"*Oh my God, what are we doing to the children?*"

For my part, I dreaded the "'Oh My God!' Club" and The People of the Slogans. They were everywhere, these *bien pensants*: NGO workers, European journalists, Mennonite pacifists, Canadians of every stripe—disparate groups united by their opposition to the invasion (and liberation) of Iraq, disdain for America and blind hatred for the Bush Administration. Together, they formed a self-righteous chorus that dripped with moral superiority and contempt for anyone unenlightened enough to believe in the war. And yet, their outrage seemed strangely selective: among the loudest to condemn the violence that the Anglo-American armies unleashed on Iraq, they maintained a near-total silence concerning the horrors of Saddam. Obsessed with the regrettable, but often unavoidable, civilian casualties caused by Coalition forces, they ignored the wholesale massacre of Iraqis by Islamic terrorists. One activist, for example, declared what the U.S. was doing in Iraq was "evil," and when I suggested she take a look at what Saddam had done the country, she said, "When are you going to get over that?" I tried to avoid such people.

But now, the crowd at Fifties made this impossible. To make matter worse, Cockburn (pronounced CO-burn) and his associates were critiquing the American "occupation" with the kind of supercilious glee typical of the anti-war crowd. Their focus was U.S. soldiers—more specifically, the GI tendency to wear heavy-duty Ray-Ban and Oakley sunglasses while on patrol. "Can you believe it?" they huffed. "Everyone knows that Arabs prize eye contact! How *stupid*, how culturally insensitive, how *American* can you get? And *these* are the people who want to bring democracy to the Middle East? *Get real . . .*"

Their conversation grated on my nerves, still raw from the terrorist attack that morning. It wasn't that the activists were mistaken: Iraqis often complained of the imperious effect sunglasses imparted to their American "liberators." No, it was more the fatuous tone and wrong-end-of-the-telescope view of the situation in Iraq. Compared to what happened at the Assassin's Gate, ridiculing soldiers' eyewear seemed trivial, picayune, offensive. Several times I considered wheeling about and asking the group if they'd spent equal energy condemning the terrorists. However, I restrained myself. Tendentious is bad enough; self-righteousness even worse. Besides, such an outburst would no doubt oblige me to move my seat and Fifties was packed. If nothing else, hunger counseled discretion.

Still, the encounter caused me to wonder about Mr. Cockburn (Canadian pop culture is not my strong suit). The next day, after completing email chores at a nearby internet café, I Googled the songster. To my surprise, I discovered a "Canadian folk legend," with twenty-five albums to his credit, an active touring schedule, and a deep and highly-publicized commitment to saving the world. His website carried his musings on a full panoply of issues, helpfully arranged into such categories as "Environmental & Animal Rights," "Globalization," "World Bank," and "Indigenous People." He took particular pride in traveling to such out-of-the-way-but-neverthe-less in-the-news trouble spots as Mozambique, Cambodia, Mexico, and Central America. The troubadour's 1983 trip to Guatemalan refugee camps in Mexico especially moved him, it seemed, for it inspired one of his biggest hits, "If I had a Rocket Launcher," a *cri de coeur* that includes the lyrics:

> I want to raise every voice—at least I've got to try
> Every time I think about it water rises to my eyes
> Situation desperate, echoes of the victims cry
> If I had a rocket launcher . . . some son of a bitch would die.

As for his presence in Baghdad, another Cockburn-dedicated site announced that the singer had embarked on a "humanitarian fact-finding mission to Iraq" that would involve "visits to hospitals, schools, orphanages and encampments for those left homeless by the war." Other items on Cockburn's busy agenda included determin-ing "the extent of the destruction, poverty and destitution that has ensued in Iraq since March," in addition to the "tens of thousands of Iraqis who have been casualties from this war and the occupation." No mention was made of the "destruction, poverty, and destitu-tion" that ensued in Iraq under Saddam, the millions of Iraqis who were made "casualties" by his regime—nor the increasing number of dead and maimed in terrorist attacks. Bruce Cockburn, meet Michael Moore.

"The calamitous situation faced by the Iraqis is a human event that needs to be understood by all," the site quoted Mr. Rocket Launcher himself. Was it any less a "calamitous situation" before the invasion? I wondered. True, many people, myself included, gave little thought to Iraq until 9-11. But unlike Cockburn, we did not style ourselves international voices of conscience. We didn't write songs and maintain websites that indulged in selective outrage. And we could differentiate between American military blunders and nihilistic murder. I regretted not laying into Cockburn the night before.

Allah provides, as the Muslims are fond of saying—and sure enough, I received a second opportunity to challenge the Canadian songbird. That afternoon, I dropped by the Hewar to reacquaint myself with Qasim, whom I'd not seen since my first trip to Baghdad. I found the old goat in the rear of the gallery's garden, standing before a raised fire pit, in which several fished were gutted, filleted and fixed to small wooden poles. I knew that sight well: Qasim was fixing another mazgouf luncheon.

"*Habibi, habibi!*" he exclaimed, giving me two pecks on each cheek. (What a culture! The men are forbidden to touch women in public, yet think nothing of kissing the cheeks of other men, or even holding their hands.) He seemed genuinely happy to see me. "You are just in time to eat with us! You will come to our group of very special guests—" and with a flourish of his hand, he indicated Bruce Cockburn and his troupe, seated behind the fire pit.

"Ah, Mr. Cockburn, I'm a big fan of your work," I lied. Then—disingenuously—I asked, "What brings you to Baghdad?"

"I am here to investigate violations of Iraqi human rights by the American army," he intoned.

"They are troubling," I agreed.

"Yes, I find them very disturbing."

Cockburn had the full-throated, masculine-but-gentle voice of an old-fashioned folk singer. His close-cropped white hair and still-handsome but well-lined face gave him a patriarchal appearance, diminished only slightly by an earring dangling from his right lobe. There was something dry and ministerial about him (according to his website, he became a Christian in 1974), a kind of crusading religiosity that believed in the power of righteousness—*his* righteousness—to step in and with common sense and good will toward all, resolve the problems of the world.

"Since you're so interested in human rights violations," I queried, "you are, of course, investigating the legacy of Saddam and the current terrorist attacks on Iraq?"

Silence. Some stirring from the three people around Cockburn, as the singer's eyes registered a flicker of discomfort. He'd come for a pleasant *mazgouf* luncheon at the Hewar, not a political debate—especially with someone rude enough to pose the one question that the anti-war left cannot answer: *Why are you so silent about the human rights abuses of Saddam Hussein, and those of the Islamic terrorists?*

"We're only here for a week," said a woman photographer from Philadelphia, apparently documenting the Cockburn mission.

"A week? How can you get an accurate picture of Iraqi suffering in a week? Especially without investigating the crimes of Saddam or the terrorists?"

"Oh, we know all about that," she replied dismissively.

"How?" I persisted. "Have you talked to Saddam's victims, gone to human rights organizations, visited the mass graves?"

"No," the photographer conceded. Then, brightening, she conjured the magic words certain to establish her credentials with any right-thinking person. "But we have been to Guate*mah*la, Me*heek*o, Neek-ar-*ah*-gwah—"

"This is Iraq!" I exclaimed, on behalf of its twenty-five million non-Hispanic residents. "We're talking about Iraqis—"

"It's the same sort of government-sponsored terrorism."

"No, it's not! Not in degree and—if you consider the jihad-ists—not in intent!" I was about to blurt out something unfortunate, like *So the suffering of all brown-skinned peoples are the same?* when Qasim interposed himself, offering some anodyne statement that I took as my cue to cease and desist. I uttered something equally innocuous and, bidding everyone a good lunch, took my leave. It was just as well: the photographer, I understood, was not a rac-ist. She was expressing, in rather stark terms, the left's blinkered view when it comes to any abuses for which America or its allies are not directly responsible. And perhaps I might have stayed and, *pace* Qasim, ratcheted up the fray a notch had I remembered that Cockburn's "Rocket Launcher" contains the stanza:

> I don't believe in guarded borders and I don't believe in hate
> I don't believe in generals or their stinking torture states
> And when I talk with the survivors of things
>   too sickening to relate
> If I had a rocket launcher . . . I would retaliate

When it came to "stinking torture states" and survivors telling of "things too sickening to relate," what country fit the bill more than Iraq? Why didn't the singer take his metaphorical RPG and "retali-ate" against the nearest Baath Party sympathizer or foreign jihadist? Instead, if you go to Cockburn's website today, you'll find multiple denunciations of a war where American soldiers took real weapons and launched real strikes against real monsters who planned and executed mass murders. What's the difference? Why, to paraphrase Osama bin Laden, is Central American blood, blood—and Iraqi blood, water?

Talent, "commitment," and career longevity aside, Cockburn embodies what Vaclav Havel called the "false moral clarity" of many on the anti-war left. During my fall trip, I'd had a long conversation with a pacifist connected with the North American Mennonite and Brethren in Christ Churches. When I broached the subject of terrorism, he cut me off: "I refuse to use the word 'terrorist' to describe those who resist the U.S. occupation. Those are terms created by the U.S. government." When I tried to explain my support for the invasion of Iraq by citing a partial list of Saddam's crimes, the Christian humanitarian rotated his wrist in an impatient gesture, as if to say, *Yeah, yeah, we know all about that—now let's get to the point.* The point being for him, of course, the abominations produced by the real criminal, George Bush.

Nor was I alone in my exasperation at the left in Baghdad. Indeed, one of my biggest surprises was how the anti-American bias of foreigners bewildered and frustrated my Iraqi friends. "European reporters don't listen to how thankful we are to America for freeing us from Saddam," Esam complained. "They ask us questions, but they really only want us to make negative comments about the U.S. They're more interested in criticizing Bush than reporting on our joy in liberation."

"The French are shit," groused Haider. "I was in Syria on April ninth. Every TV network in the world was broadcasting images of Saddam's statue coming down in Firdousi Square. But do you know what France's TV5 was showing? An anti-American demonstration on [Baghdad's] Haifa Street." As for the Arab media, like my Shia cab driver, my artist friends view it as little more than an extension of the horrors they've lived under for years. "Al-Jazeera and Al-Arabia are part of the same dark kingdom of Saddam," Naseer stated.

My friends had other, more disturbing tales of journalistic bias. Haider, for example, told me of acting as the translator for a German TV crew working outside of Baghdad in the summer of 2003.

The crew, he recounted, filmed a village trash heap, then reported, over his protests, that the smoldering compost was once "fertile farmland destroyed by Coalition bombs." In September, he accompanied a French photographer as she wandered through Baghdad looking for a scene that would dramatize Iraqi suffering resulting from the war. Unable to find a suitable tableau, she paid an Iraqi woman to kneel in the debris of a partially demolished building and raise her arms to heaven as if imploring Allah to strike down the American infidels. "The photographer had me ask the woman to remove her wristwatch so she wouldn't look too wealthy," Haider related. Mohammad recalled watching an Al-Jazeera film crew pay men loitering on Saddoun Street to throw rocks and light a car on fire. "Within a few minutes, Al-Jazeera made their own 'anti-American' demonstration," he said.

But the annoyance these young Iraqis felt toward the international media paled before the contempt they expressed toward The People of the Slogans. They would snort derisively, recalling "human shields" who vanished as soon as war appeared imminent—or the anti-sanctions group Voices in the Wilderness, whose members, now that sanctions no longer existed, were desperate to find problems in Iraq they could use to justify their existence—or Euro-activists who tried to enlist them in pro-Palestinian causes (many Iraqis hate the Palestinians, largely because Saddam, in order to curry favor with Arab leaders, showered them with money, attention and cheap Baghdad housing).

"These people never did a thing for us," Haider remarked. "They were only looking for an excuse to hang out in Baghdad. If their organizations really wanted to help Iraqis, they should have saved the money they spent sending people over here and given it to the poor."

"Those in the peace camp are the real reactionaries, representing an old way of looking at the international politics," Naseer opined, as always choosing his words with a poet's precision. "With the invasion of Iraq, Bush has forced the world to reconsider the idea of 'national sovereignty' and non-interference in the internal affairs of nations. Why is it right that the world takes no action when millions are suffering and dying under a dictatorship?"

My Baghdad friends did not find all protestors in Iraq fatuous or morally obtuse, and indeed, some in the "peace camp" did try to be open-minded and less self-congratulatory about their "mission." God knows, Iraq could use a full panoply of dedicated liberal crusaders, from labor organizers to environmental activists to feminist agitators. And let's not forget the civil rights lawyers: I'll know that democracy has finally taken root in Iraq when I hear about the first noise harassment suit filed against a mosque for awakening neighbors too loudly with the morning call to prayer.

But far too many on the left seem to confuse anti-Americanism with supporting the Iraqi people. Take, for example, the Dutch activist whom Naseer still recalls with barely suppressed anger. Just after the fall of Saddam, he related, the woman predicted that the American "occupation" would soon prove as bad, or worse, than the old regime. When Naseer replied that it was unlikely the U.S. would execute thousands of Iraqis and bury them in mass graves, or drop poison gas on whole villages, the Hollander answered, "Perhaps you need to see beyond your suffering under Saddam to view America more objectively." The corners of Naseer's large mouth drew down as he told this story. "I was so shocked and outraged I didn't know what to do," he told me.

I once asked my poet friend why, if Saddam's fall was such a positive event, did so many people—Iraqis and non-Iraqis alike—view it so negatively? To my surprise, he responded with Shakespeare.

"Think of Hamlet. In the play, the young prince is haunted by his murdered father. At the same time, his mother Gertrude wants to forget the murder in order to accommodate herself to Claudius, the murderer, and encourages her son to do the same. But Hamlet can't forget, he won't forget—and the ghost of his father haunts him, preventing him from forgetting. It is the same with many of us. We walk every day over the buried skulls of Iraqis who were murdered by Saddam—we still see the ghosts of the slain and refuse to forget them. But there are many others, Gertrudes, who close their eyes to the dead and refuse to remember them."

"Frankly," he continued after a moment, "I am baffled at the attitude of the world toward our suffering. How can people accept for so long the crimes of a dictator, then rise up to try and stop a war begun to remove that dictator from power? Anti-war activists should examine their consciences." He paused, looking at his hands folded in his lap. "And as for those 'humanitarians' who always focus on American crimes—I can't help feeling that they are digging the same trench as Saddam Hussein."

—

NASEER'S COMMENTS crystallized a question that came to obsess me: Why are there so many "Gertrudes" in the world who excuse, ignore, or deliberately obfuscate the crimes of tyrants and terrorists? I mean in particular the Moores, the Cockburns, The People of the Slogans—those who purport to care so deeply about humanity. We see their demonstrations in the streets, crowd their propagandistic films, concede their criticisms when we see, for the thousandth time, the terrible images from Abu Ghraib. They do have their points; they are not always wrong. But why don't they also condemn the terrorists in Iraq—Al-Qaeda, Ansar al-Islam, Abu Musab al-Zarqawi,

ex-Baathists, and other Saddam supporters? I write this on a day
when Al-Qaeda-related suicide bombers killed some seventy-five
people in Basra, including twenty schoolchildren. Since then, we
have witnessed further terrorist attacks, assassinations, kidnappings, beheadings—why aren't our avatars of conscience expressing
outrage over these atrocities?

Gradually, over my months in Iraq, and afterwards, I evolved an
answer. It first occurred to me in October, 2003, when Naseer and I
visited the Iraqi National Organization for Human Rights located
in Baghdad's Mustansiriya district. "I deserted from the army and
spent five years hiding from Saddam Hussein," Asad al-Abady, the
association's deputy director, told us. His was one of the milder cases
of persecution we learned about that afternoon in the organization's
small, sparsely furnished headquarters. Founded in 1996 in Jordan,
the group is one of the oldest and largest of the country's numerous
human-rights associations. Its purpose is to collect information and
personal testimony on a range of issues, from the plight of Iraqi
refugees to instances of torture, rape, and execution. The idea is
eventually to present the findings to the new ministry of human
rights and the ministry of justice.

When I asked Abady about the number of case histories his
group had accumulated, he responded by holding up a single gray
folder. "This is a Baath party list, made in 1987, of thirty-three people
whom the regime arrested in 1980 and who were at that point still
awaiting trial. Sixteen years later, we have no idea what happened
to them." He dropped the folder into a cardboard box filled with
similar folders and slid it across the floor. "If you knew the contents
of this one box alone, you would faint."

Abady let Naseer and me digest that thought for a moment, then
he took us to a dusty room on the building's second floor. Here,
illuminated by sunlight filtering through a filthy window, stacks of

other Baath party documents lay toppled by their own weight and strewn about in unequal piles. I picked a few up at random and, with Naseer translating, read a compendium of state-sanctioned criminality: murder, rape, torture, mutilation, intimidation, exile, extortion.

"We have," Abady noted, "seventeen more rooms like this in our branches across the country."

Bringing us downstairs again, the deputy director introduced us to an elderly woman named Maha Fattah Karah. Shrouded in a black *abiya*, she settled into a chair in the director's office and in impassioned Arabic began her story. In the 1980s, her husband had fled to Iran to avoid arrest by Baathists, who claimed that he had been "unfaithful" to the regime. The party then confiscated Maha's home and belongings, throwing her into the street with her three children. A few years later, Baathists arrested her eldest son on the same charge of "unfaithfulness" and executed him—taking pains, Maha noted, to charge her for the price of the bullet. Hearing about his son's death, Maha's husband returned to Iraq, only to be seized by security agents, imprisoned for five years, and executed. He was buried in a graveyard, but the regime forbade Maha or her surviving children to visit it.

At this point, she became so emotional that Abady motioned me to stop questioning her. Rising from her chair, she stretched out her palms and began to plead. "I look to America," she sobbed. "I ask America to help me. I ask America not to forget me." Then, supported by two young men, she turned and left. (By horrible coincidence, at that precise moment, the thud of a car bomb rattled the windows—the explosion had taken place, I later found out, at the Baghdad Hotel a couple miles away. Eight people died.)

Abady's office was by now crowded with men. When I asked about mass graves, a murmur passed among them. According to one of them, a doctor (and co-founder of the organization) named Abdul Hadi Mashtaq, the group had discovered three huge burial sites just south of Baghdad, each containing between fourteen and seventeen thousand skeletons. "Iraqis knew generally where these places were, but not exactly," Mashtaq recalled. "Our investigators found them and alerted the U.S. authorities."

At this point, Fadel Abbas Kazen, a lawyer who was one of the first on the scene at a killing field near the village of Emam Baker bin Ali, sat forward. "Bones and skeletal remains lay just under the surface of the earth," he related. "I watched as people began digging up bodies, some of them with clothing still hanging from the bones. Some people had been killed before being buried, but some had been buried alive." In some cases death had come so unexpectedly that women who had gone to fetch water from a nearby river were buried with basins still clutched in their hands. "Behind a nearby police station, we found another grave containing fifteen more bodies," Fadel continued. In the following days, he oversaw the reburial of some 670 skeletons. "In a thousand years, there have been few tyrants like Saddam Hussein," the lawyer finished, fingering his prayer beads. There wasn't a sound in the room.

Was he exaggerating? Perhaps. But I remember another man who approached me on the campus of Baghdad University. "Excuse me," he began politely, taking my hand in his, "but I want to thank you Americans for coming across the seas to rid us of a monster the likes of which the world has not seen since Genghis Khan."

The mind rebels at this sort of talk. It isn't reasonable. It's strange. And yet Saddam's records speak for themselves: hundreds of thousands killed in his wars; thousands buried, sometimes alive, in mass graves; barbaric tortures involving acid baths, wood chippers, electricity, power tools, and ravenous dogs. Amnesty International reports that Baathist guards sliced chunks of flesh from the bodies of women prisoners and then force-fed them to the captives. Abady told me of seeing buildings in northern Iraq filled with captive Kurdish women: men went into these buildings, filled out a form, and took women away for their own pleasure. "I watched the women being dragged away, screaming for someone to save them, to do something," he related. "But of course, there was nothing we could do."

In Iraq, you needn't rely on human rights' organizations to hear about Saddam's crimes. The evidence is everywhere. In the Shabandar, for example, I met a man I'll call Ahmed. Once a high-ranking Shia cleric, he was arrested by the Baath Party in the late 1990s for supposedly conspiring with anti-government Shia groups in Europe. Imprisoned for three years, he was repeatedly tortured. Guards tied his wrists behind his back and hung him from the ceiling, sometimes for days at a time. They starved him, beat him with heavy black cables, electrocuted him with wires connected to a hand-powered generator. When he finally regained his freedom, Ahmed told me, the right side of his body had lost most of its feeling, while an untreated disease he contracted in prison had withered his right leg to the size of his arm. "When I went into prison, I was a Muslim," he told me. "When I left, I was an atheist."

But Saddam's malevolence wasn't only in the awful statistics (five thousand dead in the 1988 poison gas attack on the Kurdish village of Halabja) or stories of individual atrocities (the 1999 murder of Mohammad al-Sadr, in which Baathists drove nails into the Shia cleric's head after raping his sister in front of him). It was also found in the endless stories of routine harassment, imprisonment, and fear expressed by nearly everyone I met. "Just talking like we're doing now," Mohammad told me one afternoon as we walked down Mutinabi Street, "could lead to the police picking me up and questioning me for hours about our conversation."

Saddam was always watching. Haider described being interviewed by a European film crew interested in his sculpture. "A
'minder' from the regime stood behind the interviewer, next to the
camera, and if they asked a sensitive question, she opened her eyes
to warn me not to answer incorrectly or else she would report me,"
he said. "Of course, if I'd hesitated, or looked defiant, she would
report that, too."

Saddam was always listening. Dr. Mashtaq told me how his son
one day blurted out "I hate Saddam Hussein" among a group of
friends and was arrested within hours, forcing the doctor to pay
more than one million dinars in ransom. Sometimes what you personally had done wasn't even the issue. Naseer told me he spent
two weeks in prison because his uncle was a communist. "I had to
cover my ears because of the screams of the women being raped,"
he said. As Abady commented, "Not since the days of the Mongols
and Tartars has there been such brutality."

I heard this refrain many times: Saddam's evil was in a category
of its own. Because his regime lasted thirty-five years, because Iraq
is a relatively small nation, because he was so open and boastful
about his tyranny—and because the outside world seemed so ready
to ignore his crimes—there seemed no way for Iraqis to escape his
grasp. "I have lived my entire life with that man in power," said Rand
Matti Petros, the twenty-six year-old manager of an Internet café
near the Orient Palace. "I wake up each morning terrified that I've
been dreaming. I still can't believe he's really gone." Remarked an
uncharacteristically somber Esam, "My generation is lost. Maybe in
twenty to thirty years Iraqi children will live normal, happy lives
outside the shadow of Saddam."

Josef Stalin once noted, "The death of one man is a tragedy,
the death of millions a statistic." It is for this reason, I think, that
the outside world found it so easy to overlook Saddam's crimes. It

represented a malevolence beyond all comprehension, so large it could only be tallied in statistics—and statistics do not readily stir moral outrage. Six million Jews? Horrible. But read about the life and death of a single, remarkably talented young girl who recorded her life in a diary, and the tears flow. It seems an appalling paradox: the more extensive the outrage, the less we object.

This lesson came back to me the morning I stood near the Assassin's Gate, watching men extract fragments of tissue and bone from the charred metal tombs of thirty innocent people. Knowing what I was seeing, yet not comprehending it—unable to grasp the enormity of the scene—I felt angry at my own superficiality. Surely, terrorist victims deserve better from their final witnesses than this. Yet my mind would not accept even these deaths without going blank. If they had perished, say, in a fire or a train wreck, the language and imagery of tragedy would have provided a framework for my imagination. But a suicide bombing is not a tragedy, it is an obscenity. And the obscene—like the divine, strangely enough—goes beyond language, beyond imagery, passing into silence and void.

But *one person*—one face, one photocopied image. Looking at Hadeel, feeling the ground give way as her smile, her truncated happiness, revealed the absolute existence of the forbidden and obscene—*haram*, as the Muslims say. My all-too-human inability to grasp her death seemed profoundly troubling. At the instant when justice called for righteous fury, I experienced an irresolute rage. At the moment I should feel wrath for her murderers, I experienced a subtle revulsion for *Hadeel herself*, as if her death were forcing me to contemplate the unreasonable, the blasphemous, the taboo. She made me confront what we strive so hard to ignore and repress: the existence of evil in the world.

And then I knew—or rather, I was reminded of a central fact: terrorism is evil. And evil diminishes. It makes us small. It reduces our hatred, indignation, and fury to futile ravings. To stand in the presence of evil is to experience a sense of moral defeat and shame. The heart urges retaliation, but there is none to strike, no foe, no "evildoer," nothing but the ghosts of the dead who, like Hamlet's father, cry for justice. Helpless in our anguish, we attack whatever is nearest to the crime—sometimes the very forces dedicated to protecting us. In the wake of the Basra bombings, for example, Iraqis threw stones at the British troops rushing to aid the wounded. Or we turn on ourselves, dismayed by our inadequacy to prevent evil in the first place. In the end, we recoil from the victims themselves, as if their fate will taint our own souls, shatter our own sense of meaning and purpose—one reason, I think, why no "human shields" ride Israeli buses. Evil paralyzes our consciences. It makes cowards of us all.

This is difficult for anyone to accept. But how much more difficult for The People of the Slogans. Their virtue enlarges them, makes them feel better, bigger, more humane. They do not want to feel small. They want to be seen, noticed; they thrive on the esteem and admiration of others, the pleasure of an ego continually gratified. There is nothing gratifying about accosting the Devil, nothing *bien pensants* gain by challenging something that neither notices nor cares about their existence, that will only humiliate and manipulate them. Better to condemn an accountable, conscientious, self-regulating entity that does notice, that does care—and will applaud and perhaps enrich them in the process. The United States of America, for example.

And so, in a flash of moral exhibitionism, the object of the humanitarian outrage is inverted: not the acid baths of Saddam, the sunglasses of U.S. soldiers; not the suicide sedans and indiscriminate slaughter by Al Qaeda, the human rights violations by an army more concerned about civilian casualties than any in history; not

the obscenity of Evil, but the imperfections of Good. I'm not arguing that we should exempt America from blame—far from it. I am
saying we should weigh the relative values of the iniquity present in
Iraq, confident that an honest assessor would chastise our nation,
but demand God's wrath against the terrorists.

Alas, however, unlike our enemies, we feel uncomfortable with
notions of Divine Justice. Wrath is no longer in our emotional lexi-
con—and that, we believe, separates us from their fundamentalist madness. Instead we applaud the well-mannered "rage" of the
world-savers who proclaim: *If I had a rocket launcher . . . some
son-of-a-bitch would die.*

—

COCKBURN AND HIS GROUP soon returned to North America and
a week later, I paid my visit to Jack at CPA headquarters. Two days
after that meeting, I found myself dining with a group of women
connected with yet another anti-war group, this one called CODE-
PINK. Now, at first blush, I had about as much business with these
ladies as I might with sharing an Eid-ul-Fitr feast with "Mookie"
al-Sadr. A self-described "women-initiated grassroots peace and
social justice movement," CODEPINK was created in November,
2002 to protest America's "pre-emptive" strike in Iraq. Their members had already made several trips to Iraq, where, to hear them
tell it, they found almost universal anarchy and total opposition to
the U.S. "[Iraqis] say it is worse under occupation that it ever was
under Saddam," CODEPINK'er Patricia Ackerman reported on the
group's website in July, 2003.

I met the group through a friend of mine, an art dealer I'll
call Deborah. Interested in seeing Baghdad, Deborah had joined
a CODEPINK-sponsored excursion to the city. Led by co-founder

Jodie Evans, Deborah and ten other women spent nearly two weeks meeting politicians, religious leaders, doctors, psychiatrists, feminists, and Iraqis whose family members had been detained or killed by U.S. troops. Only occasionally did they meet victims of Saddam, and never people whose family members had been killed by terrorists. It was, in many ways, a classic pity tour.

Because of my friendship with Deborah, Evans graciously invited me to a goodbye-to-Baghdad dinner at the end of the delegation's visit. Despite my wariness about the group's politics, I accepted, interested, in large part, in Evans herself. She was a personable, attractive, middle-aged woman with flaming red hair and a performer's talent for commanding attention. And indeed, along with associating with well-placed friends in Hollywood and California politics (among them actor Robin Williams and former governors Jerry Brown and Gray Davis, in addition to political gadfly Arianna Huffington), she is also active in numerous save-the-world groups such as the Rain Forest Action Network, Hollywood Women's Political Committee, International Occupation Watch, Unreasonable Women for the Earth, and something called Bad Babes and Their Buddies. A true, if eccentric, Person of the Slogan.

Nevertheless, I had little interest in picking a fight with Evans, as I had sought to do with Cockburn. I showed up for the dinner at the al-Mansour Hotel suffering from the third week of a devastating cold. Worse, despite Deborah's presence and Evans' hospitality, I felt awkward amidst these opponents to the war, who included, along with CODEPINK, a coterie of left-wing freelance journalists (including a fellow named Attila from Budapest) and Eman Ahmen Khammas, co-director of the vehemently anti-American Occupation Watch. Feeling cranky and unsociable, I settled down on a banquette with multiple scotch-and-sodas and sank into an deepening gloom.

The real problem was Hadeel. Or rather, her image, her smile. I still couldn't get her out of my mind. She haunted my thoughts, forming a perpetual rebuke, challenging me in my moral complacency to answer the questions posed by her death—not just *Why?* but *How can we accept this? Where is the outrage, where is the wrath?*

I'm sorry, I wanted to say to her, but we have grown too sophisticated for such primitive emotions, too refined for concepts such as the "terrible swift sword" of justice: our President can't even mention the word "crusade" without backtracking and apologizing. To even consider the existence of evil is to appear hopelessly *retardaire*, to risk being numbered among the Creationists, flat-earthers, and others with the temerity to question modern science. "How bad was Saddam *really*?" one CODEPINK'er asked me, revealing at once her own ignorance and the superficiality of her tour of Baghdad. But without a standard of morality, without an idea of evil—well, how bad *was* he?

A few minutes later another delegate approached me with a troubled expression. "Did you hear?" she whispered breathlessly. "Two members of Occupation Watch were arrested by the American army today, *and no one knows where they are.*"

The room began buzzing with the news—shock, consternation, what-are-we-going-to-do handwringing . . . once again, the American "liberators" had shown the tyranny that lurked beneath their fine promises of "democracy" and "rule of law."

"The Americans had no cause to make the arrests, they had no papers, no warrants!" the delegate raged at me, as if I represented the CPA.

Weary of activist indignation, I stood and walked to the bar. Perhaps she was right: knowing how clumsily the American military acted as police officers, I was sure she was. But still, what about the thousands of Iraqis whom Saddam arrested, executed, and buried in graves yet undiscovered? Where are they? What cause had the suicide bombers to kill Hadeel? What kind of papers or warrants did they bear that legitimized her execution? What happened to our ability to discriminate between that which is wrong, and that which is evil? *Where is our outrage, where is our wrath?*

Realizing the futility of these questions, and the rudeness of even broaching them in polite progressive company, I poured myself another scotch. I sat back down on the banquette, and let the depression roll in.

— 4 —

The "Resistance"

The Iraqis who have risen up against the occupation
are not "insurgents" or "terrorists" or "The Enemy."
They are the REVOLUTION, the Minutemen, and
their numbers will grow—and they will win.

Michael Moore[1]

SHE WAS A SUNNI MUSLIM, an attractive, thirty-something writer, one of the few women I met who eschewed a scarf in public. And she was overjoyed at the demise of Saddam. "I am so happy! Freedom at last! The world is open to me now!" she exclaimed during a small social function at an art gallery in Karada. "Can you recommend some American magazines I might send my writing to?"

I promised I'd draw up a list of suitable periodicals, then added—carelessly, for this was my first trip to Iraq—"You must not mind seeing American soldiers on the streets."

1 David Brooks, "All Hail Moore," *New York Times*, June 26, 2004.

The woman's smile vanished. Her brow darkened and she shook her head. "Oh, no. I hate the soldiers. I hate them so much I fantasize about taking a gun and shooting one dead."

Stunned by her vehemence, "But American soldiers are responsible for your freedom!" I replied.

"I know," the woman snarled. "And you can't imagine how humiliated that makes me feel."

He was a short, intense, bespectacled lawyer from Baquba, who claimed he had connections with anti-Coalition forces in the Sunni Triangle. As we drove through the desert into Baghdad, "I hate your country," he informed me. "Every time I see a U.S. tank I feel like it is crushing my skull."

Less startled by this expression—for this was my second trip to Iraq—I asked the attorney the cause of his feelings. As if explaining the most self-evident thing in the world, he replied, "America is occupying my country—as a patriot, of course I must resist." He fixed his wire-rimmed gaze on me. "Imagine if a foreign power was occupying America—wouldn't you resist?"

I think of these people each time I read about violence in the Sunni Triangle, that one-hundred-mile area stretching from Tikrit to the north, Ramadi to the east, and Baghdad to the west. I think of similar Iraqi confessions of shame, resentment, or "patriotism" each time I hear of an American soldier or Iraqi civilian killed by an IED, mortar assault, or car bomb. I feel a simmering anger over the pointlessness of these attacks and those aspects of Arab psychology that cling to humiliation and rely on violence to satisfy grievances. And my anger burns hotter when I read comments from the Western media ennobling these murderous "insurgents" by calling them the "Resistance"—or, more horribly, the "Revolution"—ignoring the thousands of Iraqis who risk their lives every day *opposing* the nihilistic bloodlust of these men.

After more than eighteen months of fighting in Iraq, there seems to be no means of dealing with this insurrection. The Kurds and the Shia (renegade cleric Moqtada al-Sadr notwithstanding) have shown a willingness to negotiate over the future of Iraq—why not the Sunnis? What do they hope to gain from their "guerrilla" war against the U.S. and against the interim government of Prime Minister Iyad Allawi? More important, what factors in the Arab Iraqi character lie behind Sunni opposition to a democratic Iraq, and why can't American politicians, military personnel and members of the media seem to understand them?

—

> Nothing is more humiliating to a man
> than to be the subject of another man's authority.
>
> Arab proverb

WE HADN'T CONSIDERED IT, those of us who supported the war. After all, it made no sense, it was *unreasonable*. And yet, the moment I spoke to that woman at the art gallery, I knew: even as they were being liberating from Saddam, Iraqis felt shamed by the fact that they couldn't do the job themselves.

"If only you'd given us more time, we would have risen up and overthrown him," a waiter at the Orient Palace lectured me a couple of days later. "It's terrible, when I think of it," a student at Baghdad University said. "A foreign army has to come across the world to free us from Saddam—who are we, then?" This sense of indignity, of loss of "face," explained the ungracious gratitude many Iraqis evinced toward the U.S.—the "Thanks America, now go home" syndrome. How naïve we were to believe that they would greet our troops with flowers, as Dick Cheney so famously and wrongly predicted. As the Center for Strategic and International Studies explained in a report on Iraq's reconstruction, "the United States should expect continuing resentment and disaffection even if the U.S.-led reconstruction efforts seem to be making positive, incremental improvements to the country according to quantifiable measures. In other words, the occupation will not be judged by the sum of its consequences, but rather *qua* occupation."[2]

In retrospect, it seems obvious. No one likes being beholden to another for his freedom. The Iraqis consider it incomprehensible that a people with a glorious Sumerian and Babylonian heritage and a country with rich natural resources had to rely on foreigners for rescue. "No wonder civilization began here," said a teacher at the Shabandar café. "We have everything—food, water, oil, minerals." This pride, however, has its negatives. Since Iraq today isn't in much of a position to fulfill its potential, its people often project their sense of superiority outward—most notably on the United States—which only reinforces their sense of national disgrace.

France may see us as a barely-restrainable "hyperpower"; the Iraqis—at least in the beginning of the "occupation"—saw us as simply omnipotent. The ease with which our armies overran their country reinforced that idea, as did America's chest-thumping over its technological know-how. As a result, many Iraqis developed a warped view of U.S. competence and intentions. Since America was all-powerful, they reasoned, we couldn't make mistakes or act incompetently: such blunders must really be part of some Bush Administration master strategy.

Take, for example, the looting and fires that wracked Baghdad

2 Center for Strategic and International Studies, "Progress or Peril? Measuring Iraq's Reconstruction" (Washington, D.C.: CSIS, 2004).

immediately after Saddam's fall. Where we might blame a catastrophic lack of Pentagon foresight, numerous Iraqis contended that
America encouraged the looting in order to demonstrate the Iraqi
people's inability to govern themselves. Approaching the status of
an urban legend was the story of GIs who broke open the National
Museum and invited passersby to help themselves to priceless antiquities. A cab driver swore to me that he had witnessed American
soldiers exhorting crowds to ransack government buildings with
hearty cries of, "Go on, people, take what you want!" I heard similar
stories about Americans urging the pillage of expensive homes in
Karada—although in my perambulations through the neighborhood, I saw no evidence of such damage. But that is incidental:
the real point of these stories isn't truth, but rather the comfort
they provide Iraqi people in shifting the blame for acts of criminal
vandalism from themselves to devious Uncle Sam.

The overestimation of U.S. capabilities also distorted Iraqi notions of what to expect from our country. Since America was omnipotent, why couldn't it gin up the electrical grid, restore peace
and tranquility, and provide employment to everyone—*today*? Here
again, the U.S. was victim both of Iraqi projections and its own high-
tech wizardry. Try to explain to an Iraqi housewife the difficulties
of repairing an electrical system decades out of date and beset by
saboteurs, and she'd cock a skeptical eyebrow. This from a nation
with weapons so smart they can look up a target's address in the
Baghdad yellow pages? No, the only reason America dropped the
quality-of-life ball was that Bush wanted to keep Iraq downtrodden
and dependent.

Not every Iraqi thought this way, of course. Still, I encountered
these sentiments often enough to recognize that they pervade the
nation's self-image and compensate for another, equally unrealistic, but even more debilitating characteristic: severe feelings of

defeat and impotence. As Raphael Patai wrote in his classic, and controversial, 1974 book, *The Arab Mind*, "The encounter with the West produced a disturbing inferiority complex in the Arab mind which in itself makes it more difficult to shake off the shackles of stagnation."[3]

A good illustration of Patai's observation was the conversation I had with Ahmed, the piano player at Fifties. Possessed of a superb knowledge of the American songbook, Ahmed would play, at my request, medleys of Sinatra songs, accompanying himself in a reedy, but serviceable, voice. One night, however, he ventured beyond "Angel Eyes" and "A Quarter to Three" to give me the low-down on the Iraq situation. "The only reason America invaded was to steal our national resources," he confided, during a break from his ivory-tickling. Ahmed's proof? America didn't actually have to invade Iraq in order to topple Saddam, he noted; all it really had to do was beam down special radiation from super-secret satellites orbiting overhead, which would scramble Baath Party communications and enable "the Iraqi people to overthrow Saddam." Why hadn't they overthrown him before? "Saddam wasn't in power just by himself, you know—he had *very powerful backers.*" And who were these backers? "The Jews," Ahmed replied. You see, Jews not only supported Saddam, the pianist maintained, but also manipulated him into attacking Iran in order to "keep the Arabs down and—"

At this point, I requested he play "Send in the Clowns," and escaped to my room.

It is tempting to discount Ahmed's analysis as typical of the anti-Semitism one finds with tedious regularity in Iraq. But it reveals many of the demons that lie beneath the surface of the Iraqi national character: historical grievances, conspiratorial thinking, and

3 Raphael Patai, *The Arab Mind* (New York: Hatherleigh Press, 2002), 332.

a kind of bi-polar superiority-inferiority dynamic. Moreover, his comments point to another, equally troubling impulse that confuses Western observers and informs the nature of the Iraqi "insurgency": an unwillingness to take the blame for Saddam.

As dissident Iraqi intellectual Kanan Makiya wrote in *The Monument*, his 1991 book about art and culture in Iraq, "The question of responsibility has to be posed completely differently in a state ruled by fear than it would in an ordinary state, because on the whole the populace does not feel itself responsible for the actions of its rulers, even when it knows that momentous life and death decisions are taken in its name."[4]

Iraqis refuse to accept that their society allowed a monster like Saddam to take power. Instead, they see him as an aberration, as if he were a maniacal gunman who suddenly burst into their homes, seized their families, and terrorized their neighbors, until the police finally stormed in and captured the lunatic. Now, standing amidst the ruins caused by the raid, they say to their rescuers, "It wasn't *our* fault this madman got in here. Thanks for getting rid of him—now, how soon are you going to repair our house?" They overlook that from 1968 to 1980, Iraq lived happily under the control of the Nazi-inspired Baath Party, while reaping the benefits of an oil-rich economy. (How many times did I hear how wonderful Baghdad was in the 1970s?) Not until Saddam seized complete control of the nation in 1979 and launched the war on Iran—and then on the Kurds, and then on Kuwait, and then on the Shia—did they realize they belonged to a madman. But by then it was too late.

At the same time, though, there are many Iraqis who, like my Baquba lawyer, don't care *why* American troops are in their country, only that they are here—and so must pay for that offense in lost and

4 Kanan Makiya, *The Monument* (London: I.B. Tauris, 2004), 128.

shattered lives. The shame that many Iraqis feel is not enough to compel them to take up arms against the Coalition—if that were the case, the volume of weaponry in Baghdad alone would make the U.S. presence untenable. (The Shia, in particular, must have enormous secret depots of small-arms ordinance just to shoot into the air to celebrate marriages.) Rather, there is another, more combustible aspect in the Iraqi personality, something that seeks healing for the wound of humiliation in violence and bloodletting. To find it, I traveled to the Sunni Triangle itself.

—

Violence is a cleansing force. It frees the native from
his inferiority complex and from his despair and inaction;
it makes him fearless and restores his self-respect.

Franz Fanon

Nam, nam, Saddam! (Yes, yes, Saddam!)
An Iraqi boy, Fallujah, January, 2004

ONE BEAUTIFUL LATE WINTER MORNING, I found myself standing on a street corner in downtown Fallujah, surrounded by a crowd of Iraqi men, each person shoving forward to express an identical sentiment: hatred for the United States of America.

"America bad, worse than Saddam. They must leave our country at once!" one man growled.

"American soldiers no good. Life was better under Saddam!" said another.

"We have no gas, no electricity, no security. When Saddam was president, everything was fine, life was good."

"Saddam was a good man. We hate President Bush! We hate America!"

The conversation didn't start this way. At first, I approached two men on the corner and we engaged in a reasonable, relatively balanced critique of the U.S. presence near their city. Gradually, though, as more people joined the group, the volume of the voices rose. Each accusation against America spawned another, harsher, castigation. Newcomers entering the discussion added even more severe views, until the entire encounter took on a radical tone. It was a phenomenon I noticed several times over there, especially in the Sunni Triangle. In heated conversation, there was a rush toward the extremes: the more vehement and violent the view, the more likely it would emerge as the consensus of a group.

Not that I was particularly alarmed this morning. Anticipating a flood of anti-American invective in this ancient smugglers den thirty-five miles west of Baghdad, I identified myself as a Yugoslavian journalist, gambling on Iraqi ignorance of southeast Europe to see the deception through. It worked. No one challenged me, or asked for any documents; in fact, nearly everyone was exceedingly polite, if agitated. Perhaps the residents didn't care *where* a reporter was from, just as long as he gave an ear to their complaints.

"The people here are angry," observed Dhia, as we drove away, passing a broken-down amusement park near Fallujah's *souk*. I nodded, resisting a temptation to ask him what he felt about America: the last thing I needed was to be alienated from my own driver in the heart of the Sunni Triangle.

I met Dhia in the fall when I asked the Armenian desk clerk at the Orient Palace to recommend someone to take me to the holy Shia cities of Karbala and Najaf. A gentle, slightly effeminate man with a soft smile and feathery voice, the twenty-nine-year-old dressed in neat slacks and polo shirts, had a good command of English, and

drove his own BMW. In our travels throughout southern Iraq, he
proved a good and trustworthy companion. When I returned to
Iraq that winter, I contacted him, asking if he could take me to the
towns of the Sunni Triangle. "No problem, Mister Steve—with me,
you will be safe," Dhia promised.

And so, under his watchful eye, I assessed the intensity of anti-
American sentiment. In Ramadi, a bustling market town of around
450,000 people, I conversed with a man preparing for the Friday
lunch rush at an outdoor café. "America should leave now, not tomorrow," he declared, chopping lamb into little kebob squares. "Iraq
is not safe because they are here. Americans shoot anyone, they
break into homes and steal money." At a tea stand, a studious-look-
ing young man shook his head. "At first we welcomed America.
Then the soldiers began killing people." Another crowd gathered,
everyone eager to tell the inquisitive Yugoslav why they despise the
U.S.: no electricity, no gas; GIs break into houses, arrest people, and
"touch" women. Life was better under Saddam. I asked nine small
boys gawking at me if the former dictator was a "good man." All
nine said yes.

One can perhaps understand why. Although totaling around
15 percent of Iraq's Arab population, the Sunnis have dominated
Iraq since the mid-sixteenth century, when the Ottoman Empire
used the sect as a bulwark against the Shia-influenced Persians to
the east. In the twentieth century, the British and Iraq's British-
controlled monarchy continued the policy of favoring the Sunnis
and their well-developed administrative skills. Under Saddam, a
Sunni himself, the religious sect reached the apogee of its power,
thriving under a system of patronage and government benefits that
awarded them top positions in all aspects of Iraqi life. In 2003,
the American war machine ended their reign; suddenly, the jobs,

pensions, and prestige the Sunnis used to lord over the Kurds and Shia were gone.

On a Ramadi street corner, I found a graying old man wearing a tattered brown sweater struggling to serve a small knot of men gathered around his portable tea stand. "I was a teacher, in my retirement," he related when the rush subsided and he had a moment to talk. "I received a nice pension from the government. When the Americans came at first I was happy—no more Saddam! Then they cut my pension. Later, they gave me $30 a month, then raised it to $60. But how can I live on that much? I had to come out of retirement. Meanwhile, there is no gas, no electricity, no salaries for the people. When Saddam was in power, we had all this. My life was fine. Now look at me. I have to sell tea to support my family."

En route to Khaldiya, we encountered a parked M-1 Abrams tank, its barrel aimed at windshield level at oncoming traffic. Dhia, however, would not enter the town itself. "They kill foreigners there," he murmured, reminding me that a few days previously, an IED killed three GIs in the area. Instead, we stopped at a roadside vegetable stand for an earful of anti-U.S. vituperation. At one point, a young man motioned toward three Bradleys lumbering down the road. "There go the Ali Baba," he spat. I noticed that Iraqis either sped up or slowed down to distance themselves from the convoy; one car actually drove off the road. No one wanted to be near a potential target of an IED or a rocket-propelled grenade.

It was painful to see America the object of so much hatred and fear, the very image of an oppressive occupier. It was worse when we found ourselves behind a trio of Humvees. Dhia crept several car lengths behind the rear vehicle, and I looked at the GI manning the roof-mounted M60 machine gun (Where was he from? What city? Where did his parents live?), reflecting on the isolation of these young men out here, how the Iraqis shun and avoid them, even as they face the threat that a roadside pile of debris will erupt into fire and shrapnel. This was not how the liberation was supposed to go.

In Fallujah, Dhia and I visit the headquarters of the Islamic Political Party of Iraq. There, I asked a Sunni cleric seated on his *diwan*, or long couch, why he thought his Shia brethren had proven more cooperative with the U.S. He offered a mirthless smile. "The Shia think America liberated them from Saddam. But America did not come to liberate, they came for oil. America must leave immediately." But without the presence of U.S. troops, wouldn't Iraq slide into terrorist violence? "Let the soldiers leave, peace will come," the cleric replied, fingering his prayer beads. "*They* are the terrorists who kill the Iraqi people."

He has a point. Heavily-armed American soldiers, untrained for the kind of constabulary work that urban combat demands, are guilty of killing Iraqi civilians. In April, 2003, for example, 82nd Airborne troops in Fallujah shot and killed eighteen, apparently unarmed Iraqis; in September, 2003, troops mistakenly killed eight policemen just west of the city. In every town through the Sunni Triangle, similar incidents have taken place. (The military claims it does not keep statistics on civilian deaths.) Moreover, the day-to-day aspects of the American presence are infuriating: roadblocks, bridge closings, curfews. House searches can be brutal: doors kicked in, furniture overturned, rooms ransacked, whole families rousted. In the Sunni Triangle, American troops truly are an occupier.

Over the next couple of weeks, Dhia and I crisscrossed the area, popping out of his car in towns west of Baghdad, as well as in Samarra, Baquba, and Tikrit (hometown of Uncle Saddam) to the north, to interview tea sellers, waiters, students, clerics, and unemployed Baathist-supporting thugs. Again and again, I heard the same litany of complaints about U.S soldiers—civilian casualties, thefts from houses, vague accusations that "they touch women." The charges sounded serious—a number of them were no doubt true. But could they *all* be true? Had each of these Iraqis actually seen or experienced such abuses, or were they simply repeating rumors?

In Fallujah one afternoon, I chatted with three guys at a corner tea stand who swore that, just the day before, they saw a U.S. soldier shoot a woman dead in the street. A week earlier, they continued, another GI killed a man and his son who were working as night guards in a garage. My heart sinking, I asked for directions to the scene of the woman's murder, and within minutes, Dhia and I were at the vacant street corner, where, by good fortune, a policeman was walking by. No, the men in the teahouse were wrong, the cop explained to my relief. The woman's slayer was a local man whose father had been murdered by her son. "Revenge," he shrugged. "She was Kurdish," he added, as if that explained something

With his intelligent eyes, ruddy complexion, and barber-shop-quartet moustache, the officer struck me as a decent fellow able to separate fact from rumor when it came to reports of American crimes. I asked him about the father and son killed at the garage.

"Oh, yes," his jaw clenching, "that was done by an American soldier."

"What happened to the soldier?"

"Nothing! Nothing ever happens to the soldiers who kill us."

"Does it happen a lot?"

The policeman's face turned crimson. "Americans have killed thousands of Iraqis since they came here. Do you hear me? Thousands! They killed my brother's thirteen-year-old son, *his only son!*" I had struck a nerve: faster and faster spilled the man's words, a kind of reverse-image of the pro-American Shia cab driver I had met in Baghdad three months earlier.

"The Americans hate the Sunnis and *insha'allah*, we hate them. Believe me, this is why the people kill the soldiers! We were kings when Saddam was president—now what? Nothing! Life is so expensive, there are no jobs—especially for Sunnis! This is what George Bush brings us! Nothing! Saddam's shoes are better than George Bush!" Trembling with rage, he thrust a finger in my face. "In Fallujah, there are 135 mosques! This is a Muslim city. It is forbidden for Americans to be here. The people of Fallujah say, 'You must leave!' Especially to the American soldiers, for they are all Zionists! And they are here with fighters from other Arab countries, Jordan, Egypt, Lebanon, Saudi Arabia. All here with Zionist America to steal from Iraq!"

Just when I feared the policeman might explode, his feverish anger seemed to break, and he blinked and looked at Dhia and me as if noticing us for the first time. Then he invited us for lunch.

It was the Iraqi temperament all over again. The policeman began reasonably enough, accusing the GIs of civilian deaths. But Arab anger is a volatile force, one that easily "sweeps over the dam of self-control and in an astonishingly short period of time transforms the entire personality," as Patai writes.[5] From denouncing U.S. soldiers, it was a short step for the cop to declare his support for Saddam, anger at the "infidel" and hatred for Zionists, the whole ascending scale of rage climaxing with his view of Iraq as the victim of a worldwide conspiracy. (Although, in fairness, his mention of the Arab fighters was a tantalizing reference to foreign jihadists operating in the Sunni Triangle.) Then, just as suddenly, he calmed down and seemed to emerge from his fury.

5 Patai, *The Arab Mind*, 169.

I felt sympathy for him, as I did for most of the Sunnis I spoke with. And yet, the same question kept nagging me: What do they want? What is the point of this "Resistance?" From Tikrit to Ramadi, whenever I asked people what they thought killing American troops would achieve, they voiced the hope that the bloodshed would drive the hated foreigner out of Iraq. When I suggested that perhaps an easier way to attain such an end would be to form a stable democratic government that would then ask the U.S. to leave—giving America no pretext to remain in the country—people looked at me with a blank expression.

Even more startling, at least for me, were the Sunni responses when I asked them what kind of government they envisioned if the U.S. suddenly did up and leave. Nearly everyone declared their interest in a new Saddam ("Only more democratic," one Baquban qualified) or a reconstituted Baath Party. Never mind that neither of these alternatives was likely, given armed Kurds to the north, armed Shia to the south, and American interests in the country, not to mention Saddam's impending trial for war crimes. Nor did these Sunnis express the slightest misgivings about agitating for the return of a dictator who modeled himself after Stalin and a political party based on the National Socialists. They felt no responsibility for the crimes of the tyrant they wanted returned to power. Rather, it was the *idea* of the resurrected "strong man" they liked. It acted like a comforting balm on their sense of "rage"—that blind, amoral, unforgiving thirst for vengeance that fed on its own indignation until it drove many to violence.

This vague, inchoate "rage against the foreigner" is nothing new in the Arab Middle East, of course. Especially in the aftermath of World War II, as David Pryce-Jones observes in his 1989 study of Arab culture, *The Closed Circle*. When Arab leaders began advocating nationalism, he writes, they "restricted themselves to the one-dimensional platform of evicting the Europeans," while at the same time refusing to "discuss what social and political institutions they might consider appropriate in the event of independence. One and all incited nationalism and then exploited it as the surest way of arousing the mob on their behalf, frightening the authorities, demoralizing the Europeans, and so levering themselves as their successors into the positions of supreme power holders. What would actually happen in the event of their seizing the state, they left undefined."[6] Fifty years later, the situation is the same, only now anonymous ex-Saddmites seek to demoralize and evict the United States in their hopes of transforming a slice of Iraq into a miniature caliphate.

But this is not all that stokes the fires of Sunni hatred. Beneath Iraqi religious and political affiliations lies a complex web of family, clan, and tribal associations that knits the country together in a tradition-based social order. Whereas in Shia-dominated Iraq, religious leaders tend to command more respect than tribal sheikhs, in the Sunni Triangle, kinship groups like the Dulaym federation, the Shammar, the al-Jaburi, and Saddam's own tribe, al-Bu Nasir, have for centuries wielded considerable, if poorly-understood, power. Although the Ottomans, the British, and even the Baathists tried to circumscribe tribal authority, it has stubbornly persisted, especially in the form of behavioral codes derived from the earliest inhabitants of the desert. This "Bedouin substratum," as Patai terms it, affirms as its highest principles hospitality, courage, loyalty and, above all, honor—a concept which itself comprises virility, dignity, and martial valor. "All these different kinds of honor," Patai writes, "interlock to surround the Arab ego like a coat of armor."[7]

6 David Pryce-Jones, *The Closed Circle* (New York: Harper & Row, 1989), 224.
7 Patai, *The Arab Mind*, 96.

And if this psychic chain-mail is breached? The Arab, he continues, "must defend his public image. Any injury done to a man's honor must be revenged, or else he becomes permanently dishonored," Pryce-Jones writes. "Shame is a living death, not to be endured, requiring that it be avenged."[8] For my part, I discovered this cultural and psychological phenomenon throughout the Sunni Triangle. While conversing with dozens of residents, I felt much less the anger of a population that was "occupied," "oppressed," or "enslaved" than the self-loathing of a people in disgrace. After decades of imperious rule, the Sunni Baathists were crushed by America—shamed, humiliated, they felt they had lost something perhaps even more precious than jobs or political power: honor.

Dishonor. This, I came to understand, was a huge factor that propelled the Sunni insurgency and gave it such an air of pointless, self-destructive violence. It is also the reason, I believe, why non-Middle Eastern observers have such trouble understanding the nature of this conflict—particularly Americans, who have no real experience with those extended families called tribes. Nor do we feel any longer a visceral connection between honor and self-respect, or the necessity of the *lex talionis* ("an eye for an eye," or, as an Arab proverb has it, *dam butlub dam*, "blood demands blood") to avenge humiliation. But the militants in the Sunni Triangle do. In order to reclaim their personal, family and clan reputations, these Iraqis seek to kill American troops, for only American blood can redeem their honor. The roadside ambushes and barbaric immolations correspond to archaic tribal codes where self-respect is restored only through violence and loss of life.

No wonder the insurgents—and many other Iraqis as well—seem to dwell on the edge of a bottomless chasm of rage: the shame

---

8 Pryce-Jones, *The Closed Circle*, 35.

they experience from the American invasion eats away at them. No wonder, too, that the insurgents' movement seems so vague. In my travels through the Sunni Triangle and my time in Baghdad I never once saw any symbols, propaganda, or call letters (FLN, NLF, IRA, and so on) that might refer to an organized "liberation front." These "resistance" fighters—or, à la Moore, Iraqi "minutemen"—seemed to have no leaders, issue no communiqués, propound no programs, or even have a name. But why should they? *Their primary interest is their own "honor."* They may claim they are "patriots" fighting for Iraq—many are, in fact, soldiers and officers from the old Iraqi Army—but at heart they see themselves as tribal warriors engaged in the venerable tradition of honor killings against the biggest tribe of all: America.

By failing immediately to occupy and pacify the Sunni Triangle during the war, the U.S. allowed the affiliation between tribal groups and the Baath Party to reform and reassert itself. Gradually, a combination of embarrassment, humiliation, disgrace, and dishonor, fueled by a genuine diminution in the Sunnis' quality of life, compelled these Iraqis to seek revenge rather than political negotiation. Attacks on U.S. soldiers produced American counter-responses, killing Iraqi civilians and initiating further cycles of honor and revenge slayings. Gradually, the Sunni's tribal mentality drew the U.S. into a new kind of war: an unreasonable war fought not for familiar goals like territory, riches, or ideology, but for the irrational, intangible prizes of honor and self-respect.

—

We must also take action against our own Iraqi citizens who choose to collaborate with the enemy. . . . If someone you know is considering taking a job with the Americans,

tell him that he is engaging in treason and encourage him
to seek honest work instead. If he refuses, you must kill
him as a warning to other weak-minded individuals.

Ted Rall[9]

As long as we're here, we're the occupying power.
It's a very ugly word, but its true.

Paul Bremer[10]

BARELY A WEEK after my last visit to Fallujah, twenty-two policemen
died when their station came under a fierce and organized assault
by some seventy attackers. I have often wondered if my mustachioed
friend with whom I lunched was among the fatalities, but I will
never know.

Nor will I ever know the identity of the assailants. Hearing about
the attack in Baghdad, I surfed the internet for additional information. I found anti-war websites —among them, the indomitable
Occupation Watch—that called the gunmen the "resistance." The
London-based news service Reuters used the term "guerrillas"; another news source mentioned "insurgents." Returning to my room, I
caught a BBC-TV newscaster who reported that the fighters were "insurgents, anti-Coalition forces, whatever you want to call them."

Of those three descriptions, the BBC's was the most accurate—if
nothing else, the reporter captured the confusion over what to call
the combatants who continue to kill American soldiers and Iraqi
civilians. Despite their VC-like stealth, are they really "guerillas"?

9 Ted Rall, "Why We Fight: A View from the Other Side," *thinkingpeace.com*,
November 12, 2003.
10 Rajiv Chandrasekaran, "The Final Word on Iraq's Future," *Washington
Post*, June 18, 2003.

Even though they appear to be rising up against a foreign "occupation," do they deserve the term "insurgents?" Although they, and others, claim they are "resisting" the Coalition, does that make them a "Resistance?"

This is not mere semantics. The terms the media use to report on Iraq profoundly affect how Americans perceive this conflict and, by extension, how much blood and treasure they are willing to sacrifice on behalf of the Iraqi people. To put it another way, the degree to which America's conception of this war remains unclear and misleading constitute victories to those who would rob the Iraqis of their future. Moral clarity is crucial in this conflict.

Unfortunately, America lost this clarity within weeks of the war's beginning. As soon as Saddam's statue fell in Firdousi Square, both pro- and anti-war camps accepted the notion that the U.S.-led Coalition was an "occupying" power. The term is accurate in a legal sense, of course, enshrined in international conventions and recognized by the UN, but supporters of the war should have avoided and, when confronted with it, vigorously contested its use. For there is another way of viewing the situation. Once, in a Baghdad restaurant, I overhead some Westerners and Iraqis discussing the conflict—when the Westerners asked what they thought of the "occupation," one Iraqi retorted, "What 'occupation'? This is a *liberation*."

Words matter. By not sufficiently challenging the term "occupation," Coalition supporters ceded crucial rhetorical ground to opponents of the war, and in the process fell into a dialectical trap. Simply put, the epithet "occupation" has a negative connotation—for example, "occupied France." Conversely, anyone who objects to being occupied and chooses to "resist" has our sympathies. (How many movies have you seen where the resistance fighters are the villains?) On an emotional level, skillfully manipulated by the Coalition's enemies, the situation in Iraq quickly boiled down to an easily grasped, if erroneous, equation: the occupation is bad; the resistance is good.

Since the Coalition represented the negative pole, its motives, means, goals, and very presence were prejudged as suspect. In contrast, since the "Resistance" reflected the positive pole, it received automatic validation, if not the admiration and actual support of people all over the world. If one side suffered the burden of proof, the other enjoyed the benefit of the doubt. "America is occupying my country—of course I must resist," the Baquba lawyer had stated, a declaration that, in the minds of the anti-war crowd from Baghdad to Seattle, seems fair, legitimate, and admirable.

In 2004, the June issue of *Harper's* featured an article entitled "Beyond Fallujah: A Year with the Iraqi Resistance." In the July 1 edition of England's *Guardian* newspaper, Seumas Milne, a bitter opponent of Iraq's liberation, wrote, "It has become ever clearer that [the insurgents] are in fact a classic resistance movement with widespread support waging an increasingly successful guerrilla war against the occupying armies." "Iraqi Resistance Breaks Away From Zarqawi," announced the July 5, 2004, *Washington Times*. The word "guerrillas" is used even more frequently: "ABC Footage Shows Iraqi Guerillas With Hostage," announced the website for ABC News on April 10. "Iraqi Guerrillas Gun Down Four Americans," declared the AP on June 21. "Guerrillas Seize Six Foreign Hostages In Iraq," read the AP headline for a July 21 article.

Let's unpack these terms for a moment. What do we mean when we say the "Resistance?" Like the word "occupation," it is technically true: the people planting IEDs, piloting car bombs, and beheading foreign workers are "resisting" the Coalition. But like "occupation," "resistance" is not a neutral word. It conjures images of heroic struggles for national liberation: the French "Resistance," for example, or the Viet Cong or Algerian FLN. The same holds true with the word "guerrillas"—it, too, evokes heroic rebels, flaunting their independence in the face of impotent U.S. rage: Che, Fidel, Uncle Ho, Daniel Ortega, Sub-Commander Marcos.

But apply these concepts to Iraq and you misrepresent the situation. The conflict there is not a mid-twentieth century colonial uprising. The anti-government fedayeen are not Fanon's "wretched of the earth." The gunmen are not "indigenous peoples" fighting an anti-imperialistic conflict. To view them through a Marxist-Chomskyite-anti-capitalist-Hollywood template is an exercise in false moral clarity. As *New York Times* columnist Thomas Friedman wrote in October, 2003: "The great irony is that the Baathists and Arab dictators are opposing the U.S. in Iraq because—unlike many leftists—they understand exactly what this war is about. They understand that U.S. power is not being used in Iraq for oil, or imperialism, or to shore up a corrupt status quo, as it was in Vietnam and elsewhere in the Arab world during the cold war. They understand that this is the most radical-liberal revolutionary war the US has ever launched—a war of choice to install some democracy in the heart of the Arab-Muslim world."[11]

And this doesn't include the hundreds of foreign jihadists operating in Iraq. Their car bombs and kidnappings and beheadings form part of the "Resistance," too. In February, Coalition authorities intercepted a letter they believed originated from Jordanian terror-master Abu Musab al-Zarqawi. Writing to unknown associates, this murderer—the man probably responsible for bombing the Jordanian Embassy, and decapitating Nicholas Berg—complained that "America has no intention of leaving, no matter how many wounded nor how bloody it becomes." Worse, he noted, the U.S. intends to pull its forces back to bases, replacing soldiers with Iraqis who "are

11 Thomas Friedman, "It's No Vietnam," *New York Times*, October 30, 2003.

intimately linked to the people of this region." He went on to write: "How can we kill their cousins and sons and under what pretext, after the Americans start withdrawing? The Americans will continue to control from their bases, but the sons of this land will be the authority. *This is the democracy, we will have no pretext.*"[12]

Zarqawi clearly prefers that democracy fail in Iraq, thus forcing the U.S. to adopt a higher profile in the country—all to justify his terror campaigns. Campaigns specifically directed, he goes on to reveal, at Iraq's Shia population, in order to spark a sectarian war between the two Muslim groups: "The solution, and god only knows, is that we need to bring the Shia into the battle because it is the only way *to prolong the duration of the fight* between the infidels and us."[13]

So here, finally, we see in all their glory the anti-Coalition forces so admired by many on the left and in the media: ex-Baathists who kill American troops out of a sense of humiliation and dishonor, and foreign jihadists who wish to see the U.S. "occupiers" remain in the country in order to justify additional attacks against their fellow Muslims. What kind of "Resistance" is this? There is nothing romantic, Che Guavaresque, or progressive about the goals of these murderers: they are thugs, fighting for the most nihilistic of causes.

How, then, should we describe this war? What words and concepts define the situation more accurately? Since Iraq is now liberated, we might replace "occupation" with a word taken from the post-Civil War era: "reconstruction," as in, "the Coalition is *reconstructing* Iraq." We might then exchange the term "guerrilla fighters"

12 "Zarqawi's Cry," trans. CPA authorities, *National Review Online*, February 14, 2004. Emphasis added.
13 Ibid. Emphasis added.

for the more precise term "paramilitaries." Rather than noble warriors fighting to liberate their people, "paramilitaries" evoke images of anonymous right-wing killers terrorizing a populace in the name of a repressive regime—which is exactly what the fedayeen and jihadists are doing. Or we could simply dust off the venerable term "fascists." It was a good enough for the anti-Republican forces in the Spanish Civil War. Why shouldn't we use it to describe similar enemies of freedom in Iraq?

I repeat—words matter. Terms like "paramilitaries," "death squads," and "fascists" clarify the nature of our enemy and underscore a fundamental point that the American media has inexcusably ignored: it is the *Iraqi people* who are under attack. *They* are the victims, *their* future is threatened, *they* are bleeding from wounds inflicted by pan-Arab Baathists and pan-Islamic jihadists. By calling these neo-fascists the "Resistance" the media reverses the relationship of assailant and defender and renders a terrible disservice to the millions of Iraqis who oppose, in ways large and small, these totalitarian forces. Hadeel gave her life resisting fascism. Yet to the Ted Ralls and Michael Moores of this world, she was a Quisling who deserved to die.

How did this happen? How did the media confuse the real forces of resistance—police officers, administrative workers, translators, truck drivers, judges, politicians and thousands of others—with men who plan car bombings, assassinate government officials, and rampage through religious shrines in their quest to reinstate tyranny? Part of the reason is the anti-American bent of the international media: many reporters will sacrifice anything—including journalistic integrity—to defame the U.S. effort in Iraq. Then there is the semantic problem of the word "occupation" and its pejorative connotation: in the rudimentary arithmetic of the media, anything that "resists" a negative must, by definition, be positive.

But there is another, more banal reason for the press' confusion we might consider. Reporters, like generals, are always fighting the last war. And in their need to fix upon a narrative, baby-boomer journalists returned to a decades-old script that pits indigenous Third World freedom fighters against aging imperialist powers. Iraq became Vietnam redux—Apocalypse Again—only with sand and *kheffiyas* instead of deltas and black pajamas. (Neoconservatives, of course, hoped the conflict would resemble World War II, with Baghdadis dancing in the streets, waving American flags, and strewing flowers on the liberators.) Or maybe—heaven help us—Gen-x reporters may have seen the conflict as a replay of *Star Wars*: after all, whenever the empire strikes back, we root for the rebels, right?

However it happened, today we suffer for our lack of clarity in this war. Unwilling to call our enemies fascists, afraid to condemn the brutal aspects of Iraqi and Arab culture, we have allowed the narrative to slip out of our control. Truth is made, not found, in Iraq. Gradually, in the war of ideas, the U.S. became the evil occupier, opposing the legitimate wishes of an indigenous "resistance." We forgot the lessons of Vietnam and the people whom our defeat abandoned to the Killing Fields, re-education camps, and desperate flotillas of boats: sometimes, the empire is on the side of right—and it is the rebels who deserve to be crushed.

5

Blood of the Shia

Every day is Ashura, and every land is Karbala.

Imam Ja'far ibn Muhammad As-Sadiq

SITUATED AT THE BOTTOM OF A FLIGHT OF STEPS, the internet café was dark, quiet and nearly empty—the perfect refuge from the turmoil taking place outside. Exhausted after hours of slogging through crowds of Shia worshipers, I sank before a computer terminal, relishing its cool, hi-tech neutrality. But even this basement oasis could not block the chanting which echoed from the streets of Karbala.

> Each drop of blood in my veins
> Yells your name
> *Ya, Hussain!*
>
> How can my soul stay in my body
> When I remember your body?
> *Ya, Hussain!*

92

My body is not as valuable, my blood
Is not as valuable as yours
Ya, Hussain!

The café lay about a quarter-mile from the main square of Karbala, a city of half a million located in south-central Iraq. On previous trips, I'd sat in the palm-lined expanse, enthralled by the colorful Shia flags and banners and the small bands of men who thumped their chests and intoned hosannas to Hussain, grandson of Mohammad. When two or three of these groups intermingled—and the cries of muezzins rose from the Mosques of Hussain and Abbas at either end of the square—a charming and devout cacophony filled the air. But today was the tenth of Moharram (March 2). Known as Ashura, it is the Shias' holiest day, commemorating an event central to their religion. Radio reports estimated the crowd at four million and growing. And rather than the quaint "holy" city I'd known, Karbala had become a turbulent sea of pilgrims, convulsed by the veneration of Imam Abu Abdullah Hussain, a Shia hero martyred fourteen centuries ago. *Ya, Hussain!*

At this moment, though, I was more interested in accessing my email. So intent was I in vaulting from the seventh to the twenty-first century that I barely registered the soft thud that sounded in the distance. My driver, Samir, ascended halfway up the basement steps, conferring with the café owner who had also heard the noise. "Mister Steven," Samir said, motioning toward the street. "Come." Drained from sensory overload, I just wanted to sit in silence for a moment. "Come," Samir insisted, as the owner began drawing shutters over his windows. "*Infeejar, infeejar.*"

Explosion, explosion.

As fast as my neck-to-ankle *dishdasha* allowed, I sprang up the café steps, emerging back into brilliant sunlight. *Crump!* A second detonation, somewhere near the main square. I took a step in that direction. Samir grabbed my arm, his expression reading *Are you crazy?* I shook myself free. "*Anni sahafee,*" I said—I am a journalist—turning back toward the city center. "*La, la,*"—no, no—Samir shouted in alarm, as a third blast erupted. But I didn't stop, I didn't look back. For I am a journalist—and I was at the scene of a story that would shake Iraq and echo around the world. Terrorists were attacking the holy Shia festival of Ashura.

———

What is raining? Blood.
Who? The eyes.
How? Day and night.
Why? From grief.
Grief for whom?
Grief for the king of Karbala.

Qaani, a nineteenth-century Persian poet

I'D MET SAMIR ON LEAP DAY, February 29. Ashura is a slow-building festival—pilgrims begin arriving in Karbala and Baghdad weeks before the event—and I wanted to investigate the scene at the great Shia mosque of Kadhimain, in northwest Baghdad. Leaving my flat, I crossed Saddoun Street and stuck out my hand. Within seconds an orange-striped Sunny Super Saloon pulled over, its driver a balding, ruddy-faced man with thick lips and a pugilist's nose. "Kadimiya," I announced, he nodded, we were off.

The cabbie was Shia, judging by the religion's distinctive chant-music blasting from his stereo. In the run-up to Ashura you heard these anthems everywhere, from trucks, cars, boom-boxes set in sidewalk kabob stands. At first, I found the undulating voices of the male chanters, backed by antiphonal all-male choirs, fascinating, hypnotic. But after the ten-thousandth depiction of the Battle of Karbala and the blood of Hussain, the psalmody became repetitive, monotonous and, to my ears, maddening. I asked the driver to lower the volume. After a moment's hesitation, he complied.

Meanwhile, he was registering details about me. Glancing, for example, at my paperback. A history of Shiism, its cover bore a rendition of Imam Hussain, gorgeously armoured on horseback. And the t-shirt I purchased in Karbala featured the noble visage of Hussain's father Ali, beneath an Arabic quotation from Mohammad: "Ali is from me, and I am from Ali." "*Inta Shia*?" the driver questioned. No, no, I replied, a trifle embarrassed. Just interested, that's all.

As we neared the Kadimiya district, Samir and I—by now we'd introduced ourselves—discussed Ashura, which reached its climax on March 2. When I mentioned I was interested in making the fifty-mile trip to Karbala, I could almost see his ears twitch. "I will take you," he announced. "Free. No money. Because you are Shia."

Yeah, yeah . . . I knew I was being hustled and felt slightly irritated. Still, I wasn't sure how I was getting to Karbala or what to do when I got there. Samir was offering his services. But was he trustworthy? I wasn't sure I liked his rough-hewn, somewhat bellicose appearance; on the other hand, I'd been in Iraq long enough to know it was impossible to judge people—or anything else, for that matter—by appearances. "Deal," I said, shaking his hand. "*Ashoofrak bukhra*." See you tomorrow.

Featuring twin gold domes and four minarets, Kadhimain is one of the most beautiful mosques in Iraq. Built by the Persian Shah Isma'il in the sixteenth century, the shrine sits over the tombs of the seventh Shia imam, Musa al-Kadhim and his grandson, Mohammad

al-Jawad. Originally, Kadhimain overlooked Baghdad from across
the Tigris River; over time, however, the city expanded until now the
masjid abuts narrow streets lined with jewelry shops, small pilgrim
hotels, and sidewalk vendors selling religious paraphernalia.

With its mosque and bustling streets, Kadimiya is one of the
most charming districts of Baghdad, and I went there frequently.
In January, I attended the commemoration of Imam Jawad's death-
day. Perhaps the only Westerner present, I stood in Kadhimain's
open-air courtyard, or *sahn*, surrounded by assemblies of chanting
worshippers, ten-foot flags of shimmering gold, red, purple, white,
and turquoise silk, large black fields of cloth embroidered with Islamic writing and religious symbols. Doffing my cowboy boots, I
ventured inside the mirrored confines of the shrine, its atmosphere
heavy with prayer and body odor, watching the faithful rub the sides
of Imam Jawad's tomb and tie small green ribbons to its silver bars.
Later, browsing among the paraphernalia-sellers near the mosque,
I bought the first of the religious posters that eventually grew into
a small collection. The vendor, surprised at my ability to identify
the characters portrayed, asked if I were Shia. When I replied, no,
Christian, he flashed an ironic smile. "For now," he said.

Today, that same street hummed with pilgrims, mostly Iranian,
judging by the Farsi I heard. A sense of joy and anticipation filled
the air, part of the general excitement gripping Baghdad as Ashura
approached. In the past, Saddam Hussein had suppressed the event.
Now, for the first time in decades, Shias could openly commemorate
it. Banners appeared on light posts, store fronts, and building walls
from Kadhimain to the Shia stronghold of Sadr City to the ecumenical streets of Karada. Multi-colored, dramatic, frequently depicted
dripping blood, the scimitar-like sweep of the Arabic calligraphy
evoked the fierce desert faith of Islam, its emphasis on aggression,

on *jihad*. With the Shias though, that spirit seemed turned inward, absorbed in some secret pain. There was a mystery at the heart of the sect, I felt. It captivated me, and I wanted to know more.

—

Mohammad is the Seal of the Prophets,
and I am the Seal of the Successors.

Ali ibn Abi Talib

I HAD TO WONDER. Why was I so interested in Shia Islam? Obviously, to understand a country where 60 to 65 percent of the population, roughly fifteen or sixteen million people, is Shia, it helps to know the creed—to know, in other words, one's Ali's from Abu Bakr's and why the Ummayad family has a higher unfavorability rating than the Bush clan. Then, too, there's Al Qaeda. Part of the terrorists' goal in attacking the U.S. is to create a Sunni-Wahabbi caliphate that will rule Saudi Arabia, destroy Israel, and cleanse Islam of Shiism, which they consider heretical. Far from an obscure theological dispute, the Sunni-Shia schism is a religious civil war with tremendous ramifications. The fields of Karbala extend to the empty space of Ground Zero.

But there were other, more personal, reasons. Some had to do with Islam itself. For most people with even a flicker of spiritual instinct, the religion of submission holds a fascination. It shrinks the space between the sacred and mundane, transports the quotidian into the realm of the divine, and streamlines the mythology of salvation. Several times a day, muezzins beckon the faithful across land and cityscape to prayer. The Koran is the incontestable Word of God; the *hadiths* (or collections of legends and stories of Mo-hammad) bestow divine injunctions for every action. The division between the inner and outer world, much clearer in Christianity, is blurred. Add the militancy of its practitioners, cultural traditions that reinforce its beliefs, and a deep resistance to criticism and self-analysis, and you have a religion that unapologetically smacks you with Allah at every turn. No wonder Muslims consider Christians misguided souls who unpack their God only on Sundays.

But it was Shiism, not Islam, that gripped my imagination. It began in early October, when I'd hired Dhia to drive me to Karbala and Najaf. As soon as we cleared the scrofulous towns south of Baghdad, I started to see tall roadside paintings of Imams Ali and Hussain, their impossibly handsome visages shrouded in green cloaks. (Green is the color of Islam.) Smaller versions of these fanci-ful depictions were plastered onto taxicab windows, hung from the rear view mirrors of passing cars, affixed to the backs of swaying pilgrim buses. Coming from a secular country which does not even allow an image of the Ten Commandments in a courtroom, I found this display of religious faith intriguing. But even more captivating were the small black flags planted near the roadside. Small fields of tattered cloth bereft of writing or images, these Shia emblems fluttered from mounds erected in the midst of desert wastes, with only palm groves or a few mud huts nearby. Who put them out there, for whom, and why? Reverent and mysterious, these lonely ensigns—reminiscent of the black standards of rebellion the Shias raised against the Abbassid dynasty in the ninth century—filled me with a spiritual pang I never felt with Christianity. This must be one compelling religion, I thought, to inspire such simple, but profound, devotion.

Later that afternoon, I became a Muslim.

Technically speaking, that is. It happened when Dhia and I visited Najaf. Located about one hundred miles south of Baghdad, this "holy" city of six hundred thousand is home to *Meshed Ali*, the Tomb of Ali, Shiism's third holiest site, after Mecca and the Dome of the Rock. Cloaked imams and lonely black flags still possessing my thoughts, I asked Dhia if he could take me inside the mosque, to deepen my knowledge of Shiism. Although Sunni, Dhia balked at leading a *kufr*, an infidel, into such sacred precincts. To appease his conscience, I rattled off a phrase I'd memorized for occasions like this: "*Ashahadu an la ilaha ill Allah, wa ashadu anna Muhammad-ur-Rasool Allah*" (I declare there is no God but Allah and that Mohammad is the Messenger of God). Called the *Kalimah*, it is the supreme testimony of Islamic faith, the utterance of which makes one Muslim. It's that simple. "You see, now I am truly *Muslim Amrikee*," I declared, trying not to sound flippant.

Cocking an eyebrow at my "conversion," Dhia nevertheless escorted me to the *masjid*, where, at a security checkpoint, he vouched for my status as a Muslim. I repeated the *Kalimah* for the guards' benefit, adding for good measure, "*Aliyaan waliullah wasiyyu Rasool-Allah*" (Ali is the friend of God and the Prophet's successor). Surprised and seemingly charmed by this American Shia and his terrible Arabic, they waved me through.

Originally founded in the tenth century, the Imam Ali Mosque was rebuilt by Shah Isma'il, the same Persian ruler who constructed Kadhimain in Baghdad. After passing the *riwaq*, or two-story portico surrounding the structure, Dhia and I emerged onto the sun-splashed *sahn*. Here, hundreds of Muslims milled about the courtyard's ladders, scaffolding and other evidence of repair and renovation, chatting, praying, reciting Koranic verses, groups of women in black *abiyas* squatting on the white concrete. In the center of the expanse sat the shrine itself, a square building featuring a golden dome, twin minarets, and exterior walls adorned with ornate blue, white, and yellow tile work. Age had burnished the mosque's surface to a honey-russet tone.

The martyr buried in the shrine, Ali ibn Ali Talib, is central to the Sunni-Shia split. Born in the Kaaba itself, Ali was Mohammad's cousin, first male convert, and eventual son-in-law. He was also—according to the Shias—the Prophet's rightful heir. Among numerous proofs adduced to support this claim, Shias note an incident that took place during the Battle of Uhud (625 AD). Although the Muslims lost that day, the Angel Gabriel was so impressed by the courage exhibited by Mohammad's cousin that he declared, "O Messenger of God, what a redeemer Ali is!" To which the Prophet announced, "Ali is from me and I am from Ali"—the very phrase on my t-shirt. No wonder it met with such approval.

Proficient in war, Ali was unfortunately not as adept in the slippery world of post-Mohammad politics. After the Prophet died in 632 without male issue, a dispute broke out over who would succeed him. Many felt that Islam's founder had intended Ali to adopt the mantle, but Mohammad's father-in-law Abu Bakr outmaneuvered the younger man to become the first leader, or caliph, of the new religion. By all accounts a quiet, pious figure, Ali waited twenty-four years before finally becoming caliph. His short imamate was characterized by constant rebellion and conflict with Mu'awiyah ibn Abu Sufyan, governor of Syria and head of the Ummayad family. Ali was assassinated in 661 by the first of Islam's interminable extremist sects, the Khawarij.

Feeling like a junior-grade Sir Richard Burton, I deposited my boots in a booth, then walked to a line of water taps, where Dhia instructed me in *wudu*, or ablutions before prayer. A child stared at me while I fumbled through the ritual, and I feared he would expose my mistakes—but no, he was just fascinated with seeing a Westerner in such an unusual setting. Refreshed, I followed Dhia into a crush of men shoving through a portal leading to the inner chamber of the shrine. Above their heads, I glimpsed a cavern lined with mirrored glass and inlaid mosaics of green and sky-blue tiles and, as the crowd pushed further into the chamber, the crypt of Ali himself. Here, in a stifling ambience of murmured prayer and excited adoration, pilgrims embraced the silver and gold tomb, men on one side, women on the other, kissing and rubbing their hands along its surface, clutching its panels as they wept. (Reportedly, the gold is fake, Saddam Hussein having long ago stripped it for his coffers.)

I wandered amidst the crowd, blinking in the harsh neon light that allowed no shadow. Suspicious glances kept flitting my way. Sidling up to me, Dhia muttered that people were asking who I was. "Perhaps I should act more Muslim?" I suggested. One eye on my friend, another on men lowering their Korans, I emulated as best I could the bending, kneeling, genuflecting motions of *salat*, or prayer. Self-conscious at first, I soon caught the devotional rhythm, my spirit steadily lifted by the dignity of the movements, and the magnificence of the setting in which I performed them. I was conscious of the millions of Shias who had come to this mosque to pay homage to Ali, conscious, too, of performing the traditions that have helped sustain and preserve their way of life for centuries. And at once, I felt the magic of Shiism encompass me, its glittering mysteries and effervescent dream-state stirring the dormant ashes of my own beliefs. It passed through me like an electrical charge and I left the mosque feeling clean, energetic, and alive.

We rule by the authority of the House of David,
and if we lack anything then the Holy Spirit sends it to us.

Imam Hussain

OUT OF ONE AND A HALF BILLION SOULS in the *Dar-al-Islam*, around
150 million adhere to Shiism (the name is a shortened version of the
Arabic "Shia-t-Ali," or "Party of Ali.") They comprise the majority
populations of Iraq, Iran, and Azerbaijan, with sizeable numbers in
such countries as Pakistan, Afghanistan, Lebanon, and Saudi Arabia. Despite the Shias' many doctrinal differences with mainstream
Islam, if you ask your average Iraqi, he'll tell you, "Shia, Sunni, no
difference. We are all Muslim."—often rubbing his index fingers
together in a sign of shared interest. Probe beneath the surface,
though, and you'll find *fitnah*—discord—aplenty between the two
sects, especially among radical Sunni-Wahabbis, whose hatred for
Shiism is near-genocidal.

Because they contend that Abu Bakr robbed Ali of his rightful
inheritance as Islam's first Caliph, Shias refuse to recognize the authority of Sunni religious leaders. Some even cast aspersions on Abu
Bakr and other Sunni favorites, including Omar, the second caliph,
and Aiesha, Mohammad's favorite wife. Rejecting the Caliphate,
the Shia instead acknowledge a lineage of twelve imams descended
from Ali. When that line ended in 874 with the disappearance of the
twelfth, or "Hidden Imam" (who will return to earth come Judgment Day, Islamic eschatology says, accompanied by Jesus who will
"break the cross and forbid the eating of pork"), they turned to
clerics chosen by God Himself.

This concept of divine appointment sounds like a recipe for
disaster—and indeed, it helped create Islamic Republic of Iran.

But the Iraqi Shias' religious establishment, called the *Hawza*, opposes Khomeini-style activism and seems more content with the traditional role of guiding, rather than directing, politics. In this ecclesiastical environment, a cleric rises in stature based on his morals, lifestyle, and number of followers who adhere to his religious interpretations. This process of advancement-through-hermeneutics involves the intricacies of *ijtihad*—or "intellectual reasoning" and limited debate in spiritual matters. While hardly creating Muslim versions of the Council of Trent, or even Vatican ii, it does mean that moderate Shiism has the potential to be more flexible and tolerant than Sunni Islam, which infamously "closed the doors to *ijtihad*" in the eleventh century.

"Sunnis are more narrow and rigid in their beliefs," Ahmed, the former Shia cleric who had been tortured by the Baathists, told me over tea at the Hewar. "Shias have a deeper sense of themselves as Muslims, and most take a liberal, transcendent view of the religion. Their approach to Islam is pure and lovely and intensely passionate." I can vouch for Ahmed's last point: several times I asked Shias to describe what their faith meant to them, only to watch them burst into tears as they tried to articulate their feelings. On a pilgrim bus from Basra to Karbala, I rode beside a one-legged man who cried the entire trip, even as he mouthed the Shia chant-music blasting through the vehicle.

As for the Sunnis, with their long association with mainstream Islam, they appear, on the surface at least, more rational in their religious practices. Especially, Sunnis insist, when compared to the Shias, whom many consider over-excitable obsessives. Ashura strikes them as overdone and not a little blasphemous, and they reject the veneration of Ali, Hussain, and the other ten imams. After all, doesn't the Koran state, "Take not with Allah another object of worship; or thou (O man!) wilt sit in disgrace and destitution"?

That's not all they find objectionable about Shiism. Meandering through the Najaf *souk*, Dhia and I discovered a video monitor playing a tape from a Shia festival in Pakistan. To the funereal beat of heavy drums and a chorus of shouts and groans, shirtless pilgrims flagellated themselves with metal whips, while others sliced their heads with swords. Rivulets of blood poured down their naked skin, even as they shrieked the name of Hussain. Stunned by the spectacle, I glanced back at Dhia. Tsk-tsking in disapproval, he said, "So many tears over someone dead for centuries—Shia minds are stuck in the past."

Macabre things happen to Shia bodies, too. Located outside of Najaf is Wadi al-Salaam (Valley of Peace). Stretching over six miles, it is the largest cemetery in the Muslim world, comprising millions of graves—including, so it is said, Abraham's and Isaac's. Shias believe that Imam Ali declared the valley to be a piece of heaven on earth, and for centuries they have carted cadavers to this spot, creating a lucrative "corpse traffic," with side businesses in tomb-building and shroud-weaving. (In the spring and summer of 2004, the cemetery became a battlefield—as did parts of Karbala and Kufa—between U.S. Marines and Jaish-i-Mahdi militiamen loyal to radical cleric Moqtada al-Sadr.)

But as I watched a funeral procession take a shroud-draped coffin across the Najaf streets toward burial in the cemetery, I had to wonder about the Shias' conception of Paradise. The Valley of Peace is in fact an endless stretch of tan-colored above-ground crypts, fashioned of brick, many crumbling with age, reminiscent of sand castles washed over by ocean waves. Despite its name, the cemetery contains no grass, trees, shade, flowers, monuments, or even mourners. Occasionally you will see a pair of youthful grave diggers or an old Bedouin dozing lizard-like in the sun. It is a silent necropolis, astonishing, decrepit, ghastly, so seemingly at odds with the high, clean desert spirit I felt in the mosques of Kadimiya, Najaf, and Karbala.

Non-Shia Muslims have long looked askance, or worse, at this veneration of tombs. In the late 1700s, the ultra-puritanical Muhammad ibn Abd al-Wahhab became convinced that Shia beliefs violated Islam's monotheistic teachings and launched a holy war on the sect. Allied with a bandit clan known as al-Saud, in 1801 al-Wahhab's followers sacked Karbala, looted the mosques of Hussain and Abbas, and slaughtered thousands. In 1803 and 1806 they led unsuccessful raids on Najaf. They conquered Mecca and Medina before eventually meeting defeat at the hands of Egyptian governor Mohammad Ali Pasha. But Shia persecution didn't stop there. The Wahabbis and al-Saud clan revived their fortunes and, in the twentieth century, established the Kingdom of Saudi Arabia, where Shia-hatred burns as hot as the desert sands.

According to its Wahabbi beliefs, Saudi Arabia considers the Shias—which comprise about 5 percent of its population, or two hundred thousand people—the essence of *shirk*, or blasphemy. In social, cultural and educational aspects, discrimination against the Shia *rafida*—or "rejectioners of religion"—is rampant. One government-sponsored agency, the World Assembly of Muslim Youth, even publishes literature claiming that Shiism is a Jewish plot to destroy Islam. There are personal stories, too. A woman in Baghdad told me about being on the Hajj in Mecca with a coterie of fellow Shias. Gathered in a tent, they were trading religious stories, some of which mocked Omar, whom the Sunnis consider Islam's second Caliph. That evening, the *mutaween*, or Saudi religious police, accosted the group, charging them with "anti-Islamic" sentiments. Only by fast talking were they able to placate the cops and avoid expulsion.

This religious bigotry turns maniacal with the Sunni-Wahhabi group Al Qaeda. In the missive Zarqawi wrote to his fellow

Islamofacists, he urges his associates to destabilize Iraq by spark-
ing conflict between the Shias and Sunnis. "Shias have declared
a subtle war against Islam," he proclaims. "Even if Americans are
also an archenemy, the Shias are a greater danger and their harm
more destructive . . . How many brothers have they killed? How
many sisters have been raped at the hands of these vile infidels?"
He vows "We will undertake suicide operations" against Iraq's Shias,
and reveals that planning for sectarian mayhem is already in the
works. As the March 2 attack on Ashura demonstrated, the terrorist
was true to his word.

—

> Dawn sheds its blood out of sadness for Hussain
> And the red tulips wallow in blood
> And carry the brand marks of their grief on their hearts
>
> Turkish poet Ergun

ALL THE WORLD SEEMED TO COME TO KARBALA. The Shia world,
at any rate.

On the ninth and tenth days of Moharram (March 1 and 2),
Samir and I traveled to the holy city (his offer of "free" transportation turning into a negotiated fee per trip of thirty-three thousand
dinars, about $19). Each day, we merged with traffic flowing south:
pilgrim buses, SUVs with luggage lashed to their roofs, pickup trucks
packed with cheering, waving people. We passed hundreds of Shias
journeying on foot: women in *abiyas*, chanting youths, tribal elders
tottering on canes, a father with his young son perched atop his
shoulders, waving a little black Shia flag. Shouts, songs, banners,
large striped tents where pilgrims rested, drank water, ate lentil

soup from iron cauldrons—the excitement was palpable. You could sense the Shias thinking—*finally, after years of Saddam's oppression, Ashura!*

A couple of miles from the city center, we hit the first security stops: ID and trunk checks by Iraqi police and black-clad al-Mahdi gunmen. The police insisted we park the cab there and walk into the city. No way, huffed Samir. With a combination of Baghdad bravado and my out-of-date arts correspondent press card, he bluffed the cops into thinking that I was a *very important American journalist* whose car *had* to be let into Karbala. Incredibly, they complied, both days permitting us park as close to the mosques as the security-conscious city allowed. I was impressed; if nothing else, my bulldog of a driver knew how to handle himself around cops.

Ashura commemorates the Battle of Karbala, the event which forever divided the Party of Ali from mainstream Islam. The real conflict was a bloody one-sided affair—a spiritual Alamo, if you will—in which forces of the Ummayad family annihilated the leader of Mohammad's Hashemite clan. And while the details of the massacre are obscure to most Westerners, to the Shias they blaze in myths, images, and passion plays, forming the core of their religion.

After Ali's assassination in 661, Mu'awiyah, the Syrian Governor—a late convert to Islam and son of one of Mohammad's bitterest enemies—claimed leadership of Islam's growing empire for the Ummayads. Refusing to defend *his* claim, Ali's oldest son, Hasan, instead accepted a pension and withdrew from the fray (in 669 AD, he was poisoned—by his wife, Shia historians believe, possibly under the orders of Mu'awiyah's).

Possibly to avoid internecine strife, Hasan's brother Hussain decided to wait until the Ummayad's death before asserting his right to the Caliphate. Mu'awiyah obliged in 680, but his corrupt son Yazid refused to relinquish power. Prompted to act, Hussain took up arms and marched out of Mecca. It was a neat bit of historical symmetry: the virtuous Hashemite grandson of Mohammad set forth to save Islam from the dissolute Ummayad grandson of one of Mohammad's chief foes.

The Imam's forces numbered about seventy-two men, women, and children, including members of his own household. They headed for the anti-Ummayad city of Kufa in southern Iraq, whose people pledged they would flock to Hussain once he arrived. But Yazid's men got there first, and through terror and bribery smothered support for the Imam. Hussain's destruction was a foregone conclusion. The Ummayads' four thousand men surrounded his little camp near a place later called Karbala (karb meaning "anguish;" bala "vexation"), depriving it of water for nine days. On the tenth day (Ashura means "ten"), they attacked. The last males to perish were Hussain's half-brother Abbas, his six-month-old baby Ali Ashgar, and Hussain himself. Yazid's men decapitated his corpse and sent the head to their exultant chief in Damascus.

The death of the Prophet's grandson shocked the Islamic world, especially those who sided with the Hashemites. (One of Hussain's sons survived to carry on the line.) For them, Hussain's fate was more than a quashed insurrection, it was a martyrdom. A myth developed around the catastrophe: sinless, infallible, realizing beforehand the fate that awaited him, Hussain marched to doom in Karbala, knowing that his death would expose the Ummayad's brutality and preserve forever the flame of pure Islam. As for the Kufans' cowardice and duplicity, it became a source of perpetual shame—one for which many Shias seek to atone by wailing lamentations and beating themselves with whips, cudgels and swords.

Caught up in the drama of the story, I entered Karbala on March 1. This was my first day, and I expected a jubilant festival—a sort of Muslim Easter which would celebrate Hussain's sacrifice as a symbol of joy, resurrection, and eternal life. Didn't the Imam's fate have Christian overtones? And those images of Ali and Hussain you saw everywhere—with their light skin, Aryan features, flowing hair and close-cropped beards, didn't they bear a resemblance to Sunday-school images of Christ? Then there were the posters I bought in Baghdad: among other scenes of Karbala, they depict Hussain clutching baby Ali, an arrow protruding from the infant's neck; Hussain cradling, Pietá-style, the dying body of his teenage son; Hussain's severed head, rapt in orgasmic death-ecstasy. The Christian riffs were unmistakable, albeit a Christianity that, in Shia imagination, conflates the myth of Mary and Christ into a single image of martyrdom and parental sorrow. A single masculine image, of course. (As an example of how intent Shi'ism is on gender-cleansing its mythology, there is a story that first person to nurse the infants Hasan and Hussain was not their mother, Fatima, but Mohammad himself, using saliva from his tongue.)

Scuttling behind Samir's broad shoulders as he cut a swath through the crowd, I marveled at the colorful banners covering the facades of storefronts and buildings. I admired the black-lined booths displaying swords, shields, and mirrored tiers of multi-colored glass vases. I gaped at the beautifully-colored silken flags embroidered with Arabic writing. And I tallied the different congeries of Shias from around the Muslim world: Iran, Yemen, Bahrain, Lebanon, Afghanistan, a contingent from Pakistan in white *dishdashas* and pillbox caps. Ashura, I thought, it's a bit strange, a little bizarre, but you still have to admire the Shias' religious fervor. It puts to shame the bloodless Presbyterianism I knew.

But there were also some bumpy moments that first day. Overhearing a comment I made in English, a tea seller refused to serve me; only after I unbuttoned my *dishdasha* to show him the Ali t-shirt did he change his mind. On another occasion, Samir and I ran across a parade of about two hundred Iraqi women—their entire bodies, down to their faces and hands, covered in black—many of them bearing Arabic signs. DEATH TO AMERICA, read one, translated by Samir; AMERICA IS THE GREAT SATAN, read another.

Then there was an incident involving Samir himself. Leaving Karbala that afternoon, we stopped to eat at his friend's restaurant just outside of town, where, during most of the meal, I had to endure waiters and customers offering me their opinions about the U.S.—America was "no good," Bush a "bad man," the invasion "only for oil," or to "help Israel," and so on. I looked to Samir for help, thinking he might admonish his pals to back off, but he avoided my eyes, eating and smoking in silence. His detachment concerned me. Did he agree with his friends? Did he, too, harbor animosities toward the U.S. And if so, how far could I trust him?

When we returned to Karbala on March 2, the climactic day of Ashura, I found my mood had darkened. Part of it was Samir: I wondered if his gruff taciturnity was in fact disguising hostility toward me. The flood of sensory input didn't help any either—the ear-splitting eulogies, chest-thumping worshippers, banners, flags, crowds grown so dense in Karbala's main square they now stood practically immobile. Something else felt immobile, too: the spirit of whole festival.

All this devotion doesn't lead anywhere, I realized. It seemed circular, repetitious. For all its religiosity, Ashura lacked symbols that lift the spiritual imagination beyond the Battle of Karbala. What it needed, I thought heretically, was an image of resurrection: Hussain rising, Christ-like, from the ashes of his failure and defeat. But the Iman is a man, not a man-god. The story of Ashura must end with his death—anything else in Islam would be *shirk*, blasphemy.

At the same time, though, I began to wonder if the Christian motifs in Shia iconography weren't exactly what they seemed: a desire to emulate Christianity and—in a case of flagrant *shirk*—deify Hussain and Ali, transform them into Christ-like incarnations of God. Ashura could use such a myth. Lacking a sense of transcendence, the festival offered the Shia no catharsis, no symbolic redemption. And so, like trauma victims, the pilgrims obsessively repeated scenes of the Karbala massacre, reliving the agonies, the suffering, their religiosity growing increasingly overwrought.

I began to see the festival with different eyes. Mirrored replicas of Hussain's bier, decorated with ornate vases and artificial flowers. Black bunting depending from the facades of the two mosques. One-hundred-foot-long banners spelling out Hussain's name in bleeding red letters. Eight-foot-long white silk flags depicting crossed swords, the blades oozing blood . . . pictures of severed hands, severed heads . . . a fountain in front of *Meshed Ali* spraying geysers of blood-red liquid . . . bloody swords flashing over the heads of milling crowds . . . men with blood-soaked bandages wrapped around their heads to stanch the bleeding from self-inflicted wounds . . . endless posters of the slaughtered innocents . . .

This an orgy of death imagery, I thought.

Meanwhile, tromping through the crowd, processions of men wearing headbands and black t-shirts marched in heavy lockstep to the beat of two bass drums, groaning in unison as each struck his back with a metal flogger. *Ya, Hussain*—UH! *Ya, Hussain*—UH!

I saw children flagellate themselves with smaller versions of the adults' metal floggers. I met a group of men sharpening on whetstones the swords they planned to use to slash their foreheads. "Come back at five this afternoon," they told me, as if advertising a performance. I felt a kind of thrill, a cruel delight, permeate the crowd as it obsessed on Hussain's suffering. And I thought of a passage from Nietzsche's *Genealogy of Morals*: "Without cruelty there is no festival . . . and in punishment there is so much that is *festive.*"

It was this cruelty submerged in Shiism that had attracted me, I realized. The black flags, the delirious belief, the emphasis of suffering, death, dismemberment—they evoked archaic passions of blood and violence that our modern age has struggled to put to sleep. Shiism awakens these Dionysian instincts, renews their potency and allure. But as fascinating as I found the religion, I knew I could not pass beyond the level of surface infatuation. I am not a Muslim, and certainly not a Shia—even if I did convert I could never experience such exquisite pain over the fate of Hussain. I could never access the deepest heart of the Shiism: piety, trauma, and the veneration of death.

—

The hardship of martyrdom is all grace and coyness:
The intoxicated understand the secret of Karbala.

Shah 'Abdu'l-Latif of Bhit (1689-1752)

BUT NOW REAL DEATH WAS STALKING ASHURA.

Still moving toward the Mosques of Hussain and Abbas, I was surprised to see the pilgrims' nonchalance. But when the fourth *Crump!* sounded seconds later, a ripple of concern passed down the street. I quickened my pace. It occurred to me that I had no idea where these bombs were located, or how many more were to come—for all I knew I was heading straight into the next explosion. By the fifth *infeejar*, I could tell the pilgrims were beginning to take notice, their concern shifting to alarm. Glancing around, I discovered that in my rush to find the source of the blasts, I'd gotten lost and did not know how to get back to the car. *Six!* There was the sixth explosion, louder yet! The thought of a panic involving four million people crossed my mind. Where was Samir? I turned, hoping to catch a glimpse of him before he was lost in the multitude, leaving me alone in Karbala.

But he was right behind me. "All right, let's go." Relieved, he seized my wrist and dragged me away from the square, no more *sahafee* nonsense now.

We zigzagged through the crowd. People seemed confused, uncertain, some heading away from the city center, others moving toward it. A pick-up truck packed with wide-eyed Iraqi police careened by. Sirens wailed. One, then two, ambulances forced their way past us. A vehicle halted next to a building, the driver shouted over a loudspeaker, two men in lab coats bounded out. "The police are asking doctors to report to first-aid stations," Samir translated.

We reached the edge of the city center, where Samir had bluffed the cops into letting us park. He pushed me toward the car, but I hesitated, trying to get a read on the situation. What did these people think? Did they know what was happening? I didn't want to leave. "Come, come," Samir insisted, his muscular arms pushing me along. I broke loose just as an ambulance shot past on a cross street. "Hospital, over there," he noted, pointing to the right.

The hospital route ran along an east-west roadway, with the route we were on continuing to the south. Samir's cab sat to the left, the only car along a long stretch of curbside. Before us, police and al-Mahdi militiamen were running, shouting, gesticulating with their AK-47s, trying to clear the roads. At that moment hundreds of pilgrims appeared to the south, their flags and pennants resembling a medieval peasant army. With a shout of *Ya, Hussain!* they charged north, colliding in the intersection with the second group trying to escape the city. Chaos and confusion followed as they jostled, pushed, and knocked into one another; I saw one old man trip and fall onto the pavement. Suddenly, sirens and flashing lights approached from the left. Cops and militiamen screamed at people to clear the roadways as the ambulances bore down—too late. With a sickening thud, a Red Crescent van struck an old woman, her *abiya* spread to the wind as she flew sideways, almost certainly dead.

"Mister Steve, come, come!" Samir shouted, unlocking the cab. But I motioned wait, wait, jumping onto a traffic island for a better view, dictating every detail into a miniature tape recorder. An armed al-Mahdi man ran toward me, *kheffiya* flapping, shouting at me in Arabic. "*New York Times!*" I exclaimed, holding up my press card. Nodding, he darted away.

Struggling to keep order, the police organized bystanders into two human chains on each side of the hospital road, creating a cordon through which a stream of ambulances passed unhindered. Even so, chanting pilgrims breached the barrier, driven by their obsession to reach the mosque of Hussain. A taxi careened down the cordon, causing people to dive out of the way, screeching to a halt only when militiamen leveled their machine guns at it. Leaping out, pale with fear, the driver threw open the cab's back door, revealing a pile of bodies, streams of blood smeared across the back seat upholstery and rear window. Behind the cab roared two flatbed trucks loaded with additional casualties, pyramids of broken human beings, bruised and bleeding. One man stirred, his arm falling over the lip of the truck bed, its shredded flesh yellowed and blackened by the explosions.

Something—the fear in the eyes of the police, Samir's agitation, the cries of Iranian women begging us to drive them from the city—told me it was time to go. I leaped off the traffic island and jumped in the cab. But the sight of two men—one a foreign-looking man, at that, dressed in a *dishdasha*—attempting to drive away from an area where no cars should have been parked, attracted attention. A crowd descended on us, blocking our passage. Alerted by the scene, a policeman ran up, demanding to know our identities. When I revealed I was an American, the mob stiffened as if electrified. Men pressed against the car. One began screaming, another reached through the open window and seized my notebook and tape recorder. I leaped out, pleading for my possessions, he threw them in my face. The crowd's temper was at a tipping point, I realized, susceptible to the slightest provocation.

That's when I heard the cop shout "*Amreeka, Amreeka!*" Samir responding "*La, la, Wahabbi, Wahabbi!*" My heart stopped. The policeman—and, I now understood, the mob as well—believed that *America* had attacked Ashura, that we had killed the pilgrims. Their anger—blind, irrational—was mounting; the cop wanted to detain me. But Samir was defending me. No, no, it was Al Qaeda, not the U.S. who had set off the bombs. The cop shouted back. Coiling himself beneath the policeman's chin, Samir seemed to spring up, roaring something in Arabic that could only have been *Let us go!* Startled, the cop drew back—then, with an angry gesture, ordered the crowd to move away as we leaped into the taxi. Within seconds, Samir was tearing down the road, blasting his horn, weaving in and out of police cars and ambulances rushing toward us to take the dead and wounded to the hospital.

It wasn't until we cleared the last checkpoint that we thought to turn on the radio. The news was horrible. Up to one hundred dead in Karbala. Terrorists had also struck the Kadhimain Mosque, killing another one hundred. (The eventual death toll of both attacks, claimed by Al Qaeda, was 271, making it the worst terror strike yet seen in Iraq.) We drove in silence for a long time. Suddenly, I did something unexpected. I started crying.

I had admired the Shias. I had marveled at the ardor of their faith, thrilled at the grandeur of their mosques, lamented the tragedy of Hussain. At the same time, I'd patronized them, too—decorated my apartment with their religious kitsch, snickered at their rituals, memorized their holy phrases as a sort of religious tourist game. But despite my ambivalence, it was *their* religion, one they had sustained for centuries, especially in such dark times as the regime of Saddam Hussein. And this Moharram—the biggest since the demise of the despot—they'd come by the millions to worship at Karbala and Kadhimain. It was to be a wonderful occasion. The fact that Al Qaeda had murdered hundreds of them seemed unbearable. Once again, terrorism had destroyed, and morally diminished, what it touched.

The ironies were almost too bitter to conceive. A religious gathering that glorified martyrdom had itself created martyrs. A festival of cruelty had turned into its own cruel festival. Ashura had become Karbala. As we drove past blue-green date groves and flat desert fields, a sense of something unspeakably vast and dark overcame me. I had witnessed people attending a religious festival commemorating the massacre of innocents become innocent victims themselves. Nietzsche was right: cruelty and sanctity are a razor's edge apart. And as I realized on my rooftop on 9-11 and before the Assassin's Gate of CPA headquarters, the *haram*, the divine obscenity, of terrorism hallows its victims, consecrates them—provided that the living bear witnesses to meaning of their deaths. I came to Iraq, in part, to bear witness for those killed on 9-11; I have tried to do so with Hadeel. Now, I realized, I will do the same for those killed at Ashura.

Drying my tears, I thanked Samir for pulling me from a tight spot. He just grunted. I had pegged him wrong in the end, although I wasn't sure why he defended me—perhaps it was because I'd hired him for the day and his personal honor depended on seeing me safely to Karbala and back. If so, there was another irony: the honor-shame dynamic which I had found so tedious had, in the end, come to my rescue. But this was too much to think about for one day. I sat back in my seat and watched the countryside roll by. After a while, Samir turned up the volume on his lugubrious Shia chant-music. For once it sounded just about right.

6

Government of Martyrs

Martyrdom is a mixture of a refined love
and a deep, complex wisdom.

Ali Shariati

BENEATH THE ELEVATED MURAL of the slain ayatollah the Shia
banners massed, their silky red and pink and purple colors standing out against the deep blue sky. South of Mustansiriya Square, the faithful were in motion, thousands of black-
clad marchers passing down Mohammad al-Qassem highway, chanting, shouting, brandishing photographs of their religious leaders:
Mohammad Baqr al-Hakim, Ali al-Hussaini al-Sistani, Moqtada al-
Sadr, and here and there the grim visage of the Ayatollah Khomeini
himself. Heating the procession's fervor to a warm, but containable,
temperature was a bearded man ensconced atop a pedestrian foot-
bridge, reciting Koranic verses through a bullhorn. Carried aloft by
earnest-looking demonstrators, banners passed along the street,
many with slogans inscribed in English:

NO TO TERRORISM

AL-HAWZA IS OUR LEADERSHIP

ELECTIONS OF RELIGIOUS LEADERSHIP IN IRAQ

WHY IS THE U.N. NOT DEMANDING FREEDOM OF
IRAQ PEOPLE?

Meanwhile, two olive-green U.S. helicopters circled overhead like observant eagles.

The January 19 demonstration was called by Grand Ayatollah Sistani, spiritual leader of Iraq's sixteen million Shias. Its objective was a show of force against America. At this time, the U.S. was pushing a plan whereby the CPA would supervise the creation of regional "caucuses" across the country, which would then select a provisional legislature by June 30. Sistani, however, favored a simpler method to choose a new Iraqi government: a hands-down, one-person, one-vote election held under UN auspices.

"Look! Look! Five million people are marching in the streets for democracy!" A man, observing me scribble in a notebook and assuming I was a *sahafee*, had broken from the parade to offer a fanciful estimate of the crowd. (Reuters placed the number at up to one hundred thousand.)

"Tell President Bush, democracy for Iraqi people!" a second man joined in. Both resumed their place in the flow of demonstrators.

The march was disciplined, peaceful, and bereft of anti-American rhetoric. If it weren't for the Arabic writing on the banners, the nearly all-male composition of the demostrators, and the bull-horned *suras*, this might have been any rally in any democratic country in the world. As it was, the upbeat ambiance was a far cry from the fervid atmosphere of resentment, hatred, and slaughter that characterized the Sunni Triangle. Unlike the Sunnis, it seemed, the Shia saw peaceful protest, rather than violence, as the best way to communicate their desires.

But, like everything else in Iraq, this was deceptive. The American plan was a laudable attempt to shift the basis of Iraqi politics from ethnic, tribal, and religious differences toward a more neutral foundation based on geography. Sistani, however, would have none of it. With Iraq's Shia population outnumbering all other religious and ethnic groups combined, he knew that the Party of Ali would emerge victorious in direct elections, reversing five hundred years of Sunni domination. The Shia, in other words, would call the shots. No wonder that among the date groves along Highway 10, the Sunnis were doing the shooting.

Not that the Shia weren't also chafing under the "occupation." "America is the source of all of Iraq's problems," declared Jasim, a thin, bespectacled student from the *Hawza*, the religious seminary at Najaf. "Of course," he continued, adjusting his wire-rimmed glasses, "it is good you ended Saddam. But you must leave soon."

"How soon?" I asked.

Jasim shrugged. "Two years. As Ayatollah Sistani says."

"And if the U.S. isn't gone by then?"

"Then we fight," Jasim replied, looking about as rugged a street fighter as Woody Allen.

But there was grit in the seminary student nonetheless. "My grandfather was killed by the British in the uprising of 1920," he told me, as we walked beside the stream of marchers. "Before he died, he gave his rifle to my father and told him to use it to protect his country from evil. Before my father died, he gave me the gun and told me the same thing. Now, if U.S. soldiers do not go home in two years, I will take up arms and kill them—although," he added prudently, "I won't use my grandfather's gun, because it would probably explode in my hands."

Youthful bravado, perhaps. Still, the Shia can be as seditious and bellicose as their Sunni brethren—perhaps more so. With their history of serving as the official religion for Islam's great caliphs and dynasties, the Sunnis are comfortable with worldly power: in their mind, a government is legitimate as long as it maintains order and security. Centuries of oppression and persecution have led the Shia, however, to consider most temporal authorities as despotic usurpers, with true legitimacy residing in their religious leaders, or the *ulema*. It was the *ulema*, for example, who pushed for the 1920 uprising against the British. In the 1960s, Khomeini fashioned the presumed superiority of the *ulema* into a concept known as *Vilayat-i Faqih*, or government by clerics, and overthrew the Shah in 1979. Now it was America's turn: in April, 2004, rebel cleric Moqtada al-Sadr initiated an insurrection against the "occupation" in an attempt to enhance his influence in post-Saddam Iraq—and, some suspect, topple the religious order of the *Hawza*.

Meanwhile, an Iraqi snake-pit exists, comprised of radical Shia groups like the *Da'wa Islamiyya* (Islamic Call) and the Supreme Council for Islamic Revolution in Iraq (SCIRI)—which maintains a private, ten-thousand-man army called the Badr Organization—all promising cooperation with the new Iraqi government, even as they denounce America and jockey for power. There are also Iranians: Hezbollah militants are infiltrating across the border, while until recently, Iraqi Ayatollah Kazem Haeri, living in Iran, provided Sadr and his insurrection with financial assistance. Adding further unpredictability is the Shia obsession with the martyrdom of Imam Hussein and resulting feelings of alienation, defeatism, and despair. "Each Shia believes that he falls and dies with Hussain," the ex-cleric Ahmed explained to me. Whether they can now rise and live again in a new Iraq is a question whose answer largely rests with their seventy-four-year-old leader, Ayatalloh Sistani.

—

MAINSTREET NAJAF was thick with cars, buses and donkey carts, elderly sheikhs in brown *abiyas* discussing the latest news, religious pilgrims, and men wearing green neck scarves walking about with Kalashnikov rifles. Two of these worthies escorted Iraqi journalist Abdul Amir el-Malik and me through a low-slung blue gate, past the *Meshed Ali*—where, two months earlier, I had "converted" to Islam—before leading us down a narrow street and depositing us at the entrance to an alleyway. On the left stood a dilapidated brick building, exposed concrete columns, pipes and wires; on the right a dusty barbershop set beside a seedy pilgrim hotel. And in the middle, more armed men.

With Abdul translating, the plainclothes guards demanded I turn everything over to them: camera, notebook, pen, miniature tape-recorder. Meanwhile, a teen-age kid swept me down with a pair of security wands. Finally, a genial fellow whose silver hair matched the barrel of his Kalashnikov gestured for me to move down the alley. It was no more than six feet wide, pinched at the top by twin rows of sagging two-story hovels, leaving only a thin strip of blue sky visible. Halfway down a slight bend, two unarmed men in athletic suits stood before a yellow brick entranceway, regarding me with flat expressions. On the ground floor of the house they guarded—with their lives, I had no doubt—the windows were shuttered, coated with ageless dust, permitting light neither to enter or leave. A beige brick facade decorated with wooden slats began on the second floor, where, directly above me, I saw an open window frame divided by two rusting iron bars and covered by a brown-striped towel: the bedroom of the chief resident of this gloomy abode, Grand Ayatollah Ali al-Sistani.

"The Ayatollah is busy and cannot speak with you," one of the sweatsuited men grunted. I wasn't surprised: Sistani, after all, had refused to meet Paul Bremer—in fact, up to that point, the Iranian-born cleric reportedly hadn't left his home in six years and speaks to the press only through representatives. No, it was enough just to stand here, beneath this unadorned window in the anchorite-like surroundings where Iraq's most revered leader lives. It was a far cry from the brutal ostentation of Saddam's presidential palaces.

When cautioned during World War II not to anger the Vatican, Stalin famously retorted, "How many divisions does the Pope have?" Sistani has no military power either, yet he keeps the Coalition at bay by controlling the invisible power of popular appeal: the Ayatollah is, quite simply, beloved of millions of Shia. In large part because he has advised his followers to tolerate the Anglo-American presence—and has refrained from issuing *fatwas*, or religious rulings against their armies—the Shia have not engaged in a Sunni-style insurrection. Mindful of the failed uprising of 1920, after which Britain turned to Iraq's more compliant Sunnis to run the country, Sistani has instead counseled patience. "The circumstances are not right to call for *jihad*," one of his representatives told an AP reporter in June, 2003. "At present we are using peaceful means to demand a constitution and a representative government. But," he added as a caveat, "it will be a different story if those demands aren't met."

My silver-haired escort stirred and looked uncomfortable. I realized that because of Abdul, who knew some people in Sistani's organization, the guards had permitted me this breach of protocol.

"Okay," I nodded to my minder. Motioning with his gun, he smiled and directed me back up the alley.

> [Sharia] has enjoined these rites on man
> while he uses atomic energy to mobilize the engine,
> just as it has enjoined them on man
> while plowing his field with a hand plow.
>
> Ayatollah Mohammad Baqr al-Sadr

BUT WHAT DOES SISTANI WANT? And the Shia—what are *their* hopes? And, most important, are either capable of achieving their goals?

When asked about politics, most Shia will tell you two things: first, they support Sistani; second, they do not favor an Iranian-style theocracy. This two-fold unanimity, at least on the Iraqi "street," is significant. They see the repression and cultural impoverishment of Iran and reject the concept of *Vilayet-i Faqih*. Then, too, as the location of the Garden of Eden, the birthplace of Abraham, and cradle of the Sumerian, Babylonian, and Assyrian civilizations, as well as the crucible of Shiism, Iraq maintains an obstinate pride when it comes to religion. "Iraq exports spiritual doctrines," journalist Yahya Batat remarked to me. "We do not import them."

But another reason why Iraq's Shia largely oppose Iran's experiment in Khomeinism is because Sistani has placed his moral authority—and that of the *Hawza*—behind an opposing doctrine. Called Quietism, it holds that clerics should remain aloof from, or above, secular affairs, interceding only when absolutely necessary. Moreover, because the *Hawza* acts as a rough equivalent of the Vatican, providing Shiism with a single voice, Sistani can proclaim his Quietist message largely free of static from dissenters. The Sunni, by contrast, suffer all sorts of loose-cannon clerics, such as the one-armed, one-eyed former sheikh of London's Finsbury mosque, Abu Hamza al Masri, who once declared that the Columbia space shuttle disaster was ordained by Allah because the joint America-Hindu-Israeli crew constituted a "trinity of evil against Islam."[1]

But Sistani's Quietism does not mean absolute detachment from politics. In response to pressure from Sistani, for example, the U.S. eventually dropped its "regional caucuses" plan in favor of the Ayatollah's demand for direct elections, scheduled for early 2005. He also refused to recognize the legitimacy of Iraq's interim constitution, in large part because it granted federal status to the Kurds, thereby giving them veto power over the permanent constitution. And there was nothing "quiet" about his memorable march to Najaf last August to put down Moqtada al-Sadr's uprising. Clearly, this is a man who, when he needs to, can take decisive action.

Unfortunately, crucial aspects of Sistani's political vision aren't so clear. Chief among them is his vision for Iraq's future. Although he has acknowledged that the nation is a multi-ethnic, multi-religious state that must respect non-Shias, how this position will work in practice—whether Sistani's Iraq will resemble Turkey or Iran—remains to be seen. The Grand Ayatollah plays his cards close to his chest.

Not so other clerics. In conversations I had with Shia imams all through Iraq, I heard a similar sentiment. "We see no conflict between secular government and Islam," said Ahmed Darwish al-Kinani, then head of the Islamic Movement of Iraq, one of many religious parties that sprang up after the fall of Saddam. "There will be problems only if the new constitution contradicts the *shari'a*." Echoing his thoughts was Aodha el-Obaydi, a sheikh in the Basra office of SCIRI. "We have one aim, one hope, one vision for Iraq, and this is Islam. We do not expect that Iraq will not become an Islamic state ruled by the *shari'a*."

1 "Astronauts were 'trinity of evil', says banned cleric," *Guardian Unlimited*, February 3, 2003.

A sobering thought. A system of religious-based laws, rules, and precepts, the *shari'a* is one of Islam's most controversial aspects. Based on the Koran and the *hadith*—and containing elements of Bedouin, Jewish, and Roman laws and traditions—the *shari'a* encompasses the totality of a Muslim's life: it is, quite literally, totalitarian. Its religious and legal injunctions are inflexible, inscribed in the Holy Book and revealed in the Prophet's life for all men, for all time—although the process of *ijtihad*, when performed by a recognized Muslim *mujtahid*, or scholar, seeks ways to adapt the commands to changing times and circumstances. "With *ijtihad*," explained Ahmed, my guide to all things Shia, "there is room to interpret and liberalize *shari'a*. It all depends on how narrow a view the *mujtahid* takes. The narrower his view, the less debate he will permit." (As noted earlier, the Sunnis discarded the concept of *ijtihad* in the eleventh century; instead, they rely on four schools of thought to deduce new applications for the divine law.)

Most interpretations of the *shari'a* agree on certain things: the necessity of the so-called Five Pillars of Islam (faith, prayer, fasting, almsgiving, and the pilgrimage to Mecca), as well as the obligation of *jihad* (often considered the sixth pillar). The precepts contain innumerable commandments to be kind, honest, upright, fair, and conscientious in personal affairs. But they also contain onerous restrictions on women's liberties, as well as bizarre dietary injunctions (no pigs, foxes, cockroaches or scorpions—although locusts are okay) and barbaric criminal statues (mutilation for thievery, death for apostasy—that is, conversion from Islam—crucifixion for "sowing terror among the people.")

The Law addresses a vast range of topics, as Grand Ayatollah Sistani himself makes clear on his website, sistani.org, which has a convenient question and answer section dealing with everyday *shari'a* dilemmas encountered by the faithful. A few points illustrate the Shia leader's thinking.

- On friendship with women: "Friendship with her is not permissible. Because in such friendship man is not immune from sin."

- On talking to a woman to seek consent for a future marriage: "Due to probably committing sins it is not permissible."

- On a Hindu man who wants to marry a Muslim woman: "It is not permissible."

- On playing chess: "It is absolutely unlawful."

- On music: "It is permissible to listen to music which is not fit for diversion or play."

- On why one can't play the lottery but can gamble on horse-racing and archery: "Lottery is a sort of gambling and there is nothing one may do to deserve the property. But horse-racing and archery are for a purpose which is called 'self-defense.' However, this is the order of Allah and we are but to follow it without asking for a reason."

- On the definition of an orgy: "It is forbidden."

- On keeping one's head under the shower for more than one minute: "It is not permissible."

- On "zina," or adultery: "Zina does not take place without penetration."

Perhaps emulating the Prophet and his comments in the *hadith*, the Ayatollah also issues a number of rulings pertaining to menses.

As for the *shari'a* and democracy, I received a stark exhibition of the basic incompatibility of the two at a western NGO in Basra. One of the tasks of this international aid organization is to teach Iraqis the basic tenets of democracy. When I asked how, exactly, the NGO goes about doing that, I was introduced to a charming, highly intelligent, Oxford-educated Iraqi man named Adil. Adil was a "Senior Trainer," meaning he instructed other Iraqis working for the NGO how to organize "council meetings" in rural areas, in order to encourage people to speak out about topics that concerned them.

"It is our hope to teach villagers how to listen to different points of view and have a free exchange of ideas," explained Adil, who like many Iraqi intellectuals had about him an arch, slightly pompous air. "Recognizing that there are no limits to free speech is an important aspect to learning about democracy."

"No limits," I repeated. "Okay, so I could stand up in the council and say 'I love Saddam Hussein?'"

Adil nodded sagely. "Of course."

"How about, 'The only problem with Halabja was that not enough Kurds were gassed?'"

"If that is your opinion. The point is free speech."

"All right. What if I stood up in the council and declared that the Koran was a book written by men, not God, and that it has gone through several revisions over time?"

Adil frowned. "That is not true," he said.

"Maybe, maybe not. But if the object of these councils is to encourage free expression of ideas—"

"But it is harmful to tell lies about the Holy Koran. Why should we allow you to tell lies that that might hurt people?"

"What if I said that 'women should be as free as men?'"

Adil looked relieved. "Why not? That is Islam."

"And that women should be free to have sex with anyone they like before marriage?"

"But—" He checked himself. "No one would say that. It is against Islam."

"Against Islam."

"Yes. Against the *shari'a*."

"So there are limits to free speech?"

"No," answered Adil, looking frustrated. "It's just that certain topics are not debatable. Such as topics that involve sacred areas."

"Who defines a 'sacred area'?"

"Everyone knows what those are. Everyone knows what is permissible and not permissible to say." Sitting up straight, he threw his shoulders back and seemed to inflate his chest. "You must understand," he began in a patronizing voice, "unlike Christianity, which has become a religion for Sundays only, Islam for us is life—and life is Islam."

"But is Islam democratic?"

"Of course. Islam *is* democracy!" I asked Adil to give me an example of a true "Islamic democracy." Turkey? Iran? Shaking his head, he answered with an inexplicable note of pride, "Islam has not seen true democracy since the death of Imam Ali"—in other words, 661 AD. "But *insha'allah*, we will bring one to pass in an Islamic state of Iraq."

Be careful you don't get what you wish for, I wanted to say, but kept silent.

No discussion of Shia beliefs would be complete with mentioning a few of the more unusual concepts that Shiism reserves for itself, such as the idea that Muhammad al-Mahdi, the Hidden Imam, is still alive and active in everyday affairs, even though he disappeared at the age of five in 874 AD. Then there is *taqiyya* ("dissimulation"), which allows Shias to lie about being Shia in circumstances when admitting their true religious affiliations might bring persecution, dishonor, poverty, or death. Many Sunnis find *taqiyya* despicable and cowardly; on the other hand, it has reportedly hampered U.S. intelligence efforts to penetrate militant Shia groups.

But perhaps Shiism most controversial practice is is *muta'a*, or "temporary marriage." (*Muta'a* means "enjoyment, pleasure, delight.") Originally intended, some sources say, to alleviate men's sexual distress during long caravan journey's, *muta'a* permits a Muslim male, either married or not, to enter into an agreement with an unmarried Muslim, Christian, or Jewish woman, whereby he enjoys all the conjugal benefits of marriage, in return for supplying her with money or property. The time period of this rent-a-wife relationship can be as short as one hour, or as long as decades. Under *muta'a*, nevertheless, women receive no rights of inheritance, the man is under no obligation to provide food or shelter for her, and any children produced by their liaison revert to the custody of the father. The Sunnis forbid *muta'a*, as they do other Shia peculiarities, believing that the second Caliph Omar abolished it during his regency. The Shia, however, marshal passages from the Koran and the *hadith* to justify the practice, while claiming that it keeps widows, unmarried women, and impoverished females from begging or prostitution. Some Shia traditions teach that whoever has practiced four *muta'as* is "secured a place in paradise."[2]

—

2 "Mut'a," *Encyclopedia of the Orient*, lexicorient.com.

> Resistance, resistance! The people of Najaf
> are with you, Moqtada—all the people are
> with you! You are our only leader!

supporters of Moqtada al-Sadr, quoted by Reuters, May, 2004

DURING ONE OF OUR CONVERSATIONS about Shiism in the palmy garden of the Hewar, Ahmed recounted yet another legend involving the Battle of Karbala—one that bodes further trouble for the future "Islamic State of Iraq." According to this tale, as Hussain lay dying on the blistering desert sands, he issued a curse against the people who betrayed him in his hour of need. "You are *munifaqeen* [hypocrites, a serious charge in Islam]," gasped the failing Imam. "After I die, you will find no mercy. Never shall you be satisfied with a ruler, and no ruler will ever be able to lead you in peace."

I'm not sure how well-known the legend is, but it's worth noting that a decade or so later, the brutal Ummayad governor and savage Shia-persecutor Hajjaj bin Yousef issued a similar anathema, declaring his subjects *ahl alshiqaq wal nifaq*, or the "people of disunity and hypocrisy." Indeed, Iraq has traditionally been a hotbed of sedition, divisiveness, and obstinacy. In his 1922 memoir, *The Insurrection in Mesopotamia*, British Lieutenant General Alymer Haldane quotes a letter from Ibn Saud, founder of modern Saudi Arabia: "As regards the tribal leaders and notables of Iraq from whom you want the improvement of the country, they do not wish that the people of Iraq should be quiet, and that there should be law and order in the land. It is impossible to change their nature, as this has been their policy of old and continues so today. Their whole idea in life is to stir up the people in order to gain profit from the Government."[3]

3 Alymer Haldane, *The Insurrection in Mesopotamia* (Ediburgh: Blackwood, 1922), 314.

There are many reasons for Iraq's volatile and recalcitrant nature—periodic onslaughts of marauding foreign armies, the Arab
"Bedouin ethos," the institutional weaknesses of Islam, and its
population's lack of modern political identity. Along with these,
however, we must add Shiism itself, in particular its attachment
to Hussain's martyrdom—the event, as scholar Moojan Momen
writes in his 1985 book *An Introduction to Shia Islam*, that gave
the religion "its impetus and implanted its ideas deep in the heart
of the people."[4] Ideas, we've seen, of sacrifice, devotion, and faith,
unsullied by governors, kings, or presidents who might seek to ex-
tinguish the flame of Allah.

But there is another side to this mindset. As I've noted, Shia
imagery extols mutilation and gore, while the commemoration of
Ashura is fixated on death. Not, however, death as a spiritual passage
to redemption, but death as a cruel and sensual spectacle. Rather
than internalize the spirit of Hussain, Shia rituals, traditions, and
imagery tend to externalize the event, degrading its message of
spiritual submission into empty displays of piety and grief. They
exhibit overzealous, theatrical signs of worship, while offering few
symbols to effect an inward transformation of the soul. What results
is a peculiar attitude that views martyrdom not as the sacrifice of
the self *to* God, but as the glorification of the self *by* God. If early
Christians believed that the blood of martyrs nourished the Church,
the Shia hold that martyr's blood embellishes their own holiness,
and that of their families, for untold generations.

This idea that God venerates those who "witness" themselves
supplies, of course, the theological justification for suicide bombing.
And though the Shia organization Hezbollah pioneered this modern

4 Moojan Momen, *An Introduction to Shia Islam* (New Haven: Yale University Press, 1985).

use of *shohada*, an important distinction exists between the Sunni and Shia varieties. The Sunni terrorist seeks honor and exaltation in a kind of suicidal sadism, killing as many of his civilian enemies as possible. The Shia *shaheed*, on the other hand, pursues his spiritual apotheosis by getting his enemies to kill *him*—a lethal exhibitionism first seen in the Iraq-Iran War, when Tehran sent waves of teenage boys, adorned with red headbands and plastic keys to Paradise, into battle zones to trigger land mines. So far, Iraqi Shia radicals have not resorted to terrorism against civilians. In addition, rather than use clandestine IEDs or car bombs against U.S. troops, Sadr's al-Mahdi militia opposed Marines in irregular combat—and paid the price. Re-enacting the fate of Hussain and his followers at Karbala, many Shias, it seems, would rather *be* killed than kill.

Spiritual martyrdom is the essence of this faith, the psychological axis around which it turns, a nearly indispensable factor in the divinity of its leaders. Take, for instance, the Imamate—the apostolic succession of twelve personages descended from the Prophet through Ali. It's no surprise that eleven of these divines were murdered, in most cases by poison.

As if condemned to maintain this tradition, contemporary imams have also met grisly fates. In 1980, Baathist thugs executed Grand Ayatollah Mohammad Baqr al-Sadr by driving nails into his head. In April, 1998, Ayatollah Murtada al-Burujerdi was shot and killed after leading prayers at *Meshed Ali*. In 1999, Grand Ayatollah Mohammad Sadiq al-Sadr and his two sons were assassinated while driving near Najaf; the deaths sparked four days of heavy clashes between the Shia and Saddam's security forces. In April, 2003, a mob hacked to death pro-American Ayatollah Abdul Majid al-Khoei outside the Tomb of Ali. Four months later, a car bomb outside the shrine killed SCIRI head Ayatollah Baqr al-Hakim; no one claimed responsibility for the deed.

Hakim's death struck a nerve with the Shia. All through Bagh-dad and southern Iraq, you see posters of his bearded, round-eyed visage; during the January 19 demonstration, it was in front of his mural in Mustansiriya Square that the marchers gathered. In the double-minareted mosque in Karada, my guide Hasam paused in his tour of the *masjid* to show me a poster of the Ayatollah and sixty of his family members, all killed by Saddam, superimposed over a bleeding map of Iraq. "We are a religion of holy martyrs," Hasam noted in a reverent voice.

Of course, not all Shia festivals are as macabre as Ashura. Eid-e Ghadir, for example, joyously celebrates the day when the Shia be-lieve that Mohammad anointed Ali as his successor. Nor are most Shia death-obsessed extremists. But even if one discounts the reli-gion's fascination with martyrdom, the myth of Hussain presents an additional political problem: to devout Shia, the Imam is an icon who combines absolute piety in the religious realm with infallibility in the secular. This ideal of perfection is, of course, impossible for any mortal to embody (as Iran's once-fervent supporters of *Vilayet i-Faqih* have discovered), exacerbating the Shias' alienation from all-too-human leaders. This "Karbala complex," as some observers call it, explains in part Shiism's history of sudden insurrections, alternating with periods of resentful acceptance of secular power. Like the man or woman searching for the ideal spouse, they find no governing authority is ever quite "right." For them, the best is always enemy to the good.

The Shia's heritage of martyrdom, insurrection, and millen-nial fantasies also helps explain the troublesome phenomenon of Moqtada al-Sadr. A mid-level cleric in his early thirties, Moqtada is neither old nor educated enough to achieve *mujtahid* status; rather, he relies for his authority on the fact that his uncle Baqr al-Sadr and his father Sadiq al-Sadr were martyred by Saddam. He also taps into some Shias' criticism of the *Hawza*. His father frequently disparaged Sistani's Quietism and his Iranian birth; today, Moqtada is suspected of wanting to overturn Sistani's authority and establish a messianic religious order of his own.

Indicted in the murder of Ayatollah Khoei, in the spring of 2004 Moqtada forestalled arrest by launching his al-Mahdi militia in a brief uprising. He had hoped that Coalition overreaction would destroy shrines in Karbala and Najaf, enflaming the masses and expanding his power base, but his gambit achieved only limited success. American troops decimated his militiamen, while causing minimal damage to holy sites; meanwhile, the Shia rejected his grab for leadership, maintaining their loyalty to Sistani. Moqtada went to ground in Najaf, where, surrounded by armed followers, he evoked the mythic image of Karbala—denouncing the U.S., for example, as "*Yazid*," and declaring that "martyrdom gives us dignity from God."

Before his uprising, Iraqis repeatedly told me not to concern myself with Moqtada—that he was a "punk," "too young and inexperienced" to command a large following. But of course, I spoke to *reasonable* people. It is the *unreasonable* Iraqis—over two million of them, for example, in Baghdad's Sadr City, a wretched Shia slum—who support Moqtada. Their support is possibly strong enough to force the new government to create a role for the cleric, despite his murder indictment and his responsibility for the deaths of numerous GIs.

It is possible, however, that Moqtada is a remnant of the Shia past—that under Sistani's guidance, the Party of Ali can transcend its fascination with alienation and death and assume the responsibilities of temporal power. Indeed, the Safavid Dynasty (1502-1736) shows that the Shia can maintain a consistent government, albeit one with strong millenarian beliefs. But Safavids were centered in Persia, not the unruly Land Between the Two Rivers. Here, the messianic pretensions of Moqtada vie with the fundamentalist designs of SCIRI and *Da'wa Islamiyya*, while in the background millions of believing Shia feed their faith on anti-Western propaganda, calls for every-more rigorous observance of the *shari'a*, and eschatological myth. "Sistani in many ways is a medieval man, but he is our best hope for stability among the religious Shia," Ahmed told me. He is also the one Shia who could possibly gainsay the prediction of Hussain and prove that even the infallible vicegerent of the Prophet can be wrong.

Uncivil Society

The democratic system that is predominant in the world
is not a suitable system for the peoples of our region.
Our peoples' makeup and unique qualities are different
from those of the rest of the world. . . . In my view,
Western democracies may be suitable in their own
countries but they do not suit other countries.

Saudi Arabian King Fahd bin Abdul Aziz

I FIRST NOTICED IT at a truck stop outside of Basra. Actually, I'd
seen it happen all over Iraq, but hadn't paid much attention
before. Now, as people peeled bananas, unwrapped cigarette
packages, finished soft drinks, then dropped their garbage where
they stood, it dawned on me: littering is a way of life in this country.
Not that this particular truck stop offered much in the way of trash
receptacles beyond a rusty oil drum and soiled cardboard boxes.
What happened to waste material was clear: about fifty feet to the
right of the dingy tea house and accompanying vendor stalls stood

a four-foot-tall heap of fly-infested refuse. A pair of dogs were rooting through the debris.

Meanwhile, across the oil-soaked gravel of the parking lot,
hordes of teenagers washed, rinsed, and wiped down motorists'
suvs, Chevrolet Caprices, Volkswagen Passats, and other cars until
they glittered in the sun. "That's Iraq for you," grunted my traveling
companion, Iraqi journalist Yahya Batat. "They turn the landscape
into a trash heap, yet make sure their cars are clean."

And not just their cars. Arriving in Basra later that day, I accompanied Yahya (pronounced ya-HEER) to his in-laws' home,
where, in true Arab custom, we were treated to a huge repast of
fish, rice, salad, assorted condiments, and bread. Also in keeping
with Arab mores, I noticed, the house was cool and comfortable,
with immaculately clean interiors. Outside, on the street, it was a
different matter. Down the block stretched small ridges of bottles,
cans, rotting animal and vegetable matter, leading to a hillock of filth
piled at the end of the road. Given the cleanliness of the house, the
contrast was startling. Even more astonishing, people went about
their business seemingly unconcerned with the trash laying about
them slowly stewing in the sun.

It was the same across Basra—across Arab Iraq, in fact: spotless
homes shielded by high concrete walls from the garbage that clot-
ted the streets. (In Kurdish-dominated Kirkuk, the streets seemed
cleaner; moreover, I saw several signs admonishing people not to
litter, something unseen in the south.) The message conveyed by this
environmental carelessness was clear: for average Iraqis, whatever
happens beyond the borders of their personal property is not their
concern. There seemed to be no sense of shared space, no idea of
the commons or urban ecology—and consequently, little desire to
form, say, voluntary clean-up associations to remove the refuse.

"Iraqis don't think that way," explained Yahya, with embarrassed resignation. "They have no sense of what you would call a 'civil society.'"

It isn't just Iraq, of course: a dearth of communal spirit is evident throughout most of the Arab Middle East. But in Iraq it is especially painful to witness, given that this was once the region's most advanced society. Now, through the presence of 150,000 Coalition troops, it is the one Arab nation with a chance to achieve a recognizable form of democracy. But are Iraqi locals up to the task? Is there a civic sense, a communitarian instinct, lying dormant beneath their traumatized national spirit? What do the terms "nation," "citizen," "sovereignty" mean to them? These questions are crucial, of course; in many ways, they are the issues facing Iraq, the Middle East, and the future of the American "War on Terror." Unfortunately, the answers are not altogether inspiring.

On the surface, Iraqis are wild for democracy. Cab drivers grin and flash the thumbs-up when you mention the subject. Tribal sheikhs smoke their Pine cigarettes down to centimeter-long nubs while debating the merits of federalism. In major Iraqi cities, scores of storefront democratic organizations have sprung up like Starbucks in the U.S., while groups you wouldn't normally associate with representative government swear allegiance to the idea. In Basra, for example, a hard-line cleric told me that his group, *Da'wa Islamiyya*, Iraq's oldest religious Shia party, was "guided by democratic principles." Samir Adil, director of the Baghdad office of Iraq's Worker-Communist Party, confirmed that his group "believes in democratic elections, the separation of religion and government—and we stand against any pan-Arab or pan-Islamic state."

This is all very encouraging, of course, except for one problem: no one seems to agree on what, exactly, democracy *is*. Iraq's notoriously refractory tribal leaders pay lip service to a system of governance that, if successful, would replace the customs and privileges their patriarchal ilk have enjoyed for centuries with impersonal laws drawn up by bureaucrats in Baghdad. My Basran friend Nour took a cynical view: "Don't be fooled, Steve. Tribal groups just see democracy as a new way to get women and money."

As for the religious parties, most argue that any new Iraqi government must base its jurisprudence on *shari'a*, which, as we've seen, is not at all compatible with Western notions of equal rights and equality under the law. The *Da'wa* sheikh I spoke to even went so far as to admit that his vision of democracy was based on "the teachings of that great man, Ayatollah Khomeini." Despite their seeming secularism, the Worker-Communist party maintains the Marxist-Leninist preoccupation with world domination: "The objective the WCPI struggles for will only come true through a socialist revolution by the working class," reads a typical statement. Given that Iraq has no industry to speak of, let alone a "working class," such evangelical fervor is probably premature. As for the secular liberal parties, "They have members, but no programs," Juliana Daoud Yussef, editor of Basra's *Al-Ahkbaar* newspaper, noted wryly.

On an individual level, Iraqis seemed equally, if understandably, confused about the nature of democracy. Take, for instance, the not-inconsequential matter of elections. "I am sixty years old, and I've never voted in my life," remarked Hanaa Edwar, secretary of Al-Amal, a woman's health care clinic in Baghdad. "How can I, or any other Iraqi, nominate our own candidates?" As another Iraqi told me, "The only time I remember participating in national elections was in 1995 and 2002, when Saddam won 100 percent of the vote." With the dictator's landslide serving as a model—not to mention the dozens of other potentates that have come and gone throughout the Arab world—no wonder many Iraqis seem to view elections as a way to establish a majoritarian tyranny. "We have to teach these people that just because you win 51 percent of the vote doesn't mean you get to go out and shoot the other 49 percent," said a member of an American NGO working in southern Iraq.

Worse, some actually perceive democratic freedoms as a kind of libertine license. Nour told me of an Iraqi man who repeatedly called the NGO where she works and made lewd and suggestive comments whenever a woman answered. Usually, the women hung up. Nour, however, stood her ground and demanded to know why the man was harassing females. "We are going to have a democracy," replied the obscene phone caller. "Now I can do what I want!" This idea of democracy-as-moral-anarchy strikes terror in the hearts of other Iraqis. One rather puritanical Baghdad cabbie groused, "What does democracy mean? That men can drink all the time and women can have sex with whomever they wish?"

But the most counterproductive attitude I detected among Iraqis was their passivity. Constantly, I heard them gripe, "No security, no electricity, no jobs—this is the democracy that America promised?" It rarely seemed to occur to many of them that *they themselves* might have to pitch in and fight to win their freedom—that in history, few people have ever been *given* their liberty. When I broached this argument, these Iraqis would blink at me in confusion. To them, it seemed, the promise of democratic citizenship meant someone else taking care of the country's yard work, while they get to swing in the hammock of constitutional liberties, freed of responsibilities.

And that's just the beginning of the problem. Among secular-minded liberals—the kind of modernizing intelligentsia and opinion-molders vital to any democracy—no one seems to agree on a definition of their own nation. (Religious hard-liners, of course, do not share that problem: Iraq is an Islamic state, period.) This is no doubt to be expected from a country famously cobbled together by Winston Churchill in the aftermath of World War I. You hear much talk about the nation's Babylonian and Sumerian past, but those kind of poetic associations are ill-suited to fashioning modern political institutions. It's hard to imagine Hammurabi or Nebuchadnezzar in a world of popular sovereignty, proportional representation, and separation of powers. Others note the resourcefulness and adaptability of the Iraqi people—and while these characteristics are real, they can hardly substitute for a national spirit around which a post-Saddam society might form. Figuring out ways to keep a ten-year-old Sunny Super Saloon on the roads hardly substitutes for a sense of patriotic duty. So the question returns, casting a shadow over this country's struggle toward democracy. What does it *mean* to be Iraqi?

I posed this question to staff members of *Al-Manarah*, Basra's largest newspaper. The response was a lot of head scratching, chin pulling, and half-articulated answers. Finally, editor Lowai Hamza Abbas essayed a reply, "Because our country contains many different people, its nature is more the likes of spectrum. The Turcoman in Kurdistan has a different view of citizenship than the Shiite in Basra." Perhaps realizing he had just outlined the impossibility of a general sense of Iraqi nationhood, he added, "While Europe spent the last decade unifying, we have experienced a century's worthy of struggle which robbed us of our concept of 'Iraq.' We need to rebuild our ideas of our nation, and who we are as a people." Suddenly, a voice rose from the back of the room: "Perhaps our common suffering makes us a people."

The reason for this collapse of identity, nearly all Iraqis say, is Saddam Hussein. As Yahya explained, "Saddam drove it into our heads, saying 'I am Iraq, Iraq is me; when I speak, Iraq speaks.' When his regime fell, so did the Iraqi people." As Lowai noted, "We are suffering the results of thirty-five years of Saddam's brutal personality—a destroyed sense of humanity." Or, as a Baghdad cabbie remarked, "Saddam turned us into a bomb. When he left, we exploded."

Iraqis gave a stark exhibition of their propensity to "explode" in April, 2003, when they rampaged through Baghdad, looting scores of buildings. As late as the spring of 2004, much of the Iraqi capital still showed scars of that frenzy—entire buildings collapsed into ruin, empty skyscrapers bearing scorch marks from the flames that gutted their interiors. What could have provoked such destruction? At the time, Bush Administration officials claimed Iraqis were wreaking a kind of blind and furious revenge on the Baath regime. Iraqis themselves blamed the Americans for not restoring law and order in the aftermath of Baghdad's fall—and believed they actually encouraged the rioting in order to "demonstrate" to the world that Iraqis were incapable of governing themselves Others accused the criminals that Saddam released from jail shortly before the Anglo-American invasion; still others claimed that Baathist insurgents, following a pre-planned script, stoked Baghdadis' rage. Then there was Defense Secretary Donald Rumsfeld's dismissive explanation: "Democracy is messy."

Esam once told me a revealing anecdote from those bleak days and nights that suggested another explanation for the self-defeating behavior of Iraqis. Walking home one night, he passed through crowds of looters stripping the guts of a burning government office, "carrying all sorts of useless things—lamps, file drawers, telephones, anything they could take." Suddenly, a friend rushed by, his arms filled with pilfered objects. Noticing Esam's empty hands, the friend asked why he, too, wasn't joining in the pillaging. "These belong to the Iraqi people, we're going to need all this in the future," Esam sensibly replied. His friend, however, thought differently. "This stuff belongs to Saddam, he bought it with money from our oil. We are just taking back what we've already purchased."

A brief, but significant, exchange. For it symbolizes, I think, a deeper motivation for the looting of not only government offices, but private businesses and museums as well. Iraqis consider oil a particularly glorious portion of the riches God bestowed upon their country; fossil fuel forms part of their identity as a people. Saddam usurped those riches to aggrandize himself, led his country into disastrous wars, and even worse, warped and mangled the nation's soul. As a result, Iraqis felt no connection to—and no sense of re-sponsibility towards—the buildings, office towers, even cultural centers constructed under the tyrant.

Destroying these aspects of Iraqi civilization was not only an act of political revenge, but an attempt to purge the country's psyche of Saddam. In the vacuum of law and order, this effort devolved into wanton, unconscious violence directed not only against the dictator, but, most important, the kind of people they had become over the last thirty-five years. The despair was total. Hospitals, art centers, animals in the Baghdad zoo—all were destroyed in an attempt to escape the nightmare of their history. Even antiquities became a target, because Saddam had made a cult of Iraq's ancient civiliza-tions, trying to draw a direct link from Babylon to the Baath party. Iraqis turned on their own archaeological treasures, as if willing themselves into extinction.

It is impossible to overestimate the psychological trauma that Saddam inflicted upon Iraq. "He turned us all into Ali Baba," a Bagh-dad cab driver once said. "You hear Iraqis say that Saddam made them so apathetic that now, if they saw a man killing another man in the street, they wouldn't stop to help," Yahya remarked. "The Iraqi mentality today is too much a part of the old Saddam mentality," commented Hanaa Edwar. "It is an aggressive, broken mentality, unfit for democracy."

You see symptoms of this "aggressive, broken mentality" everywhere in Iraq. For example, at the truck stop with Yahya, I noticed a vendor selling toys—dolls for girls, replica pistols, rifles and Kalashnikovs for boys. It's a common sight: boys running around with alarmingly realistic plastic weaponry. I asked Yahya, given Iraq's violent past, not to mention thousands of nervous and heavily-armed GIs currently stationed in the country, shouldn't parents encourage their children to play with something else? "There aren't any other kinds of toys or games," he replied, shaking his head. "You must understand. Iraq is not a society. It is a huge army camp."

The free, pleasant social institutions that bond people together and form the sinews of citizenship—clubs, associations, neighborhood groups—are missing from this country. Few recreational outlets exist. Americans may bowl alone, but Iraqis don't even have bowling alleys. One mother expressed relief to me that a new form of entertainment recently became available for children: video game "cafés." But while these games may absorb the surplus energy of children, they are hardly instruments to teach young ones teamwork, fair play, and mutual respect, let alone the non-violent resolution of problems.

On the roads, Iraqis transform driving into near-gladiatorial contest of displaced aggression. Motorists refrain from using headlights until long after dark, and when they do, often flash their high beams in the eyes of oncoming drivers, who naturally retaliate, assuring mutual blindness. The livestock that periodically wander across city streets in Basra enjoy greater rights-of-way than people. Once, Yahya and I witnessed cars roaring by a stooped and terrified old woman who had gotten caught in the middle of a major thoroughfare. "When cars stop to let that woman cross the street, then we'll have democracy," commented my friend. By the same token, intersections unsupervised by policemen inevitably become gridlocked, with each driver pushing blindly forward. As for seat belts, their use is considered unmanly. Besides, as I was told, "Why bother wearing them? The police won't check."

Or take the lengthy queues one often sees forming at Iraqi gas pumps. "We sit on a sea of oil, why don't we have enough petrol?" I constantly heard. One reason is smuggling, a huge and profitable criminal business. But another is the black market. As I discovered in Basra, cabbies waited in lines up to twelve hours to fill their tanks, with twenty liters going for around 500 dinars, or 40 cents. (Gas, subsidized by the CPA, was literally cheaper than water.) They then sold the liters for 2,500 dinars to black-marketeers, who in turn flipped the gas to motorists for three thousand. This form of "making money without working," as one Iraqi hack quipped to me, exacerbated the fuel shortage, increased gas lines and raised costs for filling the tank. But Iraqis seemed to care little; in this society of all against all, whoever got the "edge," bent the rules, shafted his neighbor, came out ahead.

It's not that Iraqis are inherently cruel, unfeeling, or irresponsible people. On the contrary, time and again I experienced extraordinary acts of solicitude, generosity, and bravery. But the alienation that festers deep in the Iraq soul—alienation from their nation, its history, their own people and ultimately themselves—has created a vacuum into which pernicious anti-democratic forces have stepped. Remarked Lowai, "In the past, people were proud to be Iraqi—now, no one has a sense of loyalty to anything beyond money, tribe, or religion." It's the last two forces that are truly wreaking havoc on Iraq's hopes. "Our future as a democracy is threatened by two dark enemies," feminist leader Yanar Mohammad told me. "Tribalism and religious fundamentalism."

The problem of this twin-headed beast bedevils most Arab cultures, of course, resulting in their startling insularity and resistance to outside influences. (For example, according to the 2002 Arab Development Report, a document written by Arab social scientists, since the ninth century the Arab world has translated about one hundred thousand books—about the average that Spain translates in a single year.) As David Pryce-Jones writes in *The Closed Circle*, "Loyalty to tribe and religious affiliation obliges the Arab and the Muslim to defy and reject true understanding and acceptance of the outsider and unbeliever." This phenomenon, he adds, "continues to prevent the transformation of the collectivity of separate families into an electorate, of group values into rights and duties [and] of the power holder into a party system with a loyal opposition."[1]

This—not the Great Satan America or Little Satan Israel, not a history of colonialism and imperialism and any other "ism" Arabs use to claim victimhood—is the real enemy facing the Iraqi people, and the Arab world as a whole: intertwining tribal and religious customs. Responsible for magnificent testaments of spirituality and great works of art, the source of the wondrous hospitality and generosity displayed so often by Arabs, this thick, visceral ambiance of religiosity and dense family ties also smothers the individual in irrational custom and law. In this environment, obligation to individual conscience, that gift of the Judeo-Protestant tradition, is replaced by obedience to external authority. Here, the orientation of the individual is outward, to the clan, the *ulema*, a Book, rather than inward, to a sense of selfhood and inner truth. Shame before others, rather than guilt before one's own conscience, is the main

1 Pryce-Jones, *The Closed Circle*, 33, 38.

engine of self-regulation. The result is too often a parochial mindset that personalizes issues, no matter how large or small, into cases of humiliation, grievance, victimization, and lust for revenge.

The twin apotheoses of this tribal-religious psychology is the honor code and *shari'a*. The first, as we've seen, derives from an obsession with shame and "losing face," and leads to pointless, endless socially-sanctioned violence—often with women as the victims—which in turn undermines the basis for a rational government. As Pryce-Jones writes, "Equality under the law, that central constitutional pillar cannot be reconciled with codes of shame and honor." Even worse, he notes, "In tribal society, violence is . . . a mechanism of social control."[2]

Shari'a was intended in part to replace pre-Islamic Bedouin codes with rules and strictures based on the most impeachable of all sources: God. But is democracy possible under a system where jurisprudence is a branch of theology; where social strictures are based on the contradictions, incoherencies, and quite often barbaric writings of the Koran and the *hadith*; where—given Islam's institutional weaknesses—interpretation of these texts is always prey to the most hard-line, the most radical of clerics? There have been—and will continue to be—attempts to shoehorn *shari'a* into a democratic mold using Islamic notions of man's "vicegerency" on earth and the complicated relationship between the *ulema* and the secular state (the first guides and advises the second). But they founder on Islam's refusal to develop an idea of inalienable individual rights and the idea of popular sovereignty. Nor should we expect such innovations under the strict eye of the Mosque. Didn't the Prophet Himself once state, "Beware of new things, for every new thing is an innovation, and every innovation a mistake"?

2 Ibid., 38, 2.

Historically speaking, however, even *shari'a* proved no match for the ancient power of tribal custom. "The pre-Islamic code of conduct survived," writes Iranian feminist Azam Kamguian, "creating a powerful value system, parallel to Islam and practically and mutually nurturing and supporting one another."[3] In his monumental *Muqaddimah*, the great fourteenth century Arab scholar Ibn Khaldun went so far as to extol *asabiyya*, or tribal solidarity, as the primary bond of human culture and the driving force of history. In her 2003 book, *The Trouble with Islam*, Irshad Manji criticizes *asabiyya* and wonders if the religion of the Prophet has become "more a faith in the ways of the desert than the wisdom of the divine, and that Muslims are taught to imitate the power dynamics of an Arabian tribe, where sheikhs rule the roost and everyone chafes under their rule."[4]

This is why Iraqi—and Arab—culture has proven so resistant to change and modernization, and why it oftentimes seems so irrational to Western perceptions. It was arduous enough for America, the most innovative and tradition-free society in history, to begin to rid itself of pernicious tribal customs, as witnessed by the carnage of the Civil War. On an individual level, each one of us is familiar with the difficulty of breaking ties of family, local culture, and ethnic identity. How much more difficult is it for an entire country, where these parochial ties are enforced by religion, social consensus and the threat of culturally-accepted violence?

In Iraq, family is everything. In a September 28, 2003, *New York Times* article, reporter John Tierney noted that nearly half of Iraqi

3 Azam Kamugian, "The Lethal Combination of Tribalism, Islam & Cultural Relativism," (Insitute for the Secularization of Islamic Society),www.secularislam.org.

4 Irshad Manji, *The Trouble with Islam* (New York: St Martin's Press, 2003), 132-33.

marriages are between first or second cousins, "a statistic that is one of the most important and least understood differences between Iraq and America." Tierney cites Rutgers anthropology professor Robin Fox: "Liberal democracy is based on the Western idea of autonomous individuals committed to a public good, but that's not how members of these tight and bonded kin groups see the world. Their world is divided into two groups: kin and strangers."[5]

The idea of severing these family bonds is inconceivable to many Iraqis. One afternoon, I conversed with Altheer, a Christian Arab waiter working at the Orient Palace. Like many Christians, he lived in the Karada district, which he loved for its close-knit sense of community. "My family is all there—mother, father, aunts, uncles, and all their children. It is so wonderful!" In response, I told him I grew up in California and moved three thousand miles to New York in large part to get away from such a constricting social milieu. "Many people who move to New York do so to get away from their families: the freedom to start over is what makes the city, and America, so great." And cold, brutal, insensitive, militaristic, and death-oriented, I could see him think—or rather feel—as a look of incomprehension bordering on fear swept his face. The idea that people would want to uproot themselves from their family matrix confused and distressed him.

Iraq's answer to tribalism and religious fundamentalism was the Baath Party. Indeed, seen in the context of the current problems roiling the Middle East, aspects of the neo-Nazi movement seem startling progressive. Article 43 of the Party's constitution reads: "Bedouin life is a primitive social status that undermines the national production and renders a large portion of the nation para-

5 John Tierney, "Iraqi Family Bonds Hinder U.S.," *New York Times*, September 28, 2003.

lyzed. It is a factor that precludes the development and progress of the nation. The party is striving to modernize Bedouin life and give Bedouins lands together with the cancellation of the tribal system and the enforcement of the State's laws on them." The constitution also "combats all kinds of denominational, sectarian, tribal, ethnic and regional fanaticism."[6] This is one reason why Iraq was one of the few secular Middle Eastern nations. Unfortunately, it was also the most tyrannical.

And indeed, it was Saddam himself who reintroduced the regressive pull of the sheikh and imam. He sought to mobilize Iraq around an ethnic basis during his war with Iran by framing the conflict as an apocalyptic struggle between Arabs and Persians. In order to put down the Shia and Kurd rebellions in the aftermath of the 1991 Gulf War, he strengthened the power of Shia, Sunni, and even Kurdish tribal leaders in return for their neutrality. In an October 20, 2002, article in the *Los Angeles Times*, Sandra Mackey, author of *The Reckoning: Iraq and the Legacy of Saddam Hussein*, described how Saddam went on to organize labor unions, art schools, trade associations and other groups to form "non-kinship groups." Writes Mackey, "As a result, Iraq today is a more tribal society than it was at the time the country was pasted together by the British."

As for Islam, in order to shore up his faltering power, Saddam in the 1990s embraced the religion, ordering avowedly secular Baath party officials to memorize the Islamic scripture and adding the words "God is Great" to the Iraqi flag. In Baghdad, he constructed the "Mother of All Battles Mosque," which boasted eight minarets, four of which resemble Scud missiles, and which houses a Koran written in large print with three pints of the dictator's own blood. In 1994, he began constructing the Grand Saddam Mosque

6 www.baath-party-org.

in Baghdad's upscale Mansour District. Planned to be the world's second largest mosque (behind Mecca) and with a dome the size of a football field, the enormous structure now stands a half-complete shell, surrounded by construction cranes, another testament to his failed dreams of glory. Failed or not, his megalomania had dire effects for Iraq. Noted Edwar, "Directly because of Saddam, tribalism and religious fundamentalism took root in Iraq where they never were before."

Not every Iraqi has succumbed to the retrograde pull of tribal Islam—or Islamic tribalism. There are thousands of Iraqis risking their lives for the new interim government, as well as numerous women's and human rights groups working at the grassroots levels. Then there are newspaper editors such as Lowai and Yussef, struggling to articulate a concept of the state as guarantor of personal freedom and equal protection. "Democracy is a process, not an end point," Yussef said. "We must try to educate the people in this process, beginning with the most fundamental ideas—such as freedom of thought and speech and the need to take responsibility as citizens."

One person who understands this full well is Dr. Abdul Mashtaq, co-director of the Iraqi National Organization for Human Rights. When I visited him in the organization's headquarters, located in Baghdad's Mustansiriya district, he was busy forming what he described as a "moderate left-of-center secular party" called "Building Democracy." A spry sixty-year-old with a distinct gleam in his eye, Mashtaq is a former Communist turned liberal patriot. "Our party will be first and foremost about Iraq—no pan-Arabism, no pan-Islamism," he explained. "We hope to form the base for a movement that will build a new, prosperous Iraq, with equality and justice and freedom for all our people."

What makes "Building Democracy" different from the numerous other secular parties I encountered was this one actually has a set of concerns, ranging from support for a federalist form of government to issues the economy, women, and—surprisingly—the environment. "Our aim is to first construct a culture of democracy, with political groups, associations and institutions," the doctor went. "And we must start with a new education for our youth—for decades they were taught about a warlike Iraq, now they must learn about a democratic Iraq."

Democracy also has a surprising ally in the Iraqi Communist Party. Eschewing the revolutionary pretensions of the Worker-Communist Party, the ICP maintains a nationalistic, Iraq-only focus. The party keeps its anti-U.S. rhetoric to a minimum, generally eschews criticism of the "occupation," and describes resisting the terrorists and criminals who prey on Iraq society as a "patriotic duty." As Ali Mehdi, director of the ICP's Basra branch told me, "We want to establish labor unions, an independent judiciary, and participate in democratic elections, where we can put forth reasonable demands— we have no interest in a 'dictatorship of the proletariat' or setting ourselves up as an alternative to the government or the police." As for capitalism, Medhi struck an unexpected note of accommodation: "Our country is in need of private enterprise, and the skills and capabilities it can bring to Iraq." No wonder an NGO official once said to me, "If I were the CPA and wanted to spread democracy through Iraq, I'd pour money into its Communist parties."

The idea is intriguing: if the U.S. used radical Islam to help defeat communism, why not use communism to help defeat radical Islam? Unfortunately, none of the smaller secular groups I spoke to claimed to receive any funds from the CPA. "We asked, but they turned us down," Dr. Mashtaq said. Instead, the U.S. seemed more interested in shoveling money to accused Iranian collaborator Ahmed Chalabi. Worse—at least from the secularists' point of view—was the make-up of the (now-defunct) Iraqi Governing Council. Overseen by the U.S., the Council contained representatives from such Islamist organizations as *Da'wa Islamiyya*, the Supreme Council for Islamic Revolution in Iraq, and even Hezbollah. The presence of these Islamists was no doubt driven by political necessity, and the Council contained many secular-minded members as well (including Hamid Majid Moussa, head of the Iraqi Communist Party). Still, the legitimacy America gave to these religious groups demoralized the secularists, as did the U.S. Army's tactic of strengthening the power and influence of tribal leaders in the Sunni Triangle as a presumed bulwark against paramilitary fighters. "America is dividing Iraq along religious and tribal lines," Samir Adil complained. "They are hastening the breakup of our country."

Perhaps. As I write this, however, the leadership of Ayad Allawi seems to be holding, with the Prime Minister making tough decisions that Iraq needs to achieve law and order (such as reinstating the death penalty and threatening to impose martial law). Even more encouraging, a poll taken in the summer of 2004 indicated that 68 percent of respondents approve of the new government, and 80 percent expect their lives to improve under it.

But faith in the Allawi government does not necessarily translate into faith in democracy. Iraq has still far to go in that area. Beneath the surface of most people's longing for freedom you'll find an almost desperate craving for a Saddam-like "strong man" ("Only more democratic," Iraqis would add). Perhaps they are not much different than citizens in Western nations. But the questions remain: can Iraqis free themselves from the tribal-religious nexus that retards the development of the entire Arab Middle East? Can they unlearn the instincts and habits they adopted to survive under the dictatorship of Saddam Hussein?

"Democracy is like an egg, you can't simply 'make' it," Yahya mused. "You need a whole culture and environment." Echoing his thoughts was Juliana Yussef. "The ground isn't ready for democracy yet. Too many people say 'It's not my business' when asked to do something for their country." Still, the editor saw room for hope. "Tribal identity and the religious parties will fade as the new government gets established and the economy begins to pick up."

My poet friend Naseer put this issue—as he did many others—into the most intelligible and inspiring context. "Our nation has undergone pan-Arabism and pan-Islamism, socialism and fascism," he averred. "We have no other alternative now but to struggle towards democracy." The stakes in this conflict could not be starker, he added. "On one hand, a return to the barbarism of the Baath regime, fueled this time by religious fanaticism—on the other, the first democracy in Iraq. No wonder the Arabs are afraid," he noted. "Iraq could be the starting point for a new Middle East, a new Arab world. And dare I say it? A new Islamic world."

I CAN'T END THIS CHAPTER without relating an important lesson the Iraqis taught me about democracy.

It was an offer I couldn't refuse: to address the Basra-based Union of Iraqi Writers and Journalists on freedom of the press. "We have no idea what independent media means," said Nour, who was organizing the event. "It's never been a part of our lives." As a freelance writer, I knew something about independence; as for the concept of a free press—well, I figured I'd wing it, so I agreed.

The lecture was well-timed. The southern Iraqi town of Basra is currently undergoing a journalism renaissance. In 1890, the city boasted seventy-three newspapers; a century later there was one, owned by Ouday Hussein. Today, Basra has around ten publications, ranging from religious broadsheets to Yussef's *al-Ahkbaar*. "Real journalism is new for Iraqis," the editor told me. "They are struggling to understand such things as truthful reporting and contrasting points of view."

Complicating matters, moreover, Nour wanted me to link the concept of a free press to another topic currently on the city's collective mind: democracy. "Just say something—anything—about independent media and building democracy," she urged me, as we approached the Union's headquarters. "You're American, you know about these things."

A little daunted—this seemed more like a job for William Safire—I entered a dingy meeting hall to a disagreeable scene. Standing before an audience of about one hundred members (all men), an angry writer was demanding that the Union expel a well-known poet from the organization because, the man claimed, the poet had participated in Saddam's Baath party. The accuser offered no evidence, nor was the accused present to answer the allegations. It was, in short, a typical Iraqi moment, gossip and character assassination taking the place of debate. "This isn't exactly a model of democratic citizenship," I muttered to a dismayed Nour. Before long, however, the audience shouted the man down, and it was my turn to speak.

How to explain the role of a free press in a free society to people who have experienced neither? As Nour translated, I started with the notion of the media as an unofficial branch of American democracy—the "fourth estate" concept. From there I moved to the First Amendment, using the *New York Times'* publication of the Pentagon

Papers as a concrete example. "Even the President of the United States couldn't stop the newspaper from publishing the truth," I said. It sounded good, but I felt I was too general and too focused on America. I decided to bring the discussion closer to home.

"Being a journalist brings responsibilities with the freedoms," I began. "Let's say I want to publish an article that claims that a famous writer once belonged to a fascist regime. I should allow the man to defend himself, and I better have proof or the man can take me to court and I could lose my job." Appreciative laughter arose from the accused poet's supporters, and I seized the moment to expound on the connection between journalistic ideals—fairness, facts, and fidelity to the truth—and democratic citizenship. But almost immediately, I began losing my audience. Where was I going wrong?

To my relief, Nour asked for questions. The first query did not surprise me. "How can America's press be free when it is owned by Zionists and Israelis?" Irritated by the constant anti-semitism one encounters in Iraq, I snapped, "How does worrying about what businesses Jews own or don't own help your lives? How does obsessing about Israel help you build a strong and prosperous democracy?" A silence fell over the room. After a moment, new questions came—but there was no more talk about "Zionists."

What effect do commercial interests have on the press? "They can be a real problem. . ." *How easy it is to make a living as a freelancer?* "Don't ask. . ."

Soon, politics intruded: *Why did America wait so long to liberate us?* "It took 9-11 to rally public support." *Why is the U.S. treating Saddam as a prisoner of war and not a war criminal?* "In a democracy, a man is innocent until proven guilty; *then* you can deal with him"—an answer which occasioned a burst of sardonic laughter. I felt my talk had regained momentum—until the inevitable occurred: a man stood and began ranting about the inaccuracies in some recent article the *Times* had published. "Just like back home," I griped to Nour, as people slipped toward the exits. But it was time to go, anyway.

"That was wonderful!" Nour enthused as I shook hands and said farewell to the journalists. But I felt a distance from them. Even though I thought I'd succeeded in expressing some idea of the importance of a free press to democracy, and trusted Nour's translation, something hadn't clicked. Leaving the meeting room, a tall, serious reporter from *al-Ahkbaar* newspaper stopped me. In English, he thanked me for my talk, then added, "but you underestimate the problems we face here. You talk about freedom, but Iraqi journalists are still not free. If we go too deep into some stories, we will anger certain people—and they will kill us."

The reporter's words startled me, and I realized at once my mistake. Swaggering a bit in my role as an American journalist, I'd forgotten that there are dangerous forces throughout Iraq who do not want the media to investigate their activities. Especially in Basra, where the placid British occupation barely suppresses the violence and intrigue. Here, Islamic hit-squads murder liquor store owners and drunks they find on the street. Iranians meddle in everything, from funding religious extremists to smuggling arms and oil across the Iraqi border. Meanwhile, family feuds and hatred for ex-Baathists create a shadow world of perpetual revenge killings. This is underside of the democratic boom in his city. How glib my comments about "being true to truth" must have seemed! How naive my emphasis on "proof" and "fairness"—particularly to journalists who could lose their lives in pursuing those ideals! Too late, I remembered something Yussef told me: "In Iraq, freedom of the press is a freedom that must be carefully applied."

I apologized to the young man for my oversight and thanked him for reminding me of how fortunate I am to be an American journalist. Taking constitutional protections for granted, I had stressed to the Iraqis the necessity of press freedom to democracy without noting the opposite: that without democracy, without the almost instinctive commitment of millions of Americans to principles of a free and responsible citizenry, true journalism (and many other occupations) would be impossible. Judging by the arrogance and pomposity of many in my profession, it's a lesson we too often overlook. "You can see what we're up against in Iraq, people don't understand what democracy means," Nour said as we left the meeting hall. "But with meetings like this, perhaps we are beginning to learn." As was this American reporter, far from home.

— 8 —

Beneath the Veil

I have not left after me any chance of turmoil
more injurious to men than the harm
done to men because of women.

The Prophet Mohammad

IN JANUARY OF 2004, street crime in Baghdad had diminished to the point that the Saddoun Street Hospital, just off Firdousi Square, no longer stationed armed men to protect itself from Ali Baba. This sense of security was not shared by those who worked next door, however, where rusting coils of barbed wire and a smooth-faced youth holding an AK-47 guarded the entrance to a one-story wooden house. For behind these walls was something more at risk than drugs or expensive medical equipment: women. Specifically, women working at the Organization of Women's Freedom in Iraq (OWFI)—and more specific yet, its director: Yanar Mohammad.

"I received this by email yesterday," said the diminutive feminist leader, ushering me into her dark office, furnished with only a desk, a glass cabinet holding some books and an uncomfortable sofa. "The message line read 'Killing Yanar Within Days.'" A man stood at the doorway, eyeing us carefully, as she handed me an English translation of the communiqué.

> May peace be upon those who follow the right path. We warn you and we offer you repentance and ask you to leave your moral perversion and psychological complex that you are spreading among the people. If you do not repent, you are not a Muslim and we need to administer a legal killing. We will legally kill you so you will go to hell where no one can protect you. Those who fight and oppose the Prophet and ruin and spoil the land deserve to be killed and crucified.
> You have been warned.
>
> Army of Al-Sahbah

Yanar shrugged. "We think it's some Wahabbi group." Despite her seeming insouciance, the message prompted her to secure a bodyguard and to change where she slept every few days. "And I'm going to start carrying a gun." Nor was that Yanar's sole warning: a few days earlier, she related, a mullah stood on a street corner, reading aloud an opinion piece about women's rights that she had written for the newspaper she founded, *Al Mousawat* (Equality). "He screamed at the people passing by, 'This woman must be stopped!'" She smiled sardonically. "You know what that means, right? Political Islam can kill like *that!*" she remarked, snapping her fingers.

It seemed ironic: once the target of looters, hospitals in Baghdad were deemed safe enough to dispense with security personnel, even as feminists received blood-curdling emails and felt it necessary to protect themselves with guns and bodyguards.

Yanar was not the only woman leader to arouse the ire of reactionary elements in Iraqi society. In September, 2003, Akila Hashimi, one of three females on the former Governing Council, was gunned down outside her Baghdad home. Although the motives for her assassination weren't clear—Hashimi had served as an advisor to Saddam's Foreign Minister Tariq Aziz—it nevertheless sent a chill through women across Iraq. Many had hoped that the Anglo-American invasion would help spur the development of Western-style feminism in the country; instead, they witnessed resurgent tribalism and religious dogma, in addition to rampant crime, fill the vacuum left by Saddam's fall. The message was clear: *women are still not free in Iraq.* "We had such hopes in the beginning—now we find we can't go out, can't socialize," Rand Petros, the manager of an Internet café near the Orient Palace, told me. "Our lives are spent in a shell traveling between home and work and back again."

It would take a heart as misogynistic as a fundamentalist cleric's not to feel outrage over the social, political, and humanitarian disaster afflicting women in Iraq. Bullied by clerics, tribal leaders, and criminal gangs, they were staying indoors, rarely venturing out, ceding their rights and freedoms before the eyes of the world. It was an unnerving spectacle, like watching people fall prey to a police state. In this case, the despotism consisted not of storm troopers and fuehrers, but archaic religious strictures and Bedouin customs clasped close to the hearts of millions of people, including their victims.

Not that I was completely unprepared for the charming manner in which Middle Eastern cultures treat women: in 2000, I traveled through Iran with Lisa, who, like Iranian women, was compelled to observe *hejab*, or the ancient tribal-Islamic tradition of covering women's hair and disguising the contours of their bodies. At first I found it intriguing, even erotic: the mystery of the veiled female, the flash of a dark Persian eye beneath the folds of a black *chador*. But one afternoon at the Caspian Sea, I watched a woman walk into the water fully clothed in a *manteau*, a kind of bulky overcoat, because she couldn't strip down to a bathing suit on a "mixed" beach. The sight was unbearably pathetic—and right there, *hejab* changed in my mind from an exotic foreign custom to a symbol of oppression. "*Exotic?*" a young woman exclaimed to me in at a dinner party in Tehran a week later. "How could you think that never being able to feel the sun on your arms, the wind in your hair, was exotic?"

Still, in the public places in Iran, you could see numerous women, even if they were wrapped in robes. In Iraq, by contrast, women were very scarce. In teahouses, art galleries, restaurants—I'd add movie theaters, but no one goes to cinemas anymore, since they're overrun with deviants, thieves, and other unwholesome types— middle-aged men predominated. Women were on the streets, of course, running errands and rushing to and from work, but they carried themselves in a grim and harried manner, as if anxious to return home. And no one went out after dark.

The condition of women becomes doubly intolerable when you consider the centrality of gender equality in the war against Islamo-fascism. It seems blindingly obvious: if Iraq emerges from its current agonies as a functioning democracy, the free world—I use the term without irony—will achieve an enormous victory against its totalitarian adversaries. But in the twenty-first century, democracy is unthinkable without the emancipation of women. As Dr. Mastaq put it, "Women are Iraq's most underdeveloped resource. If Iraq is to create a new society, women must be equal partners with men."

Thus is the moral imperative of women's rights linked with the security of the United States, and this linkage was what initially interested me in Yanar. I'd heard about this firebrand feminist before, and when I learned she was giving a talk at the Al-Aqiq Hotel on

Saddoun Street, I made sure to attend. I was not disappointed. Seated behind a small table, a vase of flowers on one side, her bodyguard on another, the five-foot tall woman spoke in Arabic and English about the threat to women posed by religious fundamentalism, what she called "political Islam."

"9-11 was one of the consequences of political Islam," she told a group consisting of fifty men and women and several TV cameras. "Why do we want to give political Islam a base in Iraq? We should be concerned that the 9-11 mentality does not show up in our country."

She took particular aim at *shari'a*, and the increasing voices calling for that harsh Islamic code to become Iraq's law regarding family, divorce, inheritance, and other "women's" matters. "This will drag us back centuries," she argued, as several women in the audience nodded. Then, in an open and candid manner that in *today's* Iraq would be unthinkable—if not suicidal—she went on to denounce *shari'a*'s endorsement of polygamy, "temporary marriages," and the power *shari'a* gives a woman's father or guardian to vet a prospective fiancé. "If I want to marry a man, no on should be able to tell me no—it is my choice." She also castigated pedophiliac marriages: "Under *shari'a*, a sixty-year-old man can marry a nine-year-old girl" (a near-blasphemous reference to the Prophet's own marriage to "his favorite wife" Aiesha)—and blasted honor killings, noting that over the last decade in northern Iraq alone, "Five thousand women have been killed for having sex without being married."

"*Shari'a* oppresses women, it is against human rights," she concluded forcefully. "We must fight for a secular government in Iraq."

I was certainly impressed. But not everyone in the audience felt the same. Out of maybe twenty women in attendance, two were in *hejab*, and they leaped to their feet and proceeded to lay into

Yanar, attacking her for her "atheistic" views (an Arab cameraman translated their comments for me), while asserting that "Islam is freedom—the Koran gives us more rights than secular feminism." Yanar responded in Arabic, initiating a long and, for me, frustratingly unintelligible argument. I asked the camera man who these women were; he said they came from something called the "Muslim Sisters' League." I made a note to drop by and visit this group as soon as possible.

The next day, I stepped around the concertina wire protecting the entrance to the OWFI, submitted to a body-and-bag search, then followed a young man into the organization's small, dark headquarters for a one-on-one interview with Yanar herself. Wearing a brown jacket and a light green high-necked sweater, her curly black hair falling loosely below her shoulders, she cut a decidedly Western look—not surprising, given her background. Born in Baghdad in 1960, she attended the city's university, where in 1993 she earned a degree in architecture. She soon emigrated from Iraq, settling in Canada in 1995. There she became active with the Communist Party, in addition to several women's groups. In May of 2003, she returned to Iraq, where she co-founded the OWFI, rapidly becoming one of the country's most outspoken and visible advocates for women's freedom, as well as a vehement opponent of "political Islam."

"When my grandmother was a teenager, she was forced to marry a mullah, who was in his forties at the time," Yanar recalled. "She had five children, and the marriage devastated her. She was anything but a role model for me." Who was her role model? She thought for a moment. "Rosa Luxembourg."

An office assistant brought in two *stiikaanat*, and we paused to sip the bitter lemon tea. Then Yanar continued. "Political Islam is not part of Iraq's tradition. We are not an Islamic society—it is the religious parties who are attempting to institute a religious government. They are just waiting for the right moment to impose their agenda on us." That moment seemed to be fast arriving, she feared. "When I attended the university, few women wore veils. Now, most of them do. Meanwhile, more and more resources and money are going into building mosques where the mullahs are asking the men to veil the women. I fear that elections will only give the fundamentalists the upper hand."

I asked about the increasing influence of tribalism. "We face the dual problem of political Islam and tribal customs," she replied. "Today, women in Iraq live under well-established patriarchal conditions that consider our role to be little more than pleasing men and bearing children." Surprisingly, though, she dismissed the long-term threat of tribalism, believing that "it will fade once economic conditions improve in Iraq."

Along with an improved economy, Yanar—like nearly every other Iraqi besides the paramilitary gunmen—yearned to see democracy established in her country. "Women make up 60 percent of Iraq's population, yet they have little voice. We need strong political representation—a Ministry of Women in the new government, perhaps." She put much faith in her group, the radical Worker-Communist Party, to spread progressive ideas through the country. (As I've mentioned, despite their small numbers—and obvious doctrinal faults—communists have the clearest concept of secular democracy and the most experience building grassroots institutions.) As for the U.S., Yanar's leftist sentiments induced her to mouth the usual criticisms about the evils of capitalism, as well as denounce the "imperialistic" invasion of Iraq—even though the fall of Saddam has given women their best chance to achieve equal rights in nearly twenty years (and allowed Yanar herself to return to Baghdad.)

But her sharpest comments were directed at the *shari'a*-breath-ing mullahs and their ilk. "Misogyny is a pillar of their teachings," she asserted. "Look at *hejab*, look at women walking around wearing gloves, with their faces covered—the Koran does not call for that. That kind of dress is a symbol of women's slavery to political Islam." She paused for a moment. Then, her intelligent, round face darkening with the force of conviction, she voiced an opinion many Iraqis express in private, what they wouldn't dare say publicly, "Religion in this country should just . . . disappear."

IF THIS WERE A NATION LIKE SAUDI ARABIA, we might ascribe the rising tide of misogyny to the moral sewage of Wahabbism. But this is Iraq, a country that until the 1980s was a model for equal rights in the Islamic Middle East. As early as the 1920s and 1930s, for example, middle- and upper-class women began attending the entering the job market; by the mid-1940s, universities in Baghdad were co-educational. In 1952, the first feminist organization—the Iraqi Women's League—was founded and in 1959, Nazhia Dulaimi, the communist head of the League, was selected to serve in the cabinet of President Abdul Karim Qasim, the first woman in the Arab world to gain such a high position. That year also witnessed the passage of the Personal Status Law, which granted women equal rights in matters of divorce and inheritance, and included provisions covering child support.

After seizing power in 1968, the Baath Party initially continued to improve the conditions of women. The 1970 Provisional Constitution, for example, declared women equal to men under the law, even as the Party worked to drive down illiteracy rates and bring more females into the work force. In 1980, one year after Saddam seized absolute power, women won the right to vote. Within a few years, their participation in the civil service rose to 40 percent. By 1987, women held 13 percent of the seats in the National Assembly; in 1990, they made up 22 percent of university teaching positions and 13 percent of administrative and managerial jobs. (It's probably worth noting that one of Iraq's top biological weapons scientists, Huda Salih Mahdi Ammash—a.k.a., "Mrs. Anthrax"—was female.)

Beginning in the 1980s, however, countercurrents against women's rights began to exert their influence. Faced with the strains of the Iran-Iraq War, the regime began to eye females more as breeders of future soldiers. "During the war, Saddam told us that it was our patriotic duty to have five children," recalled Hanaa Edwar. "Anything less than that and you were threatening Iraq's national security." Matters worsened when the war ended and men returned to their jobs, forcing women back into the home. Worse yet, UN sanctions after the first Gulf War triggered massive inflation that crippled Iraq's public sector, the largest employer of women: by one account, women in urban areas found their salaries dropping in a few years from $400 a month to less than $2 a month.

If that wasn't bad enough, Saddam got religion. As part of his efforts to placate the rebellious Shia, the dictator in the mid-1990s embraced Islam—and with it, *shari'a*. Soon, the regime was legalizing polygamy, championing veils and easing penalties on honor killings. To cite one incident, the U.S. State Department reported that in October, 2000, Iraqi security forces seized a number of women suspected of prostitution and beheaded them, many in front of their families. Their heads were displayed in front of their homes for several days.

Today in liberated Iraq, women continue to suffer a long-term health and social crisis. Since the 1990s, the country has seen, among other negative statistics, its maternal mortality rates more than double, with 50 percent of pregnant women showing signs of anemia. Female literacy rates have plunged to 45 percent, with 35 percent of girls dropping out before finishing primary school. "It's the mullahs, preaching in the mosques," Yanar asserted. "They're telling fathers to take their daughters out of school by the sixth grade."

But these figures can offer only a partial idea of the wretched conditions women suffer in the slums of Iraqi cities, where poverty, disease, and ignorance rule more effectively than the Baath Party of old. My art dealer friend Deborah, for example, told me about meeting an Iraqi family in Baghdad that consisted of one man, two wives, and twenty-two children (ten from wife one, twelve from wife two), who lived together in a small two-room apartment. In Najaf, Hanaa related, her women's group attempted to educate women about birth control. "I would meet women twenty-two years old who already had five or six children. 'What can I do?' the women would say. 'My husband wants to have children.'" (That reminded me of a Baghdad cabbie I rode with once, who told me he had nine children. "When I make babies, I feel like man!" he crowed.)

Nor can statistics impart a true notion of the backwardness of women in rural areas. "They are so ignorant, filled with incorrect information," said Dr. Qusay Abood, Basra's director of health information. "Take infant malnutrition, a huge problem in distant villages. Iraq has plenty of food," the doctor noted, "but many women use it the wrong way. During the sanctions period, there was a shortage of everything, and women somehow got it into their heads was the only reason they breast fed their babies was because they couldn't get powdered milk. Once the sanctions were lifted, they stopped breast feeding and started using powdered milk. The problem is, quite often the stuff is spoiled or poor quality and babies don't get enough nourishment."

Not all women live such harsh physical lives. Many enjoy comfortable, monogamous, and relatively secure existences—as long as they don't spend too much time out on the streets. But there is a *psychological* dimension to this oppression, a kind of psychic claustrophobia that, as Rand suggested, circumscribes the life of even middle-class Iraqi females. In Baghdad, for instance, I met a charming Pakistani woman who, raised in England, married an Iraqi man who took her back to Iraq, where she bore three children. Despite her head-to-foot *chador*, Zena seemed bourgeois and Westernized in nearly every way—until she described her life at home. Because of the kidnappings, she related, her children needed escorting to and from school, a task that naturally devolved upon her.

"I take my kids to three different schools, praying there won't be any traffic jams so I get to work on time," she related. "During the day, I try to cram in errands and such during whatever breaks I can get. Then I have to leave early to pick up children up from school, fighting traffic the whole way, so I get home before my husband comes back from his work. He wants me to have the house clean and ready for him." The situation is made worse by that not-always-welcome fixture in many Iraqi households: the mother-in-law. "Even if I come home five seconds before my husband does," Zena grumbled, "his mother expects me to wait hand and foot on her 'baby boy' as if I've done nothing all day."

Adil, the Oxford-educated "democracy trainer," expressed this view of equal rights: "Women are not oppressed in Islamic society, for here, it is not a matter of 'equality,' but 'roles.' We believe that God created men and women with separate tasks. Man's task is to work in the outside world. Woman's task is to keep the house and raise children to be good Muslim citizens." As Ahmed Darwish al-Kinani, head of the Baghdad-based Islamic Iraqi Movement told me, "Islam is specific on men's authority: man leads and woman follows. Under *shari'a*, women are treated like precious gems in a jewel box."

"It doesn't matter if they are religious or secular, poor or prosperous, the male mentality is closed," Hanaa remarked, shaking her head with an expression I was sure would be familiar to women from Karada to Malibu. "They don't want us to move forward. They speak of women's rights, but they aren't serious. Not for a moment."

—

NO ONE ANSWERED when I knocked on the front gate of the Muslim Sisters' League, so, pushing it open, I walked into the courtyard of the school-like compound, set adjacent to a small mosque. Turning a corner, I bumped into a group of women who, seeing a man suddenly in their midst, gasped and scurried away, hurriedly adjusting cloaks and veils. A moment later, a woman in a scarf and a shapeless light green smock sallied from a room, shooing me back to the street: "You cannot be here! Only women!" Standing beyond the gate once more, feeling like a blundering fool, I blurted in broken Arabic-English that I was a *sahafee Amrikee*, just looking to interview an "Islamic feminist."

"We give you five minutes," said League member Ala Abdul Qadir.

Located in the Sunni stronghold of Adamiya, the Muslim Sisters' League is an avowedly religious organization, dedicated to "teaching women about Islam," Ala explained. And being Sunni, she and a companion, Umayma Abdullah, a large woman wearing a light blue scarf and dark blue smock, started things off with some blistering comments about the "occupation."

"Bush and Bremer: no different than Saddam," Umayma stated.

"No, there is a difference," Ala retorted. "Saddam gave us security."

Conscious of time constraints, I pushed past the politics to ask them about the conditions of women in Iraq. Very bad, they both agreed: no jobs, no security, deteriorating health, the lives of rural women were a disaster, and so on. They were essentially the same complaints that Yanar and Hanaa expressed to me, with one difference. To Ala and Umayma, the solution was simple: Islam.

"The Koran gives us freedom, it liberates women from tribal customs," Ala declared. "Men in rural areas do not care what happens to women. But the Koran frees women from such backwardness. It gives women the right to an education. Do you what the first word was that Gabriel said to Mohammad? *Iqra*—'read.'"

So ingrained was my attitude about the Koran, that I had difficulty imagining the religion as anything but a bludgeon of obscure and intolerant *suras* men use to hammer women into submission. It never occurred to me that, for some, the opposite was true: by offering women limited—very limited—rights of divorce and inheritance, and even the ability to retain their family names and, under some interpretations, to vote, the Koran challenged tribal norms under which, for centuries, women had been little more than chattel. Nevertheless, though Allah declared (3:195): "Be you male or female, you are equal to one another," He also declared, in the second *sura*, "Men, wives are your tillage. Go into your tillage as ye will"—and diagnosed menstruation as a "disease."

"My faith—and my mother," Ala continued, "allowed me to choose my husband. I have the right to divorce, and the right to work." Nodding energetically, Umayma interjected, "There are many points we have in common with Western feminists."

Really? A bit flabbergasted, I sought to challenge her thesis: for example, what about calls from Islamic clerics that *shari'a* should regulate women's lives? To my further surprise, both Sisters expressed disapproval at the religious fundamentalism currently sweeping Iraq. "These religious men are mostly Shia, trying to divide their followers from the Sunni," Ala remarked. "Their idea of *shari'a* is too ambiguous. It will lead to any individual person"—and by that I figured she meant any individual *Shia* imam—"interpreting matters of marriage, divorce and inheritance however they wish."

Here was the Sunni complaint about their idiosyncratic Shia brethren. What I gathered was that the two Muslim Sisters were indeed "progressives," only they based their ideas on the *Sunni* version of *shari'a*, which largely derives from four-centuries-old schools of jurisprudence. The last thing they wanted was someone like Sistani laying down the rules for their behavior. I wasn't sure, outside of a Bedouin tent or a mosque, how their vision of Islam amounted to true gender equality, but the ladies were so pleasant I didn't feel like pressing the issue. I did ask them about Yanar Mohammad, though. Ala and Umayma both looked as if they smelled month-old *mazgouf*. "She is *against God*," they spat.

Then, smiling sweetly, Umayma changed the subject. "People have the wrong idea about Islam. The Koran makes me feel as if I dwell at the heart of Iraqi society."

And polygamy? "That is exaggerated," Ala contended. "Most men have only one wife. Who can afford more? Even so, is it better to spend money on mistresses or prostitutes than to support another wife?"

Hejab? At this, both women grinned, obviously proud of their attire. "It makes me feel comfortable, knowing that I am acting out the will of God," beamed Ala. "I feel more feminine." Added Umayma,

"We have such freedom with *hejab* because men don't stare at us. I feel sorry sometimes for Western women and the way they must dress for men. Is that freedom?"

The interview was drawing to a close. My "five minutes" had stretched to over an hour and my head was spinning with new thoughts and perspectives. Still, I was sorry to leave my delightful interlocutors.

"Look at us," said Ala, patting her chest. "Do we look oppressed? Unhappy? We both have one husband and only two children each. We drive cars, use computers, and we're learning English. People have the wrong idea about Islam. The Christians have their God, and we have ours—but we both desire dignity for women and peace in the world."

"*Insha'allah,*" Umayma added.

⸺

ALA AND UMAYMA'S AFFIRMATION of traditional Islamic mores, especially *hejab*, shouldn't have surprised me. A week earlier, I'd been in Basra, where, in the offices of a Western NGO I met Kareem, an extroverted, heavy-set middle-aged woman with the keen wit and hearty laugh of a Rosanne Barr. Despite the 70-degree weather outside, Kareem was dressed in a heavy black dress similar to Ala's, which she topped off with a black scarf.

"I am 100 percent secular," she announced in near-perfect English. "But I've worn *hejab* since 1997. And do you know why I started? The sanctions! I got tired of trying to find shampoo in the stores. With a scarf, you don't have to worry about your hair!" All very well and eminently practical, I replied, but what about the rest of the outfit—the *abiya*, the shapeless dress? "A matter of vanity and aesthetics," she answered. "Over time, I began to feel more beautiful in *hejab*." She translated her comments for three or four other *hejab*'d woman crowding around us, all of whom nodded appreciatively. "Now I feel abnormal without this attire," Kareem went on. "It gives me confidence, I feel protected."

Anwar Algebar made similar comments about the Muslim habit. A tall, striking woman, Anwar was the managing director for Basra's Radio Nahrain—960 on your AM dial. Seated behind her desk dressed entirely in black—sweater, slacks, scarf—she seemed every inch the glamorous, successful woman, what your basic female executive might look like if *hejab* became the fashion in New York. "As a professional, Islam protects me from the stares and comments of men." She sat back in her chair and fixed a direct glance at me. "I gain power by dressing like this." Then, adding yet another twist to the feminist take on the Islamic veil, she added, "Besides, *hejab* is really for the protection of men. Men are weak, you understand. The scarf guards them from temptation and keeps them from making fools of themselves."

Still, like every other issue in this country, the "women's problem" is complicated. Just when you think you have it figured out, something comes along to upset your conclusions. Case in point: Najiah Abdulsalah. I had just finished interviewing Anwar, when I stepped into the walled courtyard surrounding Radio Nahrain's office. There, smoking a cigarette on the steps beside the front door, was a slim, attractive, twenty-something woman wearing a peach-colored blouse, orange hip-huggers and backless mules, her straight black hair falling halfway down her back. Najiah was a newscaster for local Basra TV, she told me, going on the air each night at 6:00 PM. Struck by her casual attire, I asked her if she were Christian.

"Oh, no, I am Muslim," she replied. "I just believe that it is my choice to wear *hejab* or not." She exhaled a stream of cigarette smoke. "Really, I think *hejab* is an obligation of Islam but I don't care. Even if it is against God, I don't like wearing it." On the street, though, she was careful to appear properly scarved. "If I don't, I risk being attacked by the religious men." Once behind the walls of this office compound, however, she immediately doffed the restrictive garment.

"When I read the news, I don't wear a scarf," she continued (and indeed, later that night in my hotel, I switched on the TV to catch her unscarved evening broadcast). "But I'm receiving complaints from the religious parties. It is all starting to worry me."

She took a final drag off her cigarette, then ground the butt beneath her heel. "But it doesn't matter. I'm getting married to a Kuwaiti man next month and he's taking me out of the country." Good news? I asked. Najiah shrugged. "Maybe. The problem is, like a lot of Arab men, he won't let me work."

———

PARWEEN AND CHERO wanted nothing to do with *shari'a*, Sunni or Shia style. "Mixing law and religion is not good," the two Kurds agreed, as we sat drinking tea in the Women's Freedom Center in Kirkuk. "Under *shari'a*," Parween added, nestled close to her friend on a sofa, "woman is third. First is man, second is man—and then comes woman."

Chero nudged her. "Even without *shari'a*, it is still the same with Kurdish men. Men are not ready to accept women as number two."

Declaring themselves "free people of Iraq," the dark, broad-featured women were both wearing colorful sweaters and pants—no scarves here. "We talk to women," Chero said, "and try to convince them against wearing *hejab*. They must see that the Koran doesn't require it. It may have been necessary during Mohammad's time, but it is not now."

"Islam must change," Parween remarked, a comment that, at the very least, would have earned her a death threat anywhere south of Kirkuk.

Here was yet another perspective on the Islam-meets-feminism debate. To these moderate Muslims, *shari'a*, at least as it pertained to females, was a horror show of laws that granted men such conveniences as polygamy, temporary marriages, and divorce by repudiation, while denying women the ability to choose husbands, travel freely, or wear anything except cloaks to cover their bodies and hair. Not to mention countenancing such matters as inequality of inheritance, death by stoning for adultery, and honor killings.

"*Shari'a* does not allow free thinking," Parween stated. "Without free thinking there can be no women's rights. And without women's rights, there can be no democracy in Iraq."

Nor can there be any true physical well-being for women, they continued, not as long as mutually-supporting Islamic and tribal customs hold sway over their lives. "Women have very poor health in Iraq, especially when it comes to reproductive issues," Parween explained. "The problem is Iraqi society: it oppresses women's minds, so then they become ill. In Iraq, men died in wars, but women's spirits became sick—and then their bodies."

The two Kurds looked at me as I scribbled away in my notebook. I couldn't help feeling they were wondering if I—an American male—understood the obstacles they faced trying to live full and satisfying lives. Finally Parween stirred. "Tribal and religious men want women to stay in their homes," she said in a level voice. "And if women disobey, Iraqi society crushes them."

—

WOMEN AREN'T THE ONLY ONES WHO SUFFER from the misogyny of Iraqi-Arab-Muslim culture. What is usually overlooked is the impact this has on Iraqi *men*—especially younger men—who admire the freedoms and ease of interaction they see between the sexes in the West. To put it simply, the barriers between men and women constrict the male spirit almost as completely and effectively as they do the female. My Iraqi friends didn't talk much about this, preferring to maintain a kind of insouciant bravado, as if women didn't really matter, and I couldn't bring myself to raise the topic. But you could feel the loneliness and sexual frustration envelop and batter their spirits as mercilessly as the summer sun of Baghdad. "When someone from the West talks about his interactions with women," one confessed to me, "it's like he's describing color to someone who lives his life in black and white."

It wasn't just that none of them had girlfriends, wives, or women friends. (Men profess to value women's company so little in Iraq that platonic relations seem unwanted, if nearly impossible—besides, as the Prophet once stated, "If a man and a woman are alone in one place, the third person present is the Devil," and "Never will a people know success if they confide their affairs to a woman.") No, it was also the plethora of titillation that poured into this nominally Muslim country. Many were the times I'd see men sitting in the lobby of the Orient Palace watching some salacious music video broadcast from Dubai with its shimmying latex-clad sex-pots—while just beyond the window, sad-looking women in *abiyas* shuffled by in the 130-degree weather. If you didn't have access to TV Dubai, you could always go down to Mutinabi Street on Fridays: there among coffee table books on Mesopotamian Art and medical textbooks from the 1970s, you would find back issues of *FHM*, *Maxim*, and other "lad" magazines. Or you could just pop into an Internet café that features secluded video monitors: chances are, all the best pornography sites would be bookmarked.

Dating is mostly unknown, "necking" or "petting" unheard of. Casual sex can ruin a woman's life and quite possibly get her killed. Meanwhile, my Iraqi friends met a constant procession of "liberated" female journalists from the West who showered them with attention, inflating their diminished egos, yet never deepening the interactions to anything beyond professional interest in their translating abilities. As a result, they developed hopeless crushes on women who clearly weren't interested in them, or else wasted precious money on Internet "chats" with "women" supposedly living in Germany or Denmark.

Compounding the pathetic quality of my friends' not-so-merry bachelorhood was their adolescent attitude toward the opposite sex: indeed, talking to them about women reminded me of my teen days when we disguised our terror of females with defensively macho contempt. Ask the Iraqis about marrying a local girl rather than chasing Western chimeras, and they'd scoff: "All they want to do is settle down and have babies." Ask them what they want in a woman, and they'd reply, "Someone to treat us like little gods." And these were educated, sophisticated Iraqis—not the *nargheel*-smoking tribal sheikhs or bearded mullahs with heads full of charming sayings of the Prophet like "I stood at the gates of Hell and saw that the majority of people who entered were women."

I met many married Iraqi men who seemed perfectly content with their wives, if not their lives. What I'm talking about here are young Iraqis torn apart by normal sexual frustrations, exacerbated by a culture where even the most innocent gesture directed toward a woman can cause a firestorm of suspicion and misunderstanding.

On the last day of my first trip to Iraq, for example, I decided to present Rand with a bouquet of flowers to thank her for the assistance she had given me in her Internet café over the past weeks. Rand, who was attractive and single, was touched by my gift and understood its intention—but her boss, a middle-aged Iraqi woman, did not. She stormed over to us and demanded in English to know what I was doing. I told her that it was my *last day* in Baghdad (that is, I had no designs on her employee) and Rand had been so patient and helpful with me. Besides, expressing friendly gratitude like this is what I would do in the States. "You are not in the United States!" the boss snapped back at me. When I protested that it was only *flowers*, the woman—who had lived for twenty years in Detroit—glared at me: "Such things are not done here! Do you understand? Do not do this!" Embarrassed, Rand declined to accept the flowers, and I ended up giving the bouquet to the startled desk clerk at the Orient Palace, undoubtedly the first time a man had ever given him a bouquet of lilies.

At least I was returning to a wife and a relatively sane society. My Baghdad friends were stuck. Along with chronic sexual frustration and social boredom, I noticed they suffered a host of ailments stemming from the madness and stress of Iraqi life—migraines, ulcers, depression (what one called the "casual sickness"), and other signs of neurosis. They had no emotional buffers, no "love of a good woman"—amazing how much less corny that saying seems in Iraq—no gentleness to smooth the razor-sharp edges of the lives.

All of Baghdad was like that: a city whose harsh, traumatic, frightening realities lack the palliative of the female presence. After a while, the city wears down the nerves like the grinding gears of a car whose transmission has run dry of fluid. One night, about three weeks into my first trip, I became so desperate for the company of the distaff side that I went to the Al-Hamra Hotel, a well-known hangout for Western journalists. There, beside the swimming pool, I took a seat near a table where two American women were conversing. During the course of their conversation, the pair burst out laughing at some shared comment, and a chill shot through me. In all the time I'd been in Iraq, I realized, I had not heard a woman laugh. Not in a free and unguarded manner, at any rate. Their laughter struck me like music—a wonderful sound I'd taken for granted in America, but which now seemed more precious, more worth defending, in Iraq *and* at home, than anything I'd heard before. At that moment I became a feminist.

Is the White House going to push gender equality and risk antagonizing the bearded misogynists of the *Hawza*? The right maintains a reflexive opposition to feminism, but, more important, Shia Muslims represent 65 percent of Iraq's population. And we know by now how well their ideas of *shari'a* fit with women's liberation—even the kind envisioned by Ala and Umayma.

On the other hand, the silence of the left on the knotty problems of Middle Eastern culture—aside from Israel, of course—is deafening. Perhaps they'll denounce its rampant sexism, but they'll rarely describe the U.S. liberations of Afghanistan and Iraq as pro-feminist. Instead, they profess a multiculturalism that paralyzes their critical faculties and renders them incapable of denouncing even the most egregious foreign customs or conceding that sometimes, America has a better way.

One afternoon in Baghdad, I lunched with some American peace activists who vehemently denounced the U.S. "occupation" of Iraq. When I asked why they didn't similarly denounce some of the aspects of the country's society that the "occupation" might ameliorate or change, such as the rampant sexism of Iraqi culture, they looked at me as if I'd asked them to contribute to the Republican Party. True to her anti-American multicultural mindset, one leftist—old enough to remember the 1968 March on Washington, mind—replied, "Feminism has done so much to damage the American family. Do we want to wish that on Iraq?"

But perhaps the ultimate in political correctness involves a leftist repudiation of Yanar Mohammad. In the winter before the war, she told me, the International Socialist Organization of Canada put together a protest march to denounce American aggression against Iraq. All anti-war activists were invited—but not Yanar. Why not? "Because I had spoken out against political Islam and the oppression of women," she said. "They only wanted anti-Americans, not someone who also criticizes Iraq."

There are, of course, cogent objections to affirming gender equality in the Middle East. One, championed by the multiculturalists, asks who we are to judge another way of life? But when legislators force women to live in bags and courts excuse femicide under the rubric of "honor"—or when, as in 2002, fifteen young girls burn to death when Saudi religious police prevented them from escaping a flaming building because they weren't wearing their headscarves—basic moral sense compels us to judge these cultures as deficient. And not only because of the slavery that they impose on women. Let the world ask: What connection is there between terrorism and the misogyny and sexual frustration that permeate Islamic cultures?

Another argument takes up Ala and Kareem and Anwar's claims that *hejab* allows Muslim women to feel freer than Westerners by shifting male emphasis from women's appearance to their personalities. This is difficult to take seriously. As Hegel noted, to possess true freedom, feeling free is not enough: you must be objectively free in a social, political, and economic sense. Ask the Iranian woman wading fully-dressed into the Caspian Sea, or my dinner companion who complained about never feeling the sun on her body, if they are "free." Chances are they'll laugh.

More serious is the contention that women's second-tier status is too deeply ingrained in Middle Eastern cultures. Statistics support this claim: a Gallup poll taken in September of 2003 revealed that 72 percent of Baghdad males and 67 percent of the females believe that women "should follow more traditional/conservative roles than they did before the invasion." Given this regressive desire, isn't it folly to think that feminism will sprout amidst such stony soil—and dangerously counterproductive to force the issue?

I imagine people said the same before Lincoln forced the issue of the Confederacy's "tradition" of owning human beings. Besides, cultures frequently exhibit self-reflective transformation: witness the former militarized countries of Japan and Germany. In the U.S., attitudes toward race, the environment, and smoking changed completely in one generation.

But the real reason women's rights will take hold in the Middle East is because it has to. The patriarchal culture of that region is so irrational, so debilitating, so self-destructive—and so morally objectionable—that one senses it is no longer politically or historically sustainable. When even Saudi Arabia is contemplating offering physical education classes to girls, change is in the wind.

Call it my Damascene—or rather, Baghdadi—conversion to feminism. But it seems increasingly clear that women are the Achilles heel of Islamic states. More than military force, economic sanctions, and homeland security, gender equality is one of the most—if not the most—potent weapons against the social factors that breed terrorism. If we unite the progressive forces of both the left and the right around this issue, we may yet see the veil of theocratic despotism lift from Damascus to Riyadh, and beyond.

— 9 —

The Road to Basra

I looked for someone who should be journeying
thence to Bassorah that I might join myself to him.
The Seventh Voyage of Sindbad the Seaman

DESPITE ITS NAME, Baghdad's Nadha Garage is a muddy, gravel-strewn parking lot choked with exhaust fumes and packed with travelers, food vendors, families struggling with heavy baggage and scampering kids, all watched by suspicious-looking young men with no apparent reason for hanging around. Weaving through the crowd, you make your way along a row of drivers standing beside their GMCs and Chevy Caprices, beckoning to you like merchants in a *souk*: "Kirkuk, Kirkuk"—"Najaf, Mister?"—"Mosul, Sulimaniya"—"Karbala, Karbala." Pause for a second, and you're besieged by beggars, many of them spectral-looking women, bodies, hands, faces sheathed in black. Ask a driver a question and forget it: you've made eye contact and he'll cling to your side, attracting a crowd other drivers, each trying his best to take you where you don't want to go.

Leading such a small and vociferous procession—"Mister, where you go? Where, mister?"—I pass along a line of Iraqi chauffeurs until I hear the name of my destination: *Basra*, legendary port city on the Shatt-al-Arab, place of debarkation for Sindbad's fabled voyages. Instead of a swarthy seaman, however, I see a beefy, barrel-chested *sayyiq* wearing street clothes and a black checkered *kheffiya* calmly leaning against a purple Caprice. As additional drivers gather around, staring, shouting, pulling my arm—"How much, mister?"—the man and I quickly negotiate, settling within seconds on a price of twenty thousand dinars (just under $14) for the six-hour, 330-mile trip. As the disappointed drivers drift away to importune other travelers, I climb into the back of the Caprice—known in driver lingo as a "Dolphin"—and wait for additional passengers to fill the vehicle. Within minutes, a stocky, serious-looking, roundfaced man lugging a briefcase takes the front seat (it costs a little extra), while a handsome, forty-something white-haired fellow dressed in an olive green suit and yellow tie slides in beside me. Shouting something across the lot to a friend, the driver waves, jumps in the Dolphin and wheels into Baghdad traffic. We're on our way. It's that easy.

Or at least it was. Today, with control of Iraq's major highways having slipped from government control, it's difficult for foreigners to move out of Baghdad without fear of robbery, kidnapping, or worse. Back in the winter and spring of 2004, however, you could travel just about anywhere in the country, the Sunni Triangle included. Supplies of cheap gas, unemployed men, and imported cars flooding in from Dubai and Jordan meant that transportation was as plentiful in Iraq as conspiracy theories; securing a ride between major cities as simple as getting to a local "garage."

There were negatives to this vehicular convenience, of course. As previously noted, this influx of cars meant that Baghdad was more frequently shrouded in a dense *chador* of smog, while locked-down in traffic tighter than a military curfew. Even outside the city, *deyhams* a mile long or more were common—like the one we hit twenty minutes outside of the City of Peace where Highway 6 crosses a tributary of the Tigris River. During the war, Coalition JDAMS flattened the bridge, which the U.S. Army then replaced with a single steel span that permitted only one lane of vehicles to clank across at a time. "*Y'allah*, it would be so easy for the Americans to build a second lane to help us out," gripes Jabar, our driver, his comments translated by the white-haired man. "Why can't they do it?" The shotgun passenger looks up from a newspaper and shares his answer first in Arabic, earning a nod from our driver, and then in halting English for my benefit. "U.S. no good. Soldiers no good. America must go home."

Now it's my turn to sigh. It looks to be a long trip.

I'm heading to Basra this hazy February morning to check out life in Iraq's second largest city, population two million. I also plan to investigate the security situation in southern Iraq. When I first made this trip last fall, Dhia refused to drive on the roads past 2:00 PM, for fear of ambuscades by Ali Baba. And indeed, a few months back on the long and often deserted stretches of road, unidentified assailants attempted to rob the SUV carrying top *New York Times* gun John Burns. Just before my trip, assailants opened fire on a Christian group near Karbala, killing one. Particularly hazardous are the hundred miles between Amarrah and Basra, which highwaymen have claimed as their turf. Still, despite the danger, drives like this are excellent for examining day-to-day conditions outside of the major cities, in places where reporters don't normally go. It's also a great way to get to know your average Iraqi.

"My wife begged me not to take this trip," Sabah, the white-haired man, tells me. "She's terrified of the Ali Baba."

Sabah, it turns out, is a clothier (hence the snappy attire), who has been on the road for a few days, traveling from his hometown in Mosul, through Baghdad and on to Kuwait, from whence he'll catch transport to Dubai for a meeting with some business associates. He's also Kurdish, he informs me in a confidential tone, as if afraid to let the secret out. "Arabs," he whispers, eyes darting to the front seat, "are no good. Dirty. Kurds are clean."

The squalid towns of Jisr and Aziziyah roll by, automobile body shops and pools of oil and dilapidated, one-story hovels selling soft drinks and candy. Soon, the terrain opens up to flat, scrubby desertscape, broken only by dusty blue-green palm groves and clusters of crumbling habitations. There's a rough progression of building material you see the further you venture into the land—concrete and glass in the cities, brick and stucco in the suburbs, mud and thatch in the rural areas. Here, among these no-name villages, children play in the dirt among broken-down automobiles and mounds of rotting tires, the occasional cow or donkey wandering by. Here, too, women in black robes walk alongside the road, roped bundles or enormous sacks balanced atop their heads. Meanwhile, shepherd boys and girls—the girls, too young for *abiyas*, running about in colored dresses, their black hair flying free—chivvy herds of goats and sheep down rocky paths to greener pastureland.

This is also Shia territory, and before long appear the religious shrines. In fact, you start seeing them almost as soon as you leave the urban area of Baghdad—ten-foot-high murals which once displayed Saddam's mustachioed mug now featuring the bearded visages of Ali and Hussain. Meanwhile, on either side of the roadway green banners flutter from houses, black standards flap from roadside hillocks, religiosity—or at least the trappings of it—extending deep roots into the countryside. And not only the countryside: peering over Jabar's shoulder, I see stickers of the sacred Imams affixed to the car's front console, while atop the dashboard stands a little shrine consisting of a small hinged photo book with two more pictures of the saints, and a small gold-colored vase holding a lavender-colored plastic flower.

It turns out that Hassan, the briefcase-toting man, is an Arab Shia—something I ascertain by playing the naïve *sahafee Amrikee* who, out of ignorance and the general rudeness of Westerners, asks impolite questions no Iraqi would ever ask a stranger. A Baghdad-based official for the state-owned South Oil Company (headquartered in Basra), Hassan is heading back to the port to help his sister take care of her husband who got himself hurt in a "gun accident." The suggestiveness of the phrase entices my interest, but I hold off on the questions for the time being. As for Sabah, he's Sunni, he volunteers, and then, as if to prove it, wrinkles his nose as we pass yet another mural of a green-cloak Hussein, gazing out at passersby with those Shia bedroom eyes. Here we are, I think—two Shia Arabs, a Sunni Kurd, and a lapsed Presbyterian, all together on the road to Basra.

We stop for tea, pulling into the same desolate rest stop where, a week from now, I will have my epiphany regarding the Iraqi penchant for littering.[1] As men in soiled *dishdashas* work on derelict vehicles and beggar women with leather-tough faces squat in the shade of food stalls, I fall into conversation with Sabah. "Every time I come back to the south, I feel my spirit is being drained," he says. "Life here is so harsh, it causes me to lose heart." Squinting from the smoke of his cigarette smoke, he adds, "Kurds love life, music, laughter, we need happiness to make us happy"—implying, or so I take his comment, that such necessities were rare among the reli-

1 See pp. 137-38.

gion-intoxicated Shias. "Have you ever been to Kurdistan? It is so different—no garbage, many trees, very quiet." Clean, green, serene . . . there's a sadness and resignation to Sabah, I think, interwoven with a kind of simmering hostility. For once, though, this umbrage is not directed at America—in fact, when I ask the clothier what he thinks of the U.S., he nods energetically, "America good! Everyone in Kurdistan loves President Bush! We call him Abu Bush!"—Father Bush.

Not even Orange County could make that claim. And yet, Sabah was right, as I had discovered a couple of weeks earlier when I traveled among the Kurds of Kirkuk, a city of 750,000 people which, despite its historical Kurdish roots is technically not part of present-day Kurdistan (a situation local leaders are keen to remedy, especially since Kirkuk sits adjacent to one of Iraq's richest oil fields). At a meeting of the Society of Political Prisoners of Kurdistan, for example, one man shook my hand, crying, "George Bush good! Tony Blair good! Jacques Chirac no good!" Another said, "God bless George Bush! No to the Democrats!" Yet a third bellowed, "If I had money, I would give George Bush a million dollars a day for his re-election!" On a street corner I saw a mural of the Great Seal—eagle, stars and stripes, and all, with a logo painted beneath it reading, "United States and Kurdistan." It was the only pro-American image I saw in the Red Zone.

The reason for this pro-American support, of course, was the U.S. enforcement of the Northern No-Fly Zone, which kept Saddam's tanks out of Kurdistan and allowed the inhabitants to construct something closely resembling a democracy. The fact that Bush ensured that Saddam's next public appearance will be before a war crimes tribunal didn't hurt U.S. standing, either. The Kurds remember all too well the dictator's genocidal campaigns, such as the 1975 "Anfal" operation which killed over one hundred thousand people, or the 1988 poison gas attack on Halabja, which murdered five thousand (some put the figure at twelve thousand), as well as his support for terrorist organizations. At the office of the Patriotic Union of Kurdistan (PUK), one of Kurdistan's two main political-militia groups, I met a man named Pola. In the mid-1990s, he told me, the Baathists exiled him to Halabja, where he witnessed the aftermath of assaults by members of the Kurdish terrorist group Ansar al-Islam. On one occasion, the pro-Saddam paramilitaries left forty-two decapitated bodies in the town's square; on another, seventeen. Pola escaped from Halabja and made his way to the No-Fly Zone, where he joined the PUK. During the second Gulf War, he said, he helped the PUK, along with American Special Forces, destroy Ansar al-Islam bases.

"America freed me twice," he said, tears glistening in his eyes. "Once from Ansar al-Islam, and once from Saddam. In every house in Kurdistan, there is a picture of President Bush. He and America brought us freedom."

—

OUR MERRY BAND IS OFF AGAIN, a kind of dull, mid-morning bore-dom settling over us. In air-conditioned silence we pass through police road blocks guarded by sullen-looking Bulgarian and Polish troops. (How isolated they must feel! Many Iraqis know English, and can converse with GIs—but few, I imagine, speak any Eastern European languages) I whip out the my blue and gold U.S. passport, say the magic words *sahafee Amrikee*, and we pass with less hassle than through the toll booths leading into the Holland Tunnel.

As the miles roll by, I notice a number of wrecked Russian-built T-54 tanks. You see lots of these burned-out hulks in the south, some lying beside the road, others dug into emplacements positioned behind raised berms or banks of the Tigris River. Light brown, their turrets missing, or twisted on their chasses like the unscrewed lid of a jar, these abandoned machines look like a natural place for kids to play. And that's a problem, health officials warn. During both Gulf Wars, Coalition forces destroyed Iraqi tanks using armor-piercing ammunition made from depleted uranium (seventy-five tons of the stuff in Gulf War II, the Pentagon claims)—which was not so "depleted" as not to leave a radioactive residue on destroyed targets and nearby debris. "If DU enters the body, it has the potential to generate significant medical consequences," read a 1995 report to Congress issued by the U.S. Army's Environmental Policy Institute.

After Gulf War I, activists charged, rates of cancer, leukemia, and birth defects spiked in southern Iraq. Indeed, I first became aware of this problem at the Iraqi National Organization for Human Rights, where Dr. Mashtaq showed me a pamphlet distributed by his group which contained several photographs of horribly mangled babies, victims—or so the doctor claimed—of DU ammunition. "After the first Gulf War, I worked in Baghdad's Hospital for Radiation and Nuclear Medicine," he told me. "We had five hundred people there all getting cancer treatments at the same time—a very high rate. There was a corresponding rise in birth defects, as well." The jury is still out on the effects of such weaponry (the jury always seems to be out on this sort of thing), although when a fragment the size of a pencil eraser gives off radioactivity one thousand times higher than normal, or U.S. soldiers avoid DU-destroyed vehicles for fear of radiation, it's hard to believe it doesn't have some negative health effects. If so, then it's another irony of this war: in liberating the Iraqi people, the U.S. and its allies may have burdened them with additional entries in a seemingly endless inventory of woe.

Above us, the sky has begun to turn milky white, adding another soporific layer to the day. Palm groves, yet more images of

Shia icons, blocky houses sporting spindly television antennae roll by. To break the monotony, I ask Hassan about the nature of the "gun accident" that injured his brother-in-law. He stirs uneasily at first, but then, with Sabah assisting in some translation, starts to divulge the details. It is a small, rather pathetic tale, and yet for all that, a typical Iraqi saga of self-inflicted disaster, humiliation, and resentment, with a predictable emotional wind-up.

Hassan's sister Fatima, it seems, is married to one Ali, a thirty-year-old waiter at the Basra Sheraton Hotel—or rather, former waiter, for in April, 2003, looters descended on the five-floor caravansary, despoiling its 207 luxury rooms of anything portable (the *Chicago Sun-Times* ran a photograph of an Iraqi man walking from the gutted Sheraton holding eight huge sofa cushions over his head, his t-shirt emblazoned with the purple logo I HATE BARNEY.) Then they set the building on fire. The resulting catastrophe cost the hotel's three hundred employees their jobs.

Now unemployed and angry—not at the looters, of course—Ali took to grousing around the house, making a nuisance of himself, complaining about the British and Tony Blair and George Bush and going out with his similarly unemployed friends, often carrying an American-issued military pistol he picked up somewhere after the first Gulf War. Like many Iraqis, Ali participates in the national pastime of shooting weapons into the air. (The Shia especially do this, for weddings, holidays, victories in soccer games, with the result that not a few of their countrymen fall prey to projectiles whistling back to earth.) About a week earlier, Ali and his pals took to the streets in protest of some British outrage or another, registering their unhappiness by shooting into the sky—when suddenly, Ali's sidearm backfired, the round exploding in the chamber, shearing off his thumb and nearly severing his hand, which is now encased in a plaster cast he has to keep vertical at all times. The source of this excruciating mishap, Ali believed—as did Hassan, I could tell—was British perfidy. In order to warn Iraqis against taking potshots at their lightly-armed infantry patrols, the Brits—so the rumor goes—flooded Basra's *souks* with faulty ammunition purposely designed to explode in the gun, wounding or killing the shooter. Never mind that Ali's pistol was old, that desert climates are nefariously troublesome for weapons, and that it was Ali himself who decided to go shooting, no—it was the fault of the British. They were responsible for his permanent disability, his incapacity to work and support his family. Hassan was taking time off his job return to Basra and help Ali and Fatima take care of their three kids.

"British," he concluded his story, "no good. Tony Blair no good." Of course, he added, making sure Sabah translated his comments, there was a worse presence in Iraq. "Who?" I asked, although I already knew Hassan's answer.

"The Americans."

I experienced this frequently: some tale of misery and woe would wrap me up in sympathetic pain, only to hit me with a disagreeable kicker at the end. One afternoon, I journeyed out to the main campus of Baghdad University, located in the southern district of Jadiriya. I'd heard that the university's library was in dire need of books, and I wanted to ascertain exactly what kind of books and what Americans could do to alleviate the problem. The director was not in when I called, but his secretary, an Armenian Christian, and another woman, who wore a *chador*, agreed to talk with me. They were both charming—the secretary made me a couple of cups of Turkish coffee—and were overjoyed that a foreigner was expressing interest in their institution's plight. The library was in desperate straits, they said: economic sanctions, fighting near the university during the invasion, and post-war looting had devastated the collection, forcing students to study from flimsily-bound photocopies, many of which were decades out of date. Oh, and we need *every-thing*, they said: textbooks, technical manuals, microfilm, microfiche, magazines—in Arabic would be great, English okay, and everything as up-to-date as possible, please.

"I'll tell people back home right away," I vowed. "They'll be eager to help."

"We are so grateful," said the secretary. "Baghdad, as you know, has always been an international center of learning. To be brought to a condition like this is so tragic . . ."

"But no books about Israel," interrupted the woman wearing the *chador*.

I wasn't sure I'd heard correctly. "Say that again—?"

"No books by or from Israel," she repeated.

Interjected the secretary, "No, that's not right," making me proud of our shared Armenian heritage—that is, until she added, "Israel is our great enemy. You should always know what your enemy is doing, that's what my people always say."

"Maybe that is correct," *chador* responded, "but you know this is our policy. No books written by Zionists or written *about* the Zionists."

To this day, I regret not pointing out to my hosts how many American "Zionists"—but, of course, she meant Jews—were even then organizing "Books for Baghdad" relief funds.

—

SUDDENLY, JABAR SLOWS, and out of seemingly nowhere, the increasing whiteness of the sky forming a ghostly backdrop, a U.S. soldier appears, eyes obscured by sunglasses, mouth and nose wrapped in a khaki-green scarf. Concertina wire and a Bradley sit athwart the lanes before us, the GI gesturing for cars to detour down a side road, while up ahead I spy a detachment of soldiers walking along both sides of the highway. I've seen this in the Sunni Triangle—American GIs engaged in the unenviable duty of sweeping the road in search of IEDs. "Bomb," confirms Jabar in English, as he turns off the main highway

We're not yet half-way to Basra, hurtling in God know what direction. Since everyone in the car is smoking I open my window a crack; a white gritty dust coats the screen of my lap-top, rendering it nearly impossible to read. It's the edge of a dust-storm, I realize, one of the characteristic meteorological conditions in Iraq—when winds sweep like Mongol hordes across the southern deserts, driving before them air the color of blood and rust, leaving behind inch-high piles of sand in people's houses. We all remember TV scenes of the fearsome storms that temporarily halted the American army in the beginning of the second Gulf War. I myself witnessed monstrous tidal waves of sand break over Kadhimain—and again Karbala—obliterating the afternoon sunlight, forcing stores and hotels and mosques to switch on lights until the cities burned like carnival midways in a russet-toned midnight. This storm seems to be blowing away from us; the particles are thin and white, like smoke, not like the heavy cinders from some hellish fire. Fine by me, I think, traffic is fairly sparse on the two-lane road, and I hate to lose more time.

Then we approach a loop in the Tigris and come to a dead halt behind a traffic jam—cars, SUVs, trucks, a line of vehicles immobilized like flies in amber. The normal Iraqi response is to drive off the road and bypass the obstruction, which is what Jabar does, only to find everyone else has had the same idea, creating four, five rows of vehicles angling toward a single point on a raised embankment.

With our Dolphin trapped by cars pulling up behind, I set out on foot to investigate, climbing the small ridge, the wind nearly whipping my baseball hat off my head. I look down on the Tigris River, lazy brown current meandering through shoreline rushes and weeds, Iraqi women rinsing some clothing in the fawn-colored water. A narrow bridge provides the meeting point of two opposing streams of traffic: fifty, sixty cars in each direction, in fact, each funneling down the opposing riverbanks to the span where a pilgrim bus and diesel lorry face off like snorting bulls, neither about to step aside for the other—neither *able* to step aside—given the narrowness of the single lane. It's a conundrum for the hundred or so Iraqis gathered at the site of the entanglement, gesticulating, arguing, scratching their heads. There's not a cop around, just some young men with red checked *kheffiyas* wrapped around their lower faces, AK-47s slung jauntily behind their necks, looking not at all interested in exerting any sort of authority.

Despondent at the delay—this could take hours—I turn back to the car, only to find Sabah standing behind me, looking down at the fouled lines of cars with an expression of disdain on his face. "*Mooshkelay*"—problem—"always *mooshkelay* with these people." We stand together in silence for a moment, and then, figuring now is as good a time as any, I ask Sabah the reason for his seeming hostility toward Arabs. Glancing about to see that our Saracen companions are nowhere in earshot, the Kurd grinds his cigarette out beneath his shoe and answers.

It's a tale whose variations I heard many times in Kirkuk, especially from human rights activists working in the city. In the late 1960s, Sabah narrates, his father moved the family from Kirkuk to Mosul, where they eventually became involved in the "clothing business." His brother, Sabah's uncle, remained in Kirkuk, where he worked in the nearby Baba Gurgur oil fields. Life was good until the failed Kurdish uprising in the mid-1970s, when Saddam accelerated efforts (originally begun in the 1920s) to dilute the numbers of Kurds, Turkmen, and Assyrians living in the strategically important city. This process, known as "Arabization," involved the razing of thousands of villages and forced resettlement of ten of thousands of people. In the decade after the first Gulf War, Human Rights Watch estimates, the Baath regime drove some 120,000 non-Arabs from their homes, installing in their stead Shia Arabs brought up from the south.

In his uncle's case, Sabah relates, he refused to cooperate with the Baathists, his courage earning his family and him expulsion to a village near Karbala. There, he lived out the rest of his life, dying in unhappiness and poverty. He never saw Kirkuk or Kurdistan again. His children grew up with little knowledge of their Kurdish ancestry—"They don't even speak our language, only Arabic," Sabah says in anger. I begin to see the layers of animosity within him—animosity so long repressed it no longer has a focus, a direction, or even a purpose. I could only wonder what this attitude augured for the eventual unification of Iraq.

"The Iraqi people want to stay together, but we need laws in Kurdistan that will apply only to Kurds," Kurdish human-rights activist Osman Hamid told me when I visited his office in Kirkuk. "For example, our women, Kurdish women, enjoy more freedom than Arab women, and we don't want that to change. Sistani's opposition to a federal system is a danger to our way of life."

Sweeping some dust and ash from his suit, "They are no good," Sabah grumbles. "Sixty percent of the Sunnis are criminal followers of Saddam. As for the Shia, they all follow an old man whose mind is stuck in the medieval age." I ask him about Israel. He lights another cigarette and shrugs. "What's Israel? They never attacked the Kurdish people." (Sabah's sentiments are bland compared to those of one Kurdish cabbie I rode with: "Kurds are better than Arabs," he opined, "Turkmen are better than Arabs—*even Jews are better than Arabs.*")

In the midst of this rather dismaying conversation with the clothier, I notice a flurry of excitement on the bridge. A tractor-trailer across the river is backing up, creating a space for a backward chain-reaction up the riverbank, which eventually grants space to the bus to ease itself off the span. Cheers and shouts from the Iraqis on the bridge, everyone rushing back to their inert vehicles as traffic begins moving south. It's a sign, I conclude: if the Iraqis can negotiate this loggerhead, perhaps—*insha'alla*—they can work out the nettlesome difficulties of Arab-Kurd relations. As Hamid said to me, "We know the world is watching. If we can't manage our own problems, what does this mean for the future of Iraq?"

―

FORTY-FIVE MINUTES and an increasingly bluer sky later, we're back on Highway 6, plunging through the long desert miles to Basra. We pass through Amarrah—like many far southern cities, low-lying and spread-out as if in emulation of the surrounding desert—and stop at a checkpoint just outside of town. Rolling down his window, "Is it safe ahead?" Hassan asks a teen-age cop, hardly larger than his machine gun. "Yes," he shrugs, "but you should look to Allah for help." Instead of Providence, however, we trust in Chevrolet horse-power, as Jabar suddenly guns the Dolphin, the speedometer needle flatlining past the 100 MPH mark as we rush down the highway like Iraq's blistering *Shamal* wind, tail-gating cars so closely we could press another Arabic number into their license plates.

"Jabar is nervous now," Sabah mutters. Overhearing him, Hassan adds, motioning to other cars that pull over to let us pass, "Everyone is nervous now."

As on the Amman-to-Baghdad run, the Ali Babas' modus operandi is to run their own fast-moving cars up beside a driver and, brandishing weapons, force the unlucky vehicle off the road and loot it of money, equipment, and passports. (At the time, slayings were rare, which is why that recent killing of the religious activist is so distressing.) As a result, drivers had to balance several tricky defensive tactics at once: drive fast enough to dissuade potential highwaymen, yet not so fast as to damage their car in roadway ruts and divots or get so far ahead of traffic and present oneself as a target that way. (Stragglers and scouts are vulnerable.) "Why can't the British or Americans patrol this part of the road?" Jabar complains. I ask about the Bulgarians and Poles who operate in the area and he laughs: "They only eat and sleep."

The desert rushes by, flat arid wastes and windowless hovels of mud and sticks, livestock foraging in sandy flats overseen by wizened shepherds and their kids, women standing between the highway lanes selling fish from the Tigris, *abiyas* blowing in the wind like ravens' wings, electrical towers, many stooped and broken with age and disrepair. Six-story gray brick smokestacks rise from the yellow-green scrub like strange, primordial monuments, spewing clouds of pitch-black smoke across the sky. It's here the Iraqi marshlands once began, the ecological treasure only now reviving after Saddam's depredations. We sit in silence, looking with a kind of fatigued alertness at the road ahead, barely registering the misfortune of a Dolphin broken down beside the road, the driver and his passengers standing helplessly around the stricken vehicle.

BMWs sweep past us, behind the curtains draped across the windows glimpses of tribal sheikhs wearing sunglasses and brilliant

white burnooses. Soon, we're roaring by the town of Qrna, supposed
location of the Garden of Eden and the Tomb of the Hebrew prophet
Hosea ("An east wind will come, the wind of the Lord coming up
from the wilderness . . ."), set back amidst dour, dirty houses and
rusting automobile parts, now the center of Ali Baba activity.

"They will never change," Sabah mutters. "These people here all
want their cell phones and new cars and cable TV, but they want
them *here*, in this desert. Modern equipment and ancient thoughts."
He shakes his head.

Weaving, swaying, bouncing through stomach-lurching roadway
dips, Jabar drives the Chevy through the Ali Baba run. Soon, desert
landscape gives way to police checkpoints and, beyond them, the
avenues and eggshell-colored buildings of Basra. Our *sayiqq* slows,
everyone relaxes, another transit to the port complete. We pass by a
gas station with over a hundred cars lined up before the pumps, even
as two British jeeps buzz around us draped in camouflaged netting,
like Monty's army chasing the Desert Fox. I point this out but no
one seems amused. Although we've safely reached our destination,
everyone seems grumpy. "Daily existence for us is so difficult," Sabah
explains. "Bridges out, electricity on and off, endless gas lines, you
can't travel to Basra without fear of being killed." He shrugs; clearly,
he wishes he were back in Mosul.

We stop to drop Hassan off at a street corner near his home.
Collecting his luggage, he pauses by my window. "When you write
about this," he says in Arabic, Sabah translating, "mention to your
readers that it's the small details that do the most to undermine Iraqi
faith in the Coalition." He pauses, giving me a hard stare. "We're all
grateful for liberation, you understand, but how long can we remain
grateful under conditions like these?" I shake his hand, tell him I'll
do my best, and we drive off.

"Don't listen to him," Sabah whispers, seemingly forgetting what he has just told me. "All they know how to do is complain."

But that's not right, either. There is a basis for legitimate complaint from the Iraqis, Arabs as well as Kurds. Liberation has brought these people freedom from tyranny, but at a cost, the merest measure of which is increasing stress on the ties and connections that hold their lives together. This was the promise that America *didn't* articulate, I suddenly realize, that our tanks and guns and ideas of democracy would twist their way of life to the breaking point, that the little things they took for granted—ease of transportation, safety, a general predictability of conditions—would be shattered, in many cases beyond recognition.

Worse—and here's the thought, the secret, that really troubles me—even *this* tumultuous destruction may be not enough. The pressure on Iraqi society must go deeper, to its very roots. If the tribal, religious, and ethnic matrix remains untouched by American power (and it surely does not want to be touched), if only the secular bourgeois lives of people like Sabah and Hassan (and Esam and Rand and Naseer and Dr. Mashtaq) are rent asunder by our power, then we will have failed. How then can we maintain what good will we still enjoy from the Iraqi middle class? If we only split the nation into sectarian congeries, eternally at war, how have we differed from the terrorists? The sheikhs and imams, those who traffic in religious and ethnic obscurantism, must experience the plow of democracy churning up their fields as well, or the invasion, liberation, and reconstruction of Iraq will be for nothing.

Soon, it's my turn to disembark. I say goodbye to Sabah, wish him luck: he still has many days to pass among the Arabs he professes to dislike so much. Turning to Jabar, I pay him for the trip, and add a large tip. My admiration for Iraqi drivers knows no bounds:

never, in all the trips I took across the country, did I ever have a bad trip, or suffer the insecurities of a decrepit vehicle, or feel I was being cheated. Jabar was no exception. He takes the wad of dinars and places it in his shirt pocket, then, out of impulse it seems, pulls the purple plastic flower from its vase and hands it to me. A curiously gentle gesture, which I happily accept. I find myself wishing I could offer Jabar some words of encouragement, or tell him everything will work out. But of course, that is beyond my power. Beyond America, the terrorists and a fledgling Iraqi government, this country's destiny is in the hands of history—which is another way of saying *insha'allah*.

10

Nour

As for this Scheherazade,
her like is not found in the lands . . .

The Arabian Nights

A T 4:00 AM ON MARCH 2—or so the story goes—minarets across Basra suddenly broadcast an alarm for able-bodied men to seize their weapons and rush to their local mosques. From every precinct and district, men poured into the streets brandishing handguns and automatic weapons and took up positions across the city. The call to arms, fortunately, was not an insurrection against CPA authority, but a response to intelligence reports from several Shia organizations that Al Qaeda had dispatched four suicide car bombers as part of a terrorist attack. After the Ashura massacres earlier that day, the threat seemed incredible—and indeed, police and other security personnel reportedly discovered three cars loaded with explosives. The fourth was never found.

I was never able to confirm this story: some people swore they heard the alarm; CPA officials denied it took place. Still, Basra was extremely tense when I arrived on March 4. Desk clerks in the previously hospitable city refused to show me rooms; staff members at other hotels demanded to see my identification and to search my backpack. People stared. Men followed me on the street. I was ignorant of any terror warnings, nor did I stop to consider that my clothing—a black *dishdasha* and black-and-white *kheffiya*—might set off warning bells. The outfit had gotten me through Ashura and served me in Baghdad all right—why not in Basra, a town that had become my favorite place in Iraq?

As I backed out of the third hotel to give me a suspicious brush-off, an unmarked SUV suddenly screeched to a halt by the curb beside me. Down rolled the window, revealing a quartet of policemen, led by one officer-looking type seated in the passenger seat. Would I care to get inside, he asked in broken English. Sure, I replied—what else could I do?—and away we went to a police station, where, fortunately, a squad of English soldiers were hanging out. "If I were you," a Tommy said, after I convinced everyone that I was indeed an American journalist, "I'd lose the clothing. Basra's pretty edgy these days and you don't help much wandering around looking like some Wahabbi terrorist."

"'S a bloody wonder you didn't get yourself shot, mate," another soldier joined in.

No one had to tell me twice: off went the *dishdasha* and *kheffiya*. So much for my Lawrence of Arabia fantasies. The police officer offered to give me a lift to another hotel, and I accepted, wedging myself in the SUV amongst his crew. Once on the road, however, he kept turning back to me and asking questions. Why was I here? What did I plan to do? I told him *sahafee Amrikee*, but for some reason he wasn't buying it. Perhaps it was the outfit, the Ashura killings two days before, the Iranian stamp in my passport, the terrorist warning two nights previously, I didn't know—but I knew I had to allay his suspicions right away.

"Okay, here's the story, but it's kind of embarrassing," I began. "I've fallen for an Iraqi woman and I've come to be with her in Basra." The officer narrowed his eyes for a moment, then burst into laughter. After he translated my comments, the rest of the cops joined in as well. "Good, good," said the officer, giving me a lascivious thumbs-up and a smile. "Good luck to you, my friend."

Her name was Nour. I met her in early February at a meeting of the Basra Writer's Union. Dressed in a light blue scarf and matching slacks, she was a vivid patch of color amidst the drab, middle-aged men seated in the narrow, tin-ceilinged room. Women are rare in such masculine bastions, and I wondered who she was and—more important—how I could talk to her. Our eyes met, and with a forwardness that was astounding for an Iraqi woman, she stood and walked over to me. She introduced herself, and said she worked in the public communication department of an American NGO. We had a short conversation, during which I told her I was an American freelance writer, making my way through her country. "Have you eaten yet?" she abruptly asked. "I am hungry. I will treat you to lunch." She must have read the astonishment on my face, for she added, "It is part of my job, meeting foreign journalists."

She took me to the Hamdan, a clean and spacious restaurant decorated with gaudy paintings of burnoosed warriors, veiled courtesans, and other standards of Arabian fables. I was feeling a bit like a man in a fable myself: with café-au-lait-colored skin, high cheekbones, and dark, almost Persian, eyes, Nour was the most attractive woman I'd met in Iraq. Her lightly-accented English was excellent, her vocabulary large. She declined to reveal her age—and her slight build and tight-fitting *buknuk*, or tube-shaped underscarf, made it difficult to estimate—but I figured late twenties or early thirties. She welcomed the liberation of her country, she told me, and hoped that from the wreckage of the toppled Baath regime would rise a democratic Iraq. "Especially for the sake of women," she averred. "Millions live under social and religious oppression."

Beguiled by this vivacious sprite, I asked about her background. She had been born in Basra and earned a degree in English at the university. Her father died when she was fifteen, leaving her in the care of her mother and three brothers. Aside from a weekend trip to Kuwait, she had never been out of southern Iraq. Despite her foreign language skills, her greatest ambition was to become a poet. One of her poems actually landed her in some trouble a few years back, she related. Gently satirizing Saddam—in particular his claim that Kuwait was Iraq's nineteenth province—the work led the *Mukhabarat* to arrest her and hold her in a Basra prison for several months. "But that did nothing to change my love for poetry," she enthused.

As for her personal life, she volunteered that she was unmarried, although not by choice. Several years ago, her fiancé—a "famous Iraqi poet" whom I gathered was considerably older than she—was murdered by robbers one month before their wedding. "I will never love another man again," she declared with the melodrama so beloved by Iraqis. Then, almost in the same breath, she added, "But I am torn by my physical desires. I yearn to hold and kiss a man."

Was I blushing? At least five shades of red, I figured. Charming, extroverted, English-speaking, candid about her desires, she did not fit my image of a typical Muslim woman. Furthermore, she worked for a large and important NGO (because of the security situation in Basra today, I will not mention its name). For a journalist, she was a dream come true. For a man weary of the nearly insurmountable walls Arab society places between the sexes, she seemed more intoxicating than the wine proscribed by Muslim law.

It broke my heart to tell Nour that I had to leave for Baghdad the following day. We traded email addresses and promised to keep in touch. Stepping onto the street, I tried to shake her hand, but she declined. No handshake, no cheek-kiss; we said goodbye, hailed cabs and went our separate ways.

Baghdad seemed more dispiriting than usual when I returned on a cold and foggy day. Depressing me further were my friends' reactions to Nour. Jaded, accustomed to seeing the worst in human behavior, they mocked my enthusiasm. "*Sahafee Amrikee* falls for a local girl—now there's a story," one laughed. "Iraqi women are the most manipulative creatures on earth," warned another. "She'll be whatever you want her to be, it is how women here survive," said a third. I wondered about that, actually, worried that I'd seen my own idealized image of an Iraqi woman in the guise of an attractive stranger—an occupational hazard for any foreign reporter. But what if Nour were different? What if she represented something my cynical friends couldn't see? Something that stood independent of my fantasies, fears, and projections?

—

FINDING OUT WAS WORTH THE EFFORT, so five days later, I returned to Basra. Via email, Nour had already agreed to serve as my guide and translator; even better, the NGO would give her time off to assist me. We spent a week together, crisscrossing the city by cab, dropping by the countless political groups that had sprung up since the fall of Saddam—groups with names like Centre for Popular Democracy and Centre for Collection of Democracy. Assisted by her translations, I interviewed tribal leaders, Communist party officials, newspaper editors. Posing once more as a Yugoslavian journalist, I spoke to turbaned sheikhs at the Basra office of SCIRI. At Nour's

insistence I lectured the Writer's Union about freedom of the press.[1]
I made many contacts and friends and wrote several articles about
Basra for magazines back in the States. Unlike in dismal Baghdad,
I felt comfortable there.

Iraq's second-largest city and main port, Basra has had a long
and storied history, much of it having to do with war. It was founded
by Caliph Omar in 637 AD to serve as a military outpost along the
Shatt-al-Arab, the waterway that connects the Tigris and Euphrates Rivers to the Persian Gulf. (According to *The Arabian Nights*,
Sindbad began his legendary voyages from Basra.) Because of its
strategic location, a host of foreign powers—among them, the Mongols, Turks, and Persians—have attacked, occupied and sometimes
destroyed the city. In World War I, the British wrested Basra, as
well as the rest of Mesopotamia, from the Ottoman Empire. During
the 1980-1988 Iran-Iraq conflict, Tehran mounted several assaults
against the city, but never managed to take it. In the aftermath of the
first Gulf War, battles between rebellious Shia militias and Saddam's
security forces raged throughout the port, causing extensive damage.
In 2003, the British once again took the city after brief, but intense,
fighting. Since then, Basra's Shia residents have remained relatively
peaceful, unlike their Sunni brothers in and around Baghdad.

Once a beautiful, tree-lined metropolis, Basra today is a sprawl-
ing mass of dirty, low-slung cement and stucco buildings, the famous canals that once earned it the sobriquet "the Venice of the
East" now rancid garbage dumps. Because of the Shia uprising that
nearly toppled him from power, Saddam essentially cut Basra off
from government money; the city was left to rot in the fierce desert
sun that blasts its streets nine months of the year. Only 30 to 40
percent of the sewage system worked; fresh water—always a prob-

1 See pp. 155-59.

lem—was nearly nonexistent except from bottles (out of the taps, Basra had the worst water I ever tasted—or rather, *smelled*—in my life). To help nearly two million Basrans get back on their feet and repair the city's shattered infrastructure was the task of several NGOs operating there, including Nour's employer.

"Because of our work with the Coalition, many people think we have links to the CIA," Nour remarked.

"Do you?" I asked

"Do *you*?" she replied.

We started each day at 9:00 AM and interviewed people until 4:00 or 5:00 PM, finishing up at the Hamdan, where we'd drink tea in an outdoor garden beside a large cage of chattering parakeets, and a trio of sheep grazing on the lawn. Or else we'd walk along the Corniche, a promenade that runs along the Shatt-al-Arab frequented by "courting" couples. By 6:00, Nour had to be home, where her mother and brothers waited for her. She was never late.

Near the end of my second trip to Basra, something peculiar happened that deepened my feelings for Nour and changed the tenor of our interaction. One morning, two men claiming to be "intelligence agents" stopped me as Nour and I were about to leave my hotel. With my companion translating, they said they wanted some information about my activities in Basra. When they declined to provide identification, I refused to answer their questions. When they suggested I take a ride with them to their headquarters, I became alarmed. Concerned about Nour, I suggested she quit the hotel as fast as she could and get to the NGO. "Let them know what's happened." Instead, she hooked her arm around mine. "No, Steve. I'm not leaving you. We don't know who these men are, they could be trouble. You will need me." Then, with an amazed hotel staff looking on, she began to hector the men: Saddam was gone, Iraqis could no longer operate in the old ways, if they did not have identification, we were not cooperating. Realizing they had created a scene, the "intelligence agents" looked increasingly uncomfortable, denounced me as a "spy," then stormed out of the lobby. "You cannot stay here a moment longer!" Nour exclaimed, pushing me up the stairs. "Gather your belongings at once, we must find another hotel!"

I never encountered the men again, and have no idea what they wanted with me—although the incident continued to cause me worry. Mostly, though, I thought about Nour, how she had refused to leave me, how she'd stood up against the specter of what had haunted Iraqi lives for decades—mysterious "intelligence agents." She ceased being a mere friend—she had become a partner in the intrigue and danger that permeated the city of Basra.

But a chaste and scrupulous partner, nonetheless. Like most Iraqi women, Nour was hyper-conscious about respectability: she paid for everything—taxis, meals, snacks—and discouraged physical contact. ("Don't touch me in public," she'd say, a line that became a standing joke between us.) We were ever mindful of the moral and cultural barriers between us

Still, the more I got to know my companion, the keener my appreciation of her situation became. Nour did not have an easy life. Wherever she and I went, for example, people glared at us. More than curiosity, it was a cruel, malevolent stare that hoped to see Nour disgrace herself, do something scandalous or un-Islamic, in order to fuel invidious gossip and innuendo. That was normal, Nour explained. Men and women obsessed on virginity, honor, and reputation; the slightest slip could ruin a woman forever. "Reputation is everything—without it, I am lost," she would say. Like a character out of an Edith Wharton novel, she carried herself as if on stage, her every movement viewed, scrutinized, and critiqued by a hostile audience.

Once, as we walked along the Corniche, she suggested we take a boat ride down the Shatt-al-Arab. At first, the trip was idyllic: warm winds, mellow, late afternoon light, the two of us seated close together in the otherwise empty tourist boat. But the pilot, an acne-scarred teenager, insisted on turning around and staring at us, as if supervising our behavior. Irritated, I suggested to Nour that we ask the kid, or pay him, to face forward. "Oh no!" she protested. "We can't do that! Then he'll think we are doing something scandalous and he'll tell the other boatmen. I'll never be able to come to the Corniche again."

"So this means we have to sit here and let this cretin stare at us?" My anger surprised me.

"Yes, Steve, I'm sorry. We must suffer the ignorance of Iraqi men. Now do you see why I want to help change this society?"

She blamed "tribal norms" for Iraq's "ignorant men." Nour hated anything that had to do with tribes—even to the point of refusing to drink tea from a *stikaana* because of the glass's Bedouin origin. One morning, we interviewed Sheikh Abdul Wahab Abdullah Robeiey, head of a southern council of tribes whose habitats comprised some 3,400 lesser sheikhs and nine million people. Seated with ten other *abiya*-wearing men in a bare concrete room, Robeiey expressed his views on many issues involving Iraq's future, including his desire to see *shari'a* imposed on the country's women. At once, Nour leaped from her seat and shouted, "No! That cannot be!"—and proceeded to berate the tribal leader in Arabic. Not *shari'a*, secular law! Not religious government, democracy! The sheikhs sat stunned by the spectacle of a woman half their size and age challenging their authority, and even old Robeiey had to yield. "*Shari'a* is only one option; there are, of course, many others," he conceded.

"*Back*ward, *stu*pid, *rude* old men and their ignorant tribal norms," Nour groused as we left the Sheikhs' office. "They will ruin our country."

She could be surprisingly rude herself. During lunch one afternoon, I noticed she was treating our waiter in a peremptory fashion—get this, do that, hurry up, that sort of thing. When I mentioned this to her, she shrugged. "Iraqi men like to be treated roughly," she announced—and to prove it, called the waiter to our table and asked the poor man in Arabic if he liked women to abuse him. Blushing, embarrassed, no doubt terribly shamed as his fellow waiters guffawed behind him, the waiter nodded sheepishly. Nour dismissed him. "You see?" she said triumphantly.

"All I see, Nour, is that you made a fool of that guy."

She frowned, sighed, folded her hands on the table. "Steve," she began, "you must understand. Social life in Iraq is a nightmare. Gossip and rumor and attempts to destroy people's reputations are the norm, especially between men and women. Men demand that women be virgins and have pure reputations, while they carry on their polygamist affairs. In turn, women seek revenge by abusing men at home. Men are used to it, Steve, they expect abuse. It is sick," she concluded in a resigned voice. "In Iraq, the relationships between men and women are sadomasochistic."

It took me a while to realize that she was speaking from personal experience. One afternoon, as we walked along the Corniche, I asked about her brothers. "They completely dominate my life," was her surprising answer. According to "social norms," as Nour put it, these three men—high school dropouts who ran street corner vending stalls—were responsible for "guarding" her. This meant, in effect, that they never allowed her to travel out of Basra—forbidding her, for example, to move to Baghdad or another country where she might begin a new life. Nor would they allow her to pursue post-graduate studies. Their object was to marry her off and relieve themselves of the burden of "protecting" her honor and reputation. "They believe it is the will of Allah that they should do this for me," she said.

She tried to rebel once. Because of the age discrepancy between Nour and her poet fiancé, her "guardians" disapproved of the relationship. She decided to marry him anyway, then present the nuptials to her family as a fait accompli. With her fiancé's murder, however, the plot unraveled and her brothers learned of the secret engagement.

"They took turns beating me," she recounted matter-of-factly, tucking a loose bit of hair beneath her *buknuk*. "They beat me until my face was black-and-blue and they had broken my arm."

I was horrified. "Why don't you get on a bus or train or car get out of here? Go to Kuwait, Baghdad, Syria—"

"I can't, Steve." She was crying now, daubing her eyes with a wadded Kleenex. "Wherever I go, my brothers will track me down. And they will surely kill me."

Nour had two hopes for salvation. The first was Islam. "The Koran gave women real rights and freed them from tribal customs," she explained. "This is why I am a Muslim. This is why I wear a scarf." It was more than simple religious observance. One afternoon as we walked to the Hamdan, a group of thugs loitering on the corner glared at us as we passed. A white man walking with a black woman in pre-Civil Rights Mississippi could not have elicited more disapproval. The thought that Nour was the target of this resentment cause me to blurt something that astonished me: "I'm glad you wear a scarf, Nour, it protects you from these goons." She smiled. "Now you understand."

Her other hope was democracy. It was a magic word for her, a talisman that conjured security, the rule of law, and, perhaps most important, freedom from "tribal norms." She would pester me with questions about the Constitution, and I found myself at the Hamdan talking until dusk about the Bill of Rights, the separation of powers, the Electoral College. "You must give me a list of books to read!" she enthused. "We need to teach people about our new government! There are so many women who are oppressed by ignorant men in Iraq, and if we are to become a normal country, we must find a way to free them"

At times like this, I wondered if perhaps Nour was some sort of mirage, a *djinn* I'd conjured out of a wish list of characteristics I wanted so desperately to find in the Iraqi people.

"Nour, are you real? Everything I see and hear from you is just so amazing—too amazing. Is it true?"

"Of course. Why would you think otherwise?"

I remembered *The Arabian Nights*, and the way Scheherezade beguiled King Shahryar with tales of danger, romance, and magic. She, too, had to survive in a hostile environment.

"But Steve, believe me, I am not important. What is important are the millions of people who are not free in my country."

Or had I found something truly tremendous in this young woman: a glimpse of a new Iraqi soul that was struggling to break centuries-old customs and traditions and transform the nation?

—

IN EARLY MARCH, I made my third and final visit to Basra. Part of my purpose was journalistic: in conversations I'd had with English soldiers in the city, they took pride in the fact that Basra was considerably less violent than Baghdad and the Sunni Triangle. "Well, the Yanks really bollixed that up, now, didn't they?" one sergeant at the CPA compound sneered, a reflection, the Brits unsubtly implied, of their superior wisdom, tactics, and general expertise in administering "occupations." Perhaps that was true. Still, from my own encounters with "intelligence agents," to persistent stories of armed Shia militias operating under the Tommies' noses—and more specifically, of gunmen closing down liquor stores and often executing their owners—I wondered if our ally's pride was wholly merited. "If you want to investigate these matters, of course I will help you," Nour had written me by email. "But we must careful."

Nour, of course, was my other reason. A tremendous dust-storm inundating Karbala with a swirling sea of dirt and sand, the fires of the Baba Gurgur oil fields lighting the night sky on the edge of Kirkuk, Baghdad at twilight—none of these sights caused me to stop thinking of her. It was embarrassing, clichéd, and I felt uneasy about Lisa back home. But I had to get back to Basra.

After the police took me to a hotel and I checked in, I rushed to the NGO's headquarters. Nour met me there, looking glamorous in a sand-colored chiffon scarf, maroon blouse, and tan slacks. We greeted each other with the warm, easy familiarity of two friends happy to see one another again.

But reality soon intruded. Seated in the Hamdan's outdoor garden, Nour relayed a troubling incident. A few days before, she said, a man she had never seen before stopped her on the street, said, "Why are you working for the American CIA?"—and walked away.

"Who was he?"

"Someone from the criminal gangs or religious parties, I don't know." When I suggested she tell her employer or the CPA, she looked impatient. "What good will that do? Everyone is fearful these days. We know if we stand up for democracy, people will kill us—or come to our homes and kill our families."

My blood ran cold. This wasn't a game, I realized, or some romantic movie. I began to fear that I was being cavalier with Nour's safety.

"Are you sure you want to be seen with me? You'll only draw more attention to yourself."

"No, Steve. I can't let these men frighten me. Besides," she smiled and ventured to pat my hand. "You are too romantic and foolish, dear. You will need my help."

We started our investigation the next day at the Writer's Union. There, amidst the bustling of men drinking tea and trading gossip, a young, well-dressed figure approached us and, through Nour's translation, introduced himself as a local journalist eager to meet me. Flattered by his attention, I peppered him with questions about the city: How powerful were the religious militia? How many men were under arms? Who was killing the liquor store owners? The young man laughed, shook my hand and wandered off. Confused for a moment, I suddenly realized that Nour had deliberately mistranslated my questions. "Did you know that person?" she admonished me. "*I* didn't. You mustn't be so careless, dear."

Instead, she found a friend she trusted, a tall, burly fellow named Amir. Taking me aside, the unemployed actor conveyed in a low voice the general word on the street: many of Basra's smaller "religious parties" were in fact Mafia-like gangs comprised of Iranians and Saudis who were smuggling oil and dealing drugs. They were also operating a black market of out-of-date medicine and spoiled food. "Iraq is free now—free for thieves," Amir griped, glancing about for possible eavesdroppers. "We have no law here but the law of the gun."

Amir's perceptions were seconded by *al-Manarah* editor Lowai Hamza Abbas, who was, it turned out, a good friend of Nour's. Over lunch at the Hamdan, Lowza portrayed Basra as a sort of Middle Eastern version of Roaring-20s Chicago, a city where heavily-armed criminal gangs use Islam as a pretext to control entire neighborhoods. Worse, two types of terrorists had set up in Basra: Shia-hating Wahabbis from Syria, Saudi Arabia, and Afghanistan, who wanted to erect a Taliban-like state, and radical Shias organized and funded by Tehran who sought to extend Iran's control over southern Iraq. "In dismantling Saddam's regime," Lowai remarked, "the Coalition left us defenseless against criminals and terrorists. The CPA is deluded if they think they control the streets."

As if to prove Lowai's remarks, half an hour later Nour and I were seated in a plushly carpeted room of the headquarters of the *Da'wa Islamiyya*, Iraq's largest Shia organization. Posing again as a Yugoslavian journalist—with Nour translating—I engaged in a lengthy conversation about the greatness of Ayatollah Khomeini and *Da'wa*'s desire for an "Iranian-style democracy" with a quiet, self-contained, but watchful fellow who identified himself as Sheikh Asaa'di. At the end of the interview, I asked the cleric if it was true that *Da'wa* was forcing merchants to close stores that sold music CDs or alcohol.

"We have participated in that, yes," he blandly replied. "We are against immoral activities. We send the shop owners threats to close, and they obey." All very simple, it seemed. "But," he added, "we do not kill them—*that* is against Islam."

As we stood to leave, Asaa'di asked Nour something in Arabic that caused her to grab my arm. "Steve!" she gasped. "He's asking for my address and telephone number! What do I do?"

"I don't think he wants a date, Nour. Let's get the hell out of here."

In the cab taking her home, I thought of the sheikh's peculiar interest, and once again felt a pang of anxiety regarding her safety. "Don't worry, dear," she laughed, giving my hand a squeeze, then leaving her hand resting atop mine. "I have an angel who looks over me." As she did every evening, she asked the cabbie to stop at an intersection several blocks from her home. I was not to know where she lived.

"Remember now, don't touch me in public," she whispered as she collected her notebook and purse.

"Why, Nour? No one knows us here. We're just two people in a cab."

"No. Believe me, you are wrong. Basra sees everything."

That night, I worked on an article at an internet café until 10:00 PM. When I left to walk back to my hotel, I discovered the restaurants had closed. The only place I could get dinner was a tiny kebab stand, no larger than a New York hot dog cart. I gave an elderly, wall-eyed man my order and he tossed a couple of chunks of cubed lamb on the grill. As the meat sizzled, he gave me an odd look. "That woman we see you with is very pretty," he remarked in passable English. I jerked back in surprise. Nour and I had never been together in this part of town. Smiling in a half-amused, half-hostile fashion, he pressed his index fingers together in the Iraqi sign of togetherness. "We think she is your wife, yes?"

—

NAJIBAH WAS FRIGHTENED. On May 8, 2003, masked gunmen entered the liquor shop of her brother Iblahdad and murdered him. That same day, gunmen killed three other Christian wine merchants, as well. Now, in the dark back room of her small house, its wall decorated with framed pictures of the Virgin Mary, she showed Nour and me a petition she'd sent to British authorities, asking them to prosecute the killers. "They belonged to an Islamic party," she stated, eyes tearing. "But the British did nothing. They said it was not their business." Najibah's husband and his brother, sad, deflated-looking men, sat beside her, staring at the ground. They, too, had been liquor merchants; after the May killings, they closed their shops and quit the business.

"We are afraid to look for other jobs," said Najibah's husband. "We are afraid that Islamic groups will come after us. They say they want to drive all Christians out of Basra."

"We would go to Kurdistan, where it is safe," said the second man. "But we have no jobs, no money now. The Islamic parties want us to sell our houses, so they can control the real estate."

Shooing away her three eavesdropping children, Najibah added in a low voice, "Last month someone shot a bullet into our front gate. Now, I only travel by cabs when I go out, and always wear an *abiya*, although I am not Muslim."

Nour's mouth tightened, as it did when she got angry. "What does the Church say about this?"

An uncomfortable silence fell over the room. "Why don't you ask them yourselves?" Najibah replied.

The office of Archbishop Gabriel T. Kassab, spiritual shepherd of Basra's 1,150 Christian families, was only a few blocks away. By good fortune, the cleric was in, and was willing to spare fifteen minutes to talk to Nour and me. A heavy-set, graying man, dressed in a black cassock, he sat behind a desk in his small, sunny office, and confirmed his knowledge of the killings. "I am sorry for the merchants, but I cannot condone alcohol sales," he said, an assistant priest hovering beside him. "They are forbidden." When I observed that alcohol was not prohibited by Iraqi law—not yet, at least—the English-speaking clergyman shook his balding head. "It is now forbidden because the Islamic parties say so. We must be careful about this. We Christians are a minority in this land. I can do nothing."

Nour inhaled sharply. "But you are giving in to the gunmen! You are surrendering your authority to people who want to destroy democracy!"

As with Sheikh Robeiey, the sight of a young Muslim woman berating a Catholic archbishop for not opposing Islamic extremism was startling, to say the least. For his part, Kassab looked irritated. "Our church belongs to *all* Basrans, Christians and Muslims alike. Ninety percent of our kindergarten classes are *Muslims*, most of the elderly in our social programs are Muslim. And remember, eleven Muslim wine merchants have also been killed. My friends in *Da'wa* and SCIRI tell me criminals are at fault, not their people. Do I believe them?" He held up his large palms. "I must."

"For a big man, he straddles a thin fence," I said to Nour as we stepped from Kassab's church into blinding mid-day sunlight.

She wasn't listening. "I cannot believe he abandons his people like that," she murmured. "My God, Steve. It is as I told you. Everyone fears the religious parties, no one wants to stand up to them." Her brows constricted and her face took on a hardness that startled me. "No one."

She sat hunched against the door of the cab, looking out the window as we sped down Basra Street toward her NGO. She was pensive, moody: clearly, the growing threat of the violent extremists distressed her. We drove past a large concrete building that had taken a JDAM during the war, its various floors collapsed downward in a series of v's. Thinking I might cheer Nour up, I gestured toward the structure. "When I move to Basra, that's where I'm going to live."

Keeping her face averted from mine, "Why would you want to stay there?" she replied softly. "That was the headquarters of the *Mukhabarat*. That's where they held me for three days before sending me to prison."

A chill shot through me. I suddenly remembered, weeks ago, when Nour told me about her poem, the business about Kuwait, her arrest, and imprisonment. At the time, I didn't think much about it: everyone in Iraq had spent some time in prison, it seemed. But that was before I got to know her. I recalled stories of what went on Saddam's prison, what the secret police were capable of doing—what they did—how they would have viewed a helpless young woman.

"Nour," I began, forcing myself not to imagine the unimaginable. "Were you—did they—" I didn't know how to put it; suddenly, all my journalistic skills deserted me.

"Tell me it didn't happen," was all I could say.

She kept her head turned away and remained silent.

"Nour, tell me it didn't happen."

"I don't want to talk about it."

"Nour—" I couldn't let it go. The realization forced itself into my thoughts with a distress I had never experienced before. Whatever professional detachment I had, or was supposed to have, was long gone, I realized, but that seemed insignificant now. What I wanted most of all was reassurance. Not *her*, not *Nour* . . . But the more I pressed the issue, the angrier she became. The cab pulled up to our destination and we got out.

"Don't touch me in public—"

"It's too late," I said, grabbing her arm. "Look, Nour. Lie to me. Make it up, I don't care—*just tell me it didn't happen.*"

She glared at me. "All right, it didn't happen," she snapped. "Are you satisfied? Do you feel better?" I tried to respond, but she spun on a heel and disappeared behind the walls of the NGO.

I climbed back into the cab. The driver moved about fifty feet down the road, then stopped, turning back to me with a quizzical expression. In his hand was a box of Kleenex. It startled me. I didn't realize I'd been crying so hard.

—

A FEW DAYS BEFORE THIS INCIDENT, I was tending to some business at CPA headquarters when a boyish, sandy-haired American approached me. I was immediately struck by his friendly manner, and the holstered .45 strapped to his thigh. His name was Mark (we'll call him), and he was the counter-intelligence officer for the Basra area. How would I like to drop by his office at some point for an interview, he asked. I jumped at the chance and asked if I could bring along my "translator." Of course, he said.

The day after our little spat—we'd gotten over it, and I never brought the subject up again—Nour and I took a cab to the CPA's armed compound along the Shatt-al-Arab. It was my last day in Basra and, after long delays with CPA security, found ourselves in a small conference room situated inside an air-conditioned trailer. Here, leaning back in his chair, a Timberland boot pressed against the edge of his desk, Mark eyed us with professional interest. "You fascinate me," he said. "Here you are, traveling all over town, seemingly on your own, going to this organization and that—"

"Excuse me," I interjected. "How do you know this?"

"I've read the reports."

"Reports? You mean, we've been followed?"

He shrugged a shoulder. "You two stand out. People are talking about you. They're interested in what you're doing." He paused. "Do you carry a gun?"

"No." I didn't want to ask him if I should.

It suddenly dawned on me that Mark, the counter-intelligence agent, had called Nour and me into his office to investigate *us*. Turning to Nour, "You're Egyptian, right?" he asked, intrigued, I could tell, by her sharp, delicate features. Apparently unsatisfied by her denial, he called an Iraqi man into the conference room to briefly speak with her and ascertain her accent.

"By God, I will not stand for this!" she exclaimed, slamming her notebook shut and standing up. "If he does not believe me, I will leave!"

"Sit down, Nour, and stop acting like a child," I shot back. She glowered at me, huffed, then dropped back into her seat.

Flashing a bemused smile, Mark apologized for his suspicion, "But the situation here is complicated, and anyone can pass as an American or an Iraqi." He motioned behind him to an aerial map of Basra affixed to the trailer wall. "You've got *Da'wa* and sciri acting like Mafia families with their fingers in legal and illegal activities. It's not like they order someone to be shot, or a liquor store closed down—they just get the word out and some gunmen do the job for them. Then you've got these 'democratic' organizations springing up—say Ahmed and his brothers want to start a carjacking ring. What better excuse to hang out all night than by starting your own 'political party'? These gangs have taken control of whole neighborhood to use as bases for dealing liquor and drugs, prostitution, protection rackets, extortion, you name it. In my opinion, they're the biggest threat to Basra, because they're tearing apart the social infrastructure of the city."

But there were other problems, too, Mark continued. Fuel smuggling, for example. Financed largely by Iranians, criminal gangs were loading barges with pilfered crude, then piloting the vessels down the Shatt to offshore tankers, which then sailed to destinations around the world. Either that, or they were devising ingenious ways to smuggle gas out of Iraq for sale where pumps prices were higher than the cpa-subsidized price of twenty dinars a liter.

Worse, Tehran was using profits from the smuggling to meddle in Iraqi affairs. This interference included funding Islamic religious groups, as well as terrorist organizations. "Basra," he observed, "is the hub of Iranian terrorist activities in Iraq."

"You must do something!" Nour cried. "Where is the CPA? Where are the British?"

Mark spread his palms apart. "We're leaving June 30. As for the Brits, they'll tell you that crime is a matter for the Iraq police."

For the first time since I had met her, Nour looked frightened. "Don't you understand? The Iraqi police are corrupt! We have no laws, no courts, judges are afraid to rule against criminals or the religious parties. You are leaving us to the ignorant men!"

"I'm sorry," Mark replied. "But what are our options? The more we try to do for the Iraqi people, the more they hate us."

—

HE WAS RIGHT, OF COURSE: the CPA could never do enough and always did too much, a judgment that history will etch on the monument to their efforts in Iraq. I mulled this over as Nour and I drove out to our final interview at the British base in Basra's international airport, a half-hour away by cab. As the miles rolled by, she curled up beside me like a cat and dozed. I looked at her—her impeccable half-Western, half-Muslim dress, her dark eyes and smooth brown skin and marveled how she resembled a child, or some kind of Islamic doll, fragile, delicate, in need of protection. And yet, every day this woman went alone to a place of work so concerned about terrorism that its foreign employees lived behind fortified walls, security personnel manned a twenty-four-hour rooftop observation post, and her boss sat facing the door during conversations with visitors "in case gunmen break into the compound"—where no one could offer her protection against the men who had already identified her as working with the CIA.

Why did she do this? She was well-paid, of course, at least by Iraqi standards. But there was another reason: *democracy*. She believed in it, believed in the promise of America, believed in our concepts of popular sovereignty and equal rights—and saw them as her last, best chance for deliverance. I had no doubt about her now: a thousand Nours set loose in Iraq would transform the country beyond anyone's imaginings. I ventured to stroke her side and she stirred, her smile deepening. Short of destroying my marriage, I thought, I would do anything to help this woman.

The cabbie dropped us off on the road leading to the airport. Soldiers had closed the gate, and a long line of cars and trucks stretched down the tarmac, shimmering in the blistering sun. We walked to a security checkpoint and announced our presence. At the front of the line, several men squatted in the shade of an eighteen-wheeler, smoking cigarettes and talking amongst themselves. We sat on the curb opposite them to wait.

Before long, the truckers' attention shifted to us. It was clear something was annoying them, and I knew what it was: a foreigner was chatting with a young Iraqi woman whose *buknuk* and scarf indicated she was Muslim. As the minutes wore on, their stares burned holes through us. I mentioned my discomfort to Nour, but, raising her notebook to shield her eyes from the sun, she advised me to ignore the men. "Believe me," she said, stretching out her legs and crossing them at the ankles, "there's nothing you can do."

The heat intensified. The wind blew dust and grit across the asphalt, stinging our eyes. The Brits, meanwhile, evinced no inclination to open the gate. As the boredom mounted, the truckers became more agitated; finally, one of them stood and crossed the roadway toward us. Looming over Nour, he barked something in Arabic, causing her face to fall and her body to flinch as she drew her legs beneath her. As he strode back to his companions with a triumphant air, I asked her what he'd said. "He demanded that I sit more like a respectable Muslim woman," she replied in a mortified tone. Enraged at the man's effrontery, I rose to confront him, only to be halted by Nour's demurrals.

"No, Steve, please."

"Goddamn it, Nour, you can't let a total stranger tell you what to do! You're free now, you don't have to listen to these ignorant men—tell them to f— off!"

"We're not in America!" she snapped impatiently. Then, collecting herself, "Your romantic attitude will only cause me trouble."

I couldn't believe this resigned, defeated creature was Nour. And yet, she was right. What could I do? There was no proper response, no way to challenge the trucker. He had subjugated and shamed a young woman possessing ten times his intelligence and spirit by conjuring the one force our fine concepts of "democracy" and "equal rights" could not defend her against: *tribal Islam.*

Nour was noticeably subdued when two British press officers finally pulled up in a civilian car. "Sorry about the delay," said a tall, handsome captain wearing a beret and neatly-pressed desert camo. "But when you said you were coming, we thought you were flying in like all the other journalists. We weren't prepared for someone who actually lives in Basra and *drives* to the airport."

"Makes you wonder about Western reporters, doesn't it?" I said to Nour. She avoided my eyes and didn't answer.

The officers drove us into the airport and escorted us to the main terminal. Here, in a waiting lounge turned into an impromptu briefing center, a portly, avuncular major spent about forty-five minutes describing the situation in Basra as viewed by the British army. It was essentially the same woes we'd heard before: crime, religious mafias, Iranian smugglers, Wahabbi spies. And the Brits' main task in Basra? "We provide psychological stability," was the major's wan response. "When the CPA dissolves in June, we will restrict ourselves to our bases. Then, it's up to the Iraqi police to keep order."

"The police?" exclaimed Nour, who had remained silent until now. "My God, no! Look at their cars, their stations—they are all flying Islamic flags and banners. They know that once you leave, the religious parties will take over Basra and they are trying to curry favor ahead of time!"

The major gave the "Coalition shrug"—I was getting used to seeing it—and said nothing; the interview was at an end. We rose in uncomfortable silence, trying not to see Nour's distraught expression. Suddenly, she stepped in front of the beret-wearing captain, blocking his path. Looking up at the officer, who seemed nearly twice her height, "You musn't leave us," she pleaded. "We trust the British more than our own police. Please don't leave us to the criminals and religious parties. Please don't abandon us."

No one said a word. There was nothing to say. "Come on, Nour," I muttered, taking her arm. "It's time to go."

NOUR RETURNED TO THE NGO, and I went back to the hotel to finish writing an article. But I couldn't concentrate. My critical distance was shot to hell. The incident with the truckers enraged me; Nour's pleas to the English soldiers filled me with anguish.

I lay on my bed, emotionally exhausted. I felt worn out, torn by feelings I couldn't name. But at least I had the luxury of being able to wallow in such self-absorbed gusts of emotion: I was leaving. What of Nour, who had to remain locked in this madhouse called Iraq?

At 5:00 PM the desk clerk called to say she had arrived. I went downstairs to meet her wearing the black *dishdasha* and *kheffiya* that had gotten me in so much trouble. She burst out laughing. "Oh,

Steve, you look so funny!" At once, though, her amusement died. "Please, take it off. You look too much like one of the tribal men."

I changed clothes and joined her in the hotel's empty restaurant. Neither of us knew what to say. I thanked her, of course, told her I would never forget our experiences together, and she nodded. She seemed to be keeping as tight a leash on her emotions as I was on mine; both of us, I feared, were on the verge of tears. I wanted to reach out and take her hand, but that was impossible—over her shoulder, I could see the hotel staff staring at our table. In the end, all I could do was ask Nour the question I'd put to her countless time before. Why don't you find some way to leave Iraq?

She smiled wanly. "Someday, perhaps. I will find a man who will marry me with the understanding that once we leave the country, we will divorce." That bleak pronouncement hung in the air between us for a moment. Then, squaring her shoulders and brightening a bit, "Until then," she announced, "I must fight for democracy and show the world the liberal face of Islam. There is so much to do, Steve. How can I leave now?"

I walked her to the street to hail a cab. "Now, remember—"

"I know, 'Dahn tahch me in poblick,'" I answered, imitating her accent. A cab pulled up, and she climbed in.

"Okay—now—" speaking from the back seat in a crisp tone, preventing both of us from betraying any unseemly bursts of emotion, "we must have a plan, a program. I will send you articles about Iraq so you will be better prepared when you come back—"

"Yes, Nour, thank you, Nour . . ." I took her hand.

"Oh, Steve, please stop. You are such a romantic fool, and you're going to make me cry."

There were, I noticed, tears in her eyes already. Squeezing my hand, she whispered, "*Safra saaida.*" The phrase means "good travels," or "good luck."

I pressed her palm between mine, then blew her a kiss. "*Safra saaida, habibitie.*" The cab pulled away.

—

I RETURNED TO BAGHDAD THE NEXT MORNING. I thought about stopping off at Karbala or Najaf, but my heart was no longer in it. I felt empty, deflated, as if something marvelous had vanished from my life. In a sense, something had: with Nour, every moment seemed vivid. It couldn't last, of course, nor should it have.

And Nour? To me, her life seemed like a rare and precious gem nearly buried beneath the dead weight of tribalism and religious dogma. I'd seen and experienced these colorful, but sterile, customs and beliefs all through Iraq, but it wasn't until I witnessed them in comparison with a spirit as bright as Nour's (which means "light" in Arabic) that I realized how dead, how sterile they were. I wished I could release her—and the spirit of others like her. But that, I realized, was a dangerous fantasy, one that led to American misadventures in the country. America is not omnipotent; cultures do not change easily—especially the ones that should. Despite my affection and best wishes, I, like the CPA, would leave Nour to her fate.

"At least let me write something that will let people know that women like you exist in Iraq," I said to her one afternoon at the Corniche.

"Why? I am not important. What *is* important are the lives of millions of Iraqi women. Concentrate on them. Help them."

A flock of herons wheeled across the palm groves on the eastern bank of the Shatt-al-Arab, as a breeze blew her scarf across my cheek.

I will try, Nour, I thought. Starting with you.

11

Were We Right?

It was the belief that, in the modern world,
even the enemies of reason cannot be the
enemies of reason. Even the unreasonable
must be, in some fashion, reasonable.

Paul Berman

Fellow-citizens, we cannot escape history. . . .
No personal significance, or insignificance, can
spare one or another of us. The fiery trial through
which we pass, will light us down, in honor
or dishonor, to the latest generation.

Abraham Lincoln

IT'S A QUESTION EVERYONE WHO SUPPORTED—and still supports—the war must pose to themselves.

Particularly now—I write this in late September 2004—when Iraq is beset by kidnappings, beheadings, renegade Shia militiamen and an increasingly widespread insurgency that has turned western Iraq into a Wahabbi caliphate. Meanwhile, the U.S. stands increasingly alone in the conflict, with even allies like the Britain seemingly searching for the exit door. Worse, observers worry that paramilitaries will launch a "Tet"-style offensive timed for the U.S. elections in hopes of breaking the back of American support for the war. Bottom line: eighteen months after the fall of Saddam, victory hangs on the thinnest of threads.

Nor does this assessment take into account over one thousand American soldiers dead, thousands wounded and costs so high the President won't disclose the actual figures. Meanwhile, Islamic extremists are using Muslim anger at Iraq's liberation as a recruitment tool, raising new generations of *mujahideen*. Far from triggering the march of democracy across the Middle East, Operation Iraqi Freedom seems to have stoked the totalitarian fires we wished to dampen, while presenting America with its greatest foreign policy debacle since Vietnam.

Should we have invaded Iraq?

With the smoke from the World Trade Center still rising from Ground Zero, the toppling of Saddam's regime seemed to me a necessary response. Forget neo-Wilsonian "idealism": I simply wanted the Star and Stripes planted in the craw of the Middle East. Later, this thirst for retribution matured to a resolve that the civilized world must, with irresistible force and implacable wrath, eradicate the evil of Islamofascism wherever it resides. As for building a democracy in Iraq—why not? What better way to pacify the heart of the *umma Muhammadiyya*? Only a prejudiced mind could doubt that Arabs would welcome the gift of freedom.

During my first trip, my thinking broadened. I grew to appreciate the Iraqi people, to understand the suffering they had endured under Saddam. Moreover, I started to comprehend the monstrous forces that had caused this suffering—and which sought to inflict more. As my personal trauma over 9-11 faded, I began to understand that the West's legacy of individual rights, joined with a religious heritage that emphasized freedom of conscience, was the path Iraqis could take to escape their history. Helping the crooked timber of this Muslim nation to straighten itself seemed a noble purpose for American power.

At the same time, though, I encountered some portents of future problems: the unchecked looting, rampant street crime, sky-high unemployment, and daily inconveniences like on-and-off electricity wore people down. "My baby is sick," Ahmed, the piano player at the Orient Palace told me. "I give her medicine, but she doesn't get better. The medicine needs refrigeration—was it good when I bought it, with the electricity so bad? I would buy more, but how do I know that medicine isn't spoiled, too? I don't know what to do. You can't imagine," he concluded pathetically, "how a father feels when he can't care for his child."

Multiply Ahmed's pain across an entire nation and you will get an idea of the *other* side of Iraq's liberation. Still, I thought, things will improve. Of course they will—we're the United States of America!

Yet whatever America did—successes or blunders, it didn't matter—seemed only to exacerbate the more disagreeable aspects of the Iraqi character. Resentment: *We hate you for liberating us.* Grandiosity and self-loathing: *We were once the glorious Cradle of Civilization; now we are nothing.* Moral blindness: *George Bush or Saddam Hussein—what's the difference?* Conspiracy thinking: *The Americans staged 9-11 to give Bush a pretext to invade Iraq.* Anti-Semitism. Misogyny. A pervasive sense of self-loathing and defeat. Meanwhile, the killings in the Sunni Triangle continued. But again, I shrugged it off. Those Iraqis weren't reasonable like Esam or Naseer or Haider. How can unreason win the day?

I returned home in late October. Even before I touched down at JFK, I wanted to return to Iraq. For all its occasional dangers and discomforts, life—at least then, at least for foreigners—was thrilling there, infused with an intoxicating sense of purpose. *We are building a new Iraq!* Compared to that, the art world seemed irrelevant. Besides, my work was incomplete. I'd seen Iraq through an American lens: America was both the protagonist and the villain of the story. But what about the Iraqis? What role did they play?

Baghdad was more prosperous when I returned in January. Crime was down. More women were on the streets. Some of the buildings gutted by looters had been repaired; fewer taxicab windshields exhibited cracks or bullet holes. Still, Iraqi energies seemed dormant. Spirits had not caught fire. Nowhere did I feel a sense of people plunging in to determine their own destiny. The media and anti-war activists hardly helped, with their steady drumbeat of *occupier, occupier, occupier*. Logically, if Iraq were occupied, then any who assisted the occupier's aims were *collaborators*. How much more legitimate was the *Resistance*!

It was a "resistance," however, that continued to kill. Al Qaeda, Ansar al-Islam, unrepentant Baathists, a cauldron of monsters murdering more Iraqis than Americans in their strategic goal to—what? Reclaim lost honor? Destroy any chance the Iraqi people have to escape the dungeon of their history? Standing in Fallujah, Ramadi, Tikrit, listening to the Sunni hosannas to Saddam, I thought, no, this can't have substance. It's too unreasonable. How could these people discard the freedom America is presenting them?

After numerous experiences, encounters and interviews, I began to grasp in its rough outlines the Iraqi perspective. On one hand, I saw the U.S. as our critics did: as a lumbering giant full of empty promises, trigger-happy soldiers, disconnected officials, and rank incompetence. The last charge was the most shocking: nothing prepared me for a view of America as a dithering, distracted nation that couldn't fulfill its basic purpose in Iraq, *to secure the country*. (As an Iraqi once said to me, "If you're going to occupy our country, *occupy it*.")

On the other hand, I began seeing the Iraqis *as they viewed themselves*: a discordant mass, divided by ethnic, clan and religious affiliations, an ugly society, more like a military encampment, coarsened by long domination by tribal custom, Islamic fundamentalism, and autocratic brutality. The honor dynamic in the Sunni Triangle, the Shia obsession with martyrdom, the Iraqis' general misconceptions of democracy and the malignant influence of "tribal Islam"— all these began to erode my hope that a self-actualizing fire would inflame the Iraqi people. I wondered if the hope of that "fire" was too Western, too Christian (thinking of the Paraclete, tongues of flame, epiphanies), if in the end, I had followed the same footsteps of countless other Western "missionaries" seeking to rehabilitate, convert, reform, or simply wake up the Muslim world. Perhaps that awakening calls for an inward change that is not yet part of the Iraqi, or Arab, psychology. Perhaps they can only rouse themselves by fixating on an external enemy—America, say, or Zionists.

This is difficult to write, especially since one of my intentions in this book is to persuade readers that fighting for the Iraqi people is worth American blood and treasure. But we must be honest. The first step in knowledge is to see the Other as a distinct entity, not as an extension of oneself. Like many supporters of the war, I had perceived the Iraqis as I wished them to be: latent Jeffersonians, yearning for freedom and democracy. Like others, I was blinded by my personal need to account for 9-11—a desire that had sub-limated itself into political idealism. An idealism, moreover, that was reflected back to me by reasonable Iraqis, the Westernized, English-speaking people I met. Unable to speak Arabic, I, like most foreign journalists, had little access to the millions of *unreasonable* Iraqis whose lives, thoughts and spirits are ground into passivity or resentment by religious obscurantism and tribal parochialism. The people, in short, who swell the armies of Islamofascism.

But here, as I've come to see it, is the crux of the problem. In times past, Westerners could indulge in the exotic Muslim rejection of modernity as an escape from the stresses of our own industrial-ized society. But no longer. On 9-11, the despair and self-loathing at the center of the Muslim world was unleashed on America. On that day, tribal Islam became *our* problem, too. And, being our prob-lem, it demands our solution: democracy. Democracy to protect civilization from terrorism, democracy to break the bonds of tribal Islam that enslave the will, imagination, and energies of millions of Muslims. Given the malignant state of the Islamic world today, this appears to me an overwhelming necessity. As necessary in this moment of time as the freeing of America's slaves was in the mid-nineteenth century.

We have forgotten how unpopular the Civil War was in the North. Copperheads and other anti-war forces nearly unseated Lin-coln in 1864, while the outcome of the fighting was still in doubt. We have also forgotten the unsatisfactory messiness of the post-war occupation of the Confederacy—otherwise known as the Recon-struction. Victorious in war, the North ultimately lost its will to impose a true vision of universal suffrage on the South, condemning thousands of American blacks to a century of unequal rights. Like today's supporters of the liberation of Iraq, radical Republicans and Abolitionists discovered that morally repugnant ways of life do not change with the simple sweep of justice's sword. If the change required is momentous enough, the power of historical evolution must take a hand, as well.

George Bush is not Lincoln, of course. By the time this book is published, he may no longer be president. But like the Reconstruction of the South, the rebuilding of Iraq will continue in all its messiness. Neither the American or the Iraqi people find satisfaction in its progress. It will seem to be failing at times. Women's rights will probably be sacrificed in order to placate the *Hawza*. Violence will continue. But if the U.S. remains in Iraq, checking the tendency of the nation toward civil war, keeping pressure on the terrorists and shepherding the rebuilding process, then we may yet see victory pulled back from the brink of apparent disaster.

Much depends on the willingness of the American people to "stay the course." And this, in turn, depends in large part on our recognition and appreciation of those we fight and what they stand for. As I've tried to show in this book, the "insurgents" are not "freedom fighters" or noble "anti-globalization guerillas"—they are *fascists*. They represent something evil unleashed in the world. If we allow them regain power in Iraq, they will drag that nation and whatever countries they next control into the darkness of killing fields, mass graves, public executions, and other forms of spirit-breaking tyranny the likes of which Americans have little conception. We fight a modern form of slavery today, and whether the slave master appears in the guise of a secular nationalist, mouthing the cant of pan-Arab unity, or a bearded cleric, chaining the spirit to a confused and incoherent religious text, the evil is the same. Is this view simplistic? Too black-and-white?

On September 23, Iraq's interim prime minister Iyad Allawi spoke before Congress. It was a good speech—especially in Allawi's insistence that the reconstruction of Iraq is an indispensable part of the War on Terror—but more inspiring still was this image of an Iraqi willing to stand up against the Islamofascists who are murdering his people. Almost immediately, though, the cynical niggling arose from the chattering classes. John Kerry advisor Joe Lockhart, denounced Allawi as an "American puppet." "Allawi Backs Bush Campaign," declared the *Financial Times*; the AP characterized Allawi's linking of the Iraqi conflict to the War on Terror as "echoing one of Bush's campaign themes"; "Dance of the Marionettes" read Maureen Dowd's *New York Times* column.

The irresponsibility of these reactions is breathtaking. How demoralizing they must seem to the Iraqi people—nearly 70 percent of whom support Allawi as their leader! How comforting to their enemies! As Iraqis suffer daily attacks by paramilitary death squads, the leader of the nation's true resistance comes to speak to the American people—and the world's cultural elite treats him like a GOP stooge. Perhaps in the future we will look at these "sophisticated" voices in the same way we view "peace Democrats" and anti-abolitionists during the Civil War, the "America-Firsters" of the 1930s and 1940s and "peaceniks" of the Cold War era. What was it about fighting the enemies of human freedom and dignity that was so difficult for them to comprehend?

I hope to return to Iraq soon. In a perfect world, U.S. and Iraqi forces will secure the nation, and I will not travel alone. Rather, I'll form part of an inundation of American support for the nation's reconstruction which marshals the power of Democrats and Republicans, liberals and conservatives, idealistic Jeffersonians and hard-nosed Hamiltonians alike. A civilian army that will bear texts like the *Declaration of Independence* and the *Federalist Papers* (as well as *Roberts Rules of Order*, and while we're at it, a little Locke, Paine, and Toqueville) to help teach Iraqis about the possibilities of freedom. A crusading force that includes feminists to assist in the liberation of women, environmentalists to help repair Iraq's ruined landscape, lawyers to defend civil liberties. Business entrepreneurs and corporate executives to introduce capitalist efficiency and populism. Christian evangelists to carry out the dangerous work of introducing religious pluralism to Islam. Journalists, academics, and artists willing to dispense with multiculturalism to critique a culture long overdue for reform and renovation. A revolutionary vanguard that mobilizes the progressive energies of the West in an effort that does not shirk from, but rather affirms the hazards of vying against malignant cultural norms. I know this idealism is out of fashion in conservative circles (it has almost perished on the left), where "realists" are attempting to discredit the vision of democratizing the Middle East—and that mystifies me. If America stands for its core values of individualism, human rights and the pursuit of happiness, we shall surely triumph against our Islamo-fascist enemies, in Iraq and elsewhere.

Were we wrong in Iraq? Yes, in one major sense, beyond even the shortage of troops, failure to anticipate a Baathist-led insurrection and Abu Ghraib: we did not, and still don't, understand the regressive, parasitical, unreasonable presence of tribal Islam—the black hole in Iraqi and Arab cultures that consumes their best and most positive energies. Because of our blindness, we find ourselves fighting an enemy we do not see, comprehend, or even accurately identify.

Fortunately, however, while that failure looms, history may yet reveal other, more important, events as our perspective lengthens. Take, for example, the end of Saddam. Thousands of people now live who would have perished under that regime; millions have something they had thought lost forever to the Baathists: their future.

How will they use that gift? In ways, I imagine, that will make the destiny of the Arab world more unpleasant for our enemies than for us.

Should we have invaded Iraq? History will tell if it helped or harmed us in the overall struggle against Islamofascism. I believe it *can* help, if the U.S. prosecutes it correctly. More importantly, though, when I consider the people I met in that country—among them Esam, Ahmed, Haider, Naseer, Yanar, Dhia, Samir, Rand, Dr. Mashtaq and, above all, Nour—I can only say yes, we were right. Saddam is gone. They have a chance for freedom. They have an opportunity, however distant it seems now, to enjoy the same freedoms you and I take for granted. As long as the United States of America does not abandon them, does not let the seeds of democracy shrivel and die.

Would this answer satisfy an American family whose loved one died in Iraq? Probably not. But if—*if*—Iraq does begin a "reverse domino" effect that brings a measure of emancipation to the enslaved people of the Middle East, then the blood and treasure spent so dearly by the U.S. will not have been in vain. Just as important, it will give meaning to the three thousand lost on 9-11.

I end where I began, on that tragic morning when the world changed. Like most Americans, I cannot think of 9-11 without experiencing a terrible emptiness, a sense of loss that will never heal. We all have our private reactions to what happened. In my case, I hoped to carry on in a manner that would give meaning to the lives lost that day. For me, that meant grappling with the concept of evil, and its existence both in the world and in myself. It meant going to Iraq, where I saw the irrational and brutal sides of human nature, alongside the generous and brave. It meant becoming a feminist, and growing more resolute in my opposition to Islamofascism. I saw the limits of America and learned to appreciate my country even more, in all its political, cultural, and spiritual diversity. Most of all, though, I discovered a larger capacity within myself to care for people I hardly knew and may never see again.

I went to Iraq largely because of 9-11. No one can undo that event, of course. But I feel I have used the sacrifice of the lives lost that day in a manner that honors them—to learn, to grow, to mature and to love. *Insha'allah*.

Bibliography

Ahmad, Fazl. *Husain the Great Martyr*. Lahore, Pakistan: Sh. Muhammad Ashraf, 1999.

Ali, Ameer. *A Short History of the Saracens*. London: MacMillan & Co., 1955.

Anonymous. I*mperial Hubris: Why the West is Losing the War on Terror*. Washington, D.C.: Brassey's, Inc., 2004.

Armstrong, Karen. *Islam: A Short History*. New York: The Modern Library, 2000.

Berman, Paul. *Terror and Liberalism*. New York: W.W. Norton & Company, 2003.

Bewley, Aisha. *Mu'awiya, Restorer of the Muslim Faith*. London: Dar Al Taqwa, Ltd.

Bodansky, Yossef. *The Secret History of the Iraq War*. New York: ReganBooks, 2004.

Dodge, Toby. *Inventing Iraq: The Failure of Nation Building and a History Denied*. New York: Columbia University Press, 2003.

Elshtain, Jean Bethke. *Just War against Terror: The Burden of American Power in a Violent World*. New York: Basic Books, 2003.

Haldane, Alymer L. *The Insurrection in Mesopotamia*. Ediburgh, Blackwood, 1922.

Harris, Lee. *Civilization and its Enemies: The Next Stage of History.* New York: Free Press, 2004.

The Koran, translated by N.J. Dawood, London: Penguin Books, 1997.

Ledeen, Michael A. *The War Against the Terror Masters*. New York: Truman Talley Books, 2002.

Lewis, Bernard. *The Crisis of Islam: Holy War and Unholy Terror*. New York: The Modern Library, 2003.

_____. *What Went Wrong? Western Impact and Middle East Response*. New York: Oxford University Press, 2002.

L-Ghita, Muhammad Husayn al Kashifu. *The Origin of Shi'ite Islam and its Principles*. Kuwait: Committee Ahl al-Bait Charity.

Makiya, Kanan. *The Monument*. London: I.B. Taurus, 2004.

Manji, Irshad. *The Trouble with Islam: A Muslim's Call for Reform in Her Faith*. New York: St. Martin's Press, 2004.

Momen, Moojan. *An Introduction to Shi'i Islam: The History and Doctrines of Twelver Shi'ism*. New Haven: Yale University Press, 1985.

Patai, Raphael. *The Arab Mind*. New York: Hatherleigh Press, 2002.

Pipes, Daniel. *Militant Islam Reaches America*. New York: W.W. Norton & Company, 2002.

Pryce-Jones, David. *The Closed Circle: An Interpretation of the Arabs*. Chicago: Ivan R. Dee, 2002.

Qutb, Sayyid. *Milestones*. Kuwait: International Islamic Federation of Student Organizations, 1978.

_____. *In the Shade of the Qur'an, Surahs 1-2*, translated by M.A. Salahi. Leicester, England: The Islamic Foundation, 1999.

Souad. *Burned Alive: A Victim of the Law of Men*. New York: Warner Books, 2004.

Schwartz, Stephen. *The Two Faces of Islam: The House of Sa'ud from Tradition to Terror*. New York: Doubleday, 2002.

Stowasser, Barbara Freyer. *Women in Qur'an, Traditions, and Interpretation*. New York: Oxford University Press, 1994.

Wahab, Muhammad bin Abdul. *Kitab at-Tauhid*, translated by Compilation and Research Department Dar-us-Salam. Riyadh, Saudi Arabia: Dar-us-Salam Publications, 1996.

Warraq, ibn. *Why I am Not a Muslim*. Amherst, New York: Prometheus Books, 1995.

Index

This book was designed and set into type
by Mitchell S. Muncy,
with cover design by Stephen J. Ott,
and printed and bound
by Phoenix Color Corp.,
Hagerstown, Maryland.

The text face is Minion Multiple Master,
designed by Robert Slimbach
and issued in digital form by Adobe Systems,
Mountain View, California, in 1991.

The index is by IndExpert, Fort Worth, Texas.

The paper is acid-free and is of archival quality.

39